GOD

Wants
You To *Roll*

Also by John Phillips III

Slippery

GOD

Wants
You To *Roll*

The $21 Million "Miracle Cars" Scam—How Two Boys
Fleeced America's Churchgoers

John Phillips III

CARROLL & GRAF PUBLISHERS

NEW YORK

GOD WANTS YOU TO ROLL

The $21 Million "Miracle Cars" Scam—How Two Boys Fleeced America's Churchgoers

Carroll & Graf Publishers
An Imprint of Avalon Publishing Group Inc.
245 West 17th Street
11th Floor
New York, NY 10011

AVALON
publishing group incorporated

Copyright © 2005 by John Phillips III

First Carroll & Graf edition 2005

Library of Congress Cataloging-in-Publication Data is available.

ISBN: 0-7867-1443-3

9 8 7 6 5 4 3 2 1

Interior design by Maria Torres
Printed in the United States of America
Distributed by Publishers Group West

This book is dedicated to my father, *John D. Phillips,*
Attorney at Law, the best writer I know and a man to whom I
owe a debt the size of a '62 Eldorado Biarritz convertible

Contents

Acknowledgments

My deepest thanks to Assistant United States Attorneys J. Daniel Stewart and James Curt Bohling. Both men made available every piece of information the law allowed and always took time to explain the twists and turns of their investigations and of the legal maneuvering that emerged during the trial. Thanks to United States Postal Inspector J. Steven Hamilton and Department of the Treasury Special Agent Gary A. Marshall, both of whom toppled the scam and were ever eager to answer questions. Thanks to former Division of Gambling Control Special Agent Elijah Zuniga, who has a super-sleuth's nose, a wise man's wits, and a pit bull's determination. From those five men, U.S. taxpayers got *way* more than they deserved.

Special thanks to Susanne Vandenbosch and Angela P. Snapp, who put a few thousand pages of my interviews and notes into chronological order, and kudos to Patti Eldridge Maki, the Michigan wolverine of copyediting. Thanks to Tom Cosgrove for laying out the family tree and initial photo pages. Thanks to Brock Yates for a veteran's advice. Thanks to writer Neil A. Grauer for supplying magician Ricky Jay's quote, from his story "The Wizard of Odd," in the *Smithsonian,* June 2004.

And loving, endless gratitude to Julie Renee Gothrup, who plucked the words from my heart.

DRAMATIS PERSONAE

THE "HEIR"
ROBERT GOMEZ
(aka "Buddha," aka "Robert Bowers")
[alleged adoptive father: John Bowers]

THE "ESTATE EXECUTOR"
JAMES R. NICHOLS
[parents: Rose and Sam Nichols]

THE "NEVER-SEEN ESTATE LAWYERS"
Vince McNeil, Shawn Houston, Howard Gaines

#1 "NATIONAL FINDER"
GWENDOLYN BAKER
Memphis

#2 "NATIONAL FINDER"
CORINNE CONWAY
Kansas City/Higginsville

#3 "NATIONAL FINDER"
KIM KRAWIZCKI
Philadelphia

THE BIG INVESTORS:
Robert Fluellen, Ohio
David Harp, Arkansas
Matt Jones, Washington
Randy Lamb, Kansas
Greg Ross, California
Ricky Siglar, Kansas
Neil Smith, Missouri

HIGGINSVILLE CHIEF OF POLICE
CINDY SCHROER, Higginsville, Missouri

SPECIAL AGENT IN THE CASINOS
ELIJAH ZUNIGA, Los Angeles, California

INVESTIGATING FEDERAL AGENTS
GARY MARSHALL & STEVEN HAMILTON
Kansas City

ASSISTANT U.S. ATTORNEYS
DAN STEWART & CURT BOHLING
Kansas City

KANSAS CITY ATTORNEYS
FOR THE DEFENDANTS
BRUCE SIMON (for Robert Gomez)
TOM BRADSHAW (for James R. Nichols)

PART I

Confidence tricks are born, but they never die. They flourish, fade, and then spring back to life in new clothes. They're stories, and, like stories, they stick to effective formulas. The unclaimed-estate swindle is one of the oldest forms of con, and it was enjoying a particular vogue in America at the end of the 19th century. Belief blossomed in the existence of the Sir Francis Drake estate and a multitude of other fictitious inheritances. The estate scheme touched the democratic suspicion that inherited wealth is fortuitous and arbitrary and deserved by anybody as much as anybody else.

—**Richard Rayner,** *Drake's Fortune*

1

BUDDHA AND THE PORNOGRAPHER

A t four P.M., a few days after Christmas 2001, a black Rolls-Royce inched silently into the VIP parking area of the Hustler Casino in Gardena, California. It slipped into the slot nearest the side door, the only reserved space without someone's name stenciled on the curb. Before the car stopped moving, an African American bodyguard—trim, muscular, six and a half feet tall, and armed—leapt from the back seat to the pavement. He scanned the lot, looking for any face he didn't recognize. The bodyguard unfolded a gold-plated wheelchair with a velvet seat cushion and swung the device to the front passenger door. He opened the door, bent deeply at the waist, then picked up a man with dull red hair—picked him up as if he were lifting nothing heavier than a sack of groceries. He placed the man gently in the gold wheelchair, then spent five seconds ensuring he was comfortable. Two more security officers arrived, both in uniforms, both carrying walkie-talkies, both armed.

As the man in the wheelchair and his bodyguard rolled through the side door and into the circular fifty-thousand-square-foot casino—a structure intended to resemble a gold crown—a half-dozen card dealers looked up. They straightened their vests and bow ties. This was, after all, their boss, Larry Flynt, America's best-known purveyor of porn but also a devoted gambler. He owned this casino and had named it after the periodical that had earned him some $500 million.

Most of the Hustler employees liked Mr. Flynt. He was easygoing, soft-spoken, unerringly polite. The pornographer's wife ran the gift shop—T-shirts, ashtrays, shot glasses, X-rated magazines—and his father often spent entire days shuffling around the gaming tables in a kind of senile fog. "It looks like a casino, but we called it Flynt's Day Care Center," joked a former dealer. On the second floor, Flynt kept a secure apartment, where he'd occasionally retreat to nap or snack on his favorite food, fried chicken. His wife usually remained upstairs while he gambled, although sometimes she'd fuss with the merchandise in Shorty's gift shop, driving the clerk crazy. On the casino floor, however, the Flynts never overstayed their welcome. Larry rarely gambled later than two A.M.

Few casino patrons realized that a celebrity was in their midst. Those who had, however, stood and walked in Flynt's direction, hoping to exchange greetings or to collect an autograph. All were out of luck. Flynt's towering bodyguard was pushing the wheelchair too fast, and although Flynt himself was smiling, the bodyguard was scowling like a serial killer. It was impossible to misinterpret his message. Flynt had been shot by a stranger once before. It would not happen again, certainly not in the man's own casino.

The bodyguard wheeled Flynt to a table in an alcove of the poker area, where yet another security guard waited. That guard attached thick velvet ropes to gold stanchions so no one else could enter, although anyone could watch. The poker table was custom-made to Flynt's specifications—twelve inches taller than normal, up high, where a man in a taller-than-average wheelchair could get his face right into the cards. Already seated at the table, also in abnormally tall chairs, were three professional gamblers ready to play seven-card stud. Each had been formally invited. No walk-ins gambled with Big Larry.

The bodyguard stood directly behind his boss, then folded his hands across his abdomen, Secret Service–style. He was capable of standing motionless and glaring for hours on end.

On the table in front of each gambler sat tall stacks of white chips. These were the hundred-dollar chips, and each man knew he'd require at least a hundred, maybe three times that amount. In fact, the Hustler's poker manager had already brought Flynt a pile worth $30,000. The pornographer was not a skilled gambler, often losing as much as $50,000 per week. He played instead for the love of the game and for a chance to socialize with gamblers who *were* skilled, who sometimes revealed tricks of the trade. And on those occasions when Flynt won, he never cashed out his chips. He just handed them back to the cage manager. This was, after all, his own casino, which he'd recently spruced up at a cost of $30 million—the circular fountain out front, a sushi bar, a massage parlor, flocked wallpaper, gold-framed mirrors, plasma-screen TVs, crystal chandeliers nearly as big as Toyotas, and a Diamondvision billboard out near the street.

Seated at Flynt's table was Ted Forrest, a handsome, dark-haired professional from Canada, now living in Las Vegas, *the* acknowledged master of seven-card stud. Across from Forrest sat Barry Greenstein of Rancho Palos Verdes, California, then the leader in *Card Player* magazine's Player of the Year competition. And between the two veterans slouched an impossibly young-looking Latino with a shaved head, pencil-thin mustache, tinted glasses, and immense stomach. Everyone knew him as Buddha, and it was easy to see why. The young man reeked of cologne. He wore a golf shirt, pressed khaki slacks, Cole Haan loafers, and a seventeen-hundred-dollar maroon leather jacket he'd purchased at the Bellagio in Vegas. When he wasn't smiling, he was talking.

Buddha stood deferentially as Flynt rolled up to the table. "God, Larry, it's so great to see you," he gushed. "You look so healthy, as always, oh, sure. Put a bad beat on anybody lately? How's your wife and dad?"

The minimum bet was set at $1,000, although it quickly escalated to $4,500. The four men played earnestly, like the pros they were, but there was a gaiety to the proceedings. Flynt's philosophy was that the game was played for fun, not profit. Each man was quick to laugh at big bust-outs. Someone made fun of Buddha's cologne.

That was fine with Buddha, who, in any event, did not take seven-card stud seriously. His game was pai gow poker, "real gambling," he called it, not the domain of first-timers or tourists. "I'm Buddha, *king* of pai gow," he told anyone who would listen. In fact, that phrase was custom-stamped on his Lincoln's license-plate frame.

Buddha began to gamble "full tilt"—the insider's term for reckless wagering, for relying on emotion and hunches rather than logic. He played impatiently, almost psychotically. Sometimes he'd get a bad hand and laugh so hard his breasts would jiggle. But just as often, a murderous look would contort his face, and he was liable to explode.

"What kind of motherfucking asshole would *hand* me shit like this?" he suddenly blurted, tugging at one of his double chins. Buddha was famous for abusing dealers, especially if they made the mistake of being female. He sometimes joked that he'd made every woman dealer in Southern California cry at least twice, and it was close to the truth.

Flynt frowned. Despite his seamy profession, he remained an

old-school Midwesterner at heart, with a residual sense of pro-priety. He didn't abide cursing, wouldn't tolerate it at the tables, and was, ironically, chivalrous about defending his female employees.

"We are gentlemen playing a gentleman's game," Flynt softly reminded, saying it to his cards, not to Buddha directly. He tapped his left hand against the table, causing two immense gold rings to click ominously, like a dog snapping its teeth. Forrest and Greenstein stared nervously at their knuckles.

"Sure, Larry, *of course,*" Buddha apologized, realizing he might have offended his idol. "Just funning around. You know me. These small pots we're bettin' here, I mean, why should *I* care who wins, right? I'm the king of pai gow. I'm just glad to be here, in my favorite casino. You're the man, Larry, *my* man, sure. You know that."

Flynt did not reply. But he turned and glanced at his body-guard, standing as stiff and upright as a bridge abutment. Other players at the table knew the meaning of the look—tantamount to the high-school principal phoning your parents. One more out-burst and Buddha would be quietly but firmly led from the VIP table to the "tourist" side of the velvet ropes. He'd have to finish his night's gambling with the local schmoes who walked in off the street wearing dirty Nikes and fake gold chains. It would be a humiliation that most professional gamblers would find nearly unbearable. But such incidents rarely worried Buddha. He'd been suspended or expelled by virtually every casino, sometimes for as long as a month. The bans never lasted, though. When Buddha was putting in what he called his "nine to five"—nine *P.M.* to five *A.M.*—the casinos stood to increase their take by $30,000 daily, often more. And there'd occasionally be whopping tokes, or tips, for any dealer who dealt him a series of winning hands. *No one* could forget the night that Buddha, after a few big wins, grabbed twenty $5,000 chips and placed them in the hand of a third-party banker named Ray Garcia. *"There,"* he had said. "Now you don't have to work for them anymore."

From the Hustler VIP table, Buddha beckoned to a friend who'd come to watch him take on Flynt. She was standing outside the velvet ropes, not sure whether she was welcome. Her name was Linda Janowski, forty-six, the finance director at nearby South Bay Toyota, where she earned more than $200,000 a year. Janowski was smart and witty and possessed a bombshell figure that caused men to stare.

"Linda, these guys are ganging up on me!" Buddha joked. He went over to hug her. "Call security and have them videotape this game. I'm being raped!"

Janowski loved to watch Buddha, who was as colorful, profane, and flamboyant as any man in her experience. She wasn't Buddha's girlfriend—he had no girlfriends—but he often staked her at blackjack, just for fun, and he just as often showered her with gifts. There was expensive jewelry, a huge Sony TV, Lakers tickets, suites at the Bellagio—gifts Buddha himself had been bequeathed by casinos courting his play. At that very moment, in fact, he was wearing a gaudy Rolex, courtesy of . . . well, this one came from Larry at the Hustler, if he remembered correctly. He had seven more at home.

"They totally kissed his ass," Janowski remembered. "And the reason was, at pai gow poker, he was the biggest whale in California. He was Godzilla. I once saw him start with $40,000 and go up to half a million. He was good. Fearless. Also incredibly fast."

But when Buddha fooled around with seven-card stud, he was reckless about "tells"—facial expressions and body language that gave away his hand. "He'd sometimes kick his legs," Janowski recalled, "or give me this huge wink. Just crazy stuff, so obvious. He'd do it just to be funny. He could be a real clown."

Janowski wasn't sure where Buddha got his money. No one was. Maybe he was simply the world's luckiest gambler. All anyone knew for sure was that Buddha enjoyed a steady influx of cashier's checks, money orders, and wire transfers. Just that day, a wire transfer for $50,000 had arrived, earmarked for deposit in Buddha's player's account. In fact, incoming five-figure checks and wires were so frequent that the Hustler cage managers took little notice. Only when the cash arrived in *six*-figure sums—denominations larger than the managers had ever seen—would the execs upstairs become fidgety. They'd call Big Larry first to get an okay before young Buddha was permitted to convert the funds into chips.

Flynt wondered about it himself, off and on, but Buddha assured him that he was simply living off a vast inheritance. Flynt didn't dig any deeper and wasn't obliged to. "He was an extremely warm and decent person," Flynt told a reporter from the *New Times*. "He was just a kid, and to be as experienced as he was at gambling . . . well, he was a phenomenally good player."

Buddha said he was "the heir to a rich white man's estate, a New Yorker who adopted me when I was six." The adoptive father had reportedly worked for the engineering division of Mission Foods in Irving, Texas, and was worth $411 million. It sounded fishy to Janowski, but what else was she to believe? Buddha never left his Long Beach country-club estate without a two-inch roll of bills, half of them hundred-dollar bills. When he came home, he'd toss his "leftovers"—orphaned bills and stray poker chips—into a bowl cradled in the arms of a Buddha statue in front of his fireplace. "With what he flipped in there as loose change," Janowski recalled, "I could have paid my rent for four months."

A few months after his game with Flynt, when Buddha strolled into the Hustler one evening, he was greeted by a nice little surprise. Another check had arrived. This one was a beaut. It was for $518,731.22. It had been sent by a Pastor John Alexander of Atlanta, Georgia.

"That was just such an enormous sum, you know, it took my breath away," said Eleanor Gonzales, a Hustler cage manager. "So we called Mr. Flynt. He got somebody to investigate, but there were no stops, no holds, and I guess they found out that the account, at the Bank of America, held more than enough to cover it."

The check didn't have Buddha's name on it. Attached instead was an inscrutable handwritten note signed by Pastor Alexander. It read, "The enclosed amount . . . reflects the balance of my account that has been used to collect refunds owed to Robert Gomez per instruction of James R. Nichols."

Gonzales and Flynt read the note over and over, trying to divine its meaning. Was it some sort of code? Refunds for what? Who was this Nichols guy? Why was a church sending a half-million-dollar check to a professional gambler who habitually cursed at women card dealers? When Gonzales and her coworkers failed to answer even one of those questions, they did the next best thing. They handed to Robert "Bobby" Gomez, aka Buddha, $518,731.22 in poker chips.

All Buddha said was: "Hey, last night I put a *terrible* beat on Larry at seven-card stud. Think I should get a bodyguard, too?"

Then he drove his new Lincoln Town Car to the Wiener-schnitzel, ate three dogs, and had two more wrapped to go.

2

SECURITY GUARDS IN LONG BEACH

James Randall Nichols was an African American with caramel-colored skin. He was as handsome as Denzel Washington but more athletically blessed—tall, a slim 170 pounds, thin hips and waist, powerful chest, square shoulders, and a voice as deep and mellifluous as Barry White's. He was aggressively polite, referring to all adults as "sir" or "ma'am." He was serious and solemn, with a crushing handshake. He rarely spoke unless first spoken to, and even then his response was measured, almost halting, as he selected words with patience and precision. It was difficult not to like him. Moreover, it was difficult not to believe he was college-educated.

In fact, he was not. Nichols—always James, never Jim—attended Western Avenue Baptist Elementary School, Benton High School, James Christian Academy, and one year of community college. He was the sixth of seven children of Sam and Rose Nichols, and grew up in a fastidiously maintained brick ranch house on Kemp Avenue, in Carson, California. His father drove a truck. His mother was a nurse's aide.

From the day he was born, James never wanted for clothes or food or material possessions, but his parents were strict and deeply religious, faithful members of Christ Christian Home Missionary Baptist Church. As soon as he could walk and speak, James attended that church as often as five times weekly—Bible-study class, prayer meetings, choir practice, mid-week services, then formal Sunday school. He was an usher, also a drummer for the choir, and was adored by the church elders, especially the colorfully named Reverend Houston Buggs. When he was four, James once asked a member of the congregation if the Reverend Buggs were God Himself. Everybody roared. What a kid.

Adults were drawn to James because he was polite and inquisitive. When he turned fifteen, he read the Bible, front to back, in five days. Afterward, he said to his mother, "There were some inaccuracies compared with what my church taught me to believe, such as certain martyrs, disciples, how the Bible is dragged underground." She encouraged him to read more. "So I studied the *Lost Books of Moses,* the Dead Sea Scrolls, the *Return of the Dead Sea Scrolls,*" he recalled. "Then I read books on paganism, satanic worship, the Muslim faith, and others. I wanted to get an idea of who my enemy was."

When his mother wasn't looking, he was reading *Car and Driver* and *Road & Track* and *Motor Trend.* "I knew every car model," he recalled. "My favorite old car was a '65 Mustang 289 2 + 2 GT—that fastback Shelby shape, so beautiful. My favorite new car was a BMW M3. I promised myself I'd own one someday."

It was Sam Nichols's philosophy to impose what he called "tough love" on his sons. The regimen included ousting each boy from the house when he turned eighteen. "The idea was to get some life experience, some maturity, find out the value of a dollar," James explained. "You could come back a year later, no problem, as long as you put in a legitimate effort for 365 days and didn't get in trouble or rely on handouts."

James prepared for his year of tough love. He got an apartment in nearby Torrance and landed a job with Langner Security as a security guard for office complexes in Long Beach. It was boring work, especially the night shift, and it paid only minimum wage. "The job was basically to watch for trespassers or people parking illegally in private lots," he recalled. "Usually, nothing happened. You just walked around the office buildings in the dark, and if you saw anything suspicious, well, your instructions were simple. Dial 911. Get the real cops."

In fact, that's exactly what eighteen-year-old James wanted to be—an officer with the Los Angeles Police Department. He'd been in touch with the department's human-resources division, who described the written and oral tests he'd need to pass and what physical standards would be imposed. James studied when no one was looking—at four in the morning, no one ever *was*—and he lifted weights. But he couldn't take his rookie tests until he was twenty and a half. It was frustrating and, above all, tedious. "There'd be nights when I'd almost be frantic, thinking to myself, My brain is wasting away, just shriveling," he said. "It was like babysitting toddlers for too long, you know, when you start to pray for some intellectual stimulation."

In September 1994, James Nichols's prayers were answered. That's when the security company hired a pudgy Latino kid, a graduate of Canyon Verde High School in El Segundo. Just nineteen, the boy had been assigned the swing shift, craved overtime, and didn't mind sixteen-hour tours. The company gave him a dull white Chevy sedan to drive, and he circled the office buildings and warehouses, looking for loiterers and listening to the radio—not to the Hispanic stations but to mainstream middle-American soft rock. "I liked listening to the ads, how those guys talked," he explained. He was a happy-go-lucky type, gregarious, sometimes clownish, as funny as a stand-up comic. Everybody loved the guy, at least until he started boasting, which began after about ninety seconds of conversation.

His name was Robert Gomez, second son of Mercedes Flores, a Mexican immigrant who spoke almost no English, a woman so poor she collected discarded cardboard to sell to recyclers.

One night, Gomez was assigned to relieve Nichols. "When we first met," Gomez remembered, "James stared at my head, just gawked. So I told him, 'Look, when I was young, I got a weird punk-rocker haircut, and my dad about threw a fit.' He took me back to the barber and said, 'Shave all this boy's hair off!' And I kinda liked it, liked rubbing my smooth head. So I've cut it like this ever since."

James thought that was hilarious. In fact, the two boys hit it off immediately, soon joking they were the "black and brown Starsky and Hutch." In part, Nichols was tickled that he hadn't made this particular friend through the church, like all the others in his eighteen years. This new guy was wild, loud, a dirty-mouthed show-off—everything the Reverend Houston Buggs had warned against.

"We hung out like two new adult guys," Nichols remembered. "Went to certain restaurants we liked, like Acapulco's. Went to the gun club together, bowled on occasion. Very chummy. Robert told me that his family didn't quite like him too much around that time, that he'd been kicked out of the house. Turned out that wasn't true, but Robert liked to make up certain dramatic scenarios. And if he couldn't live them out, he would make up a new one. I'd never met anyone like that."

Gomez made intimate confessions to Nichols—how he'd been in and out of high school special ed for "behavioral problems, fights, goofy stuff I did." One of those goofy things was a night of beer, followed by a trip to a tattoo parlor. Gomez emerged with eight small Asian figures on his arms. "They have to do with karma," he explained to Nichols. "I'm a big believer in karma," although Nichols knew that Robert often confused karma with predestination.

Unlike Nichols, Gomez was not much of a reader, yet he became absolutely addicted to crossword puzzles and word jumbles, which he played with the concentration of a Zen master. He believed they helped him focus, helped increase his attention span, which he realized was meager. Gomez enjoyed going to the movies and to malls with Nichols. He liked watching James, who was so handsome and so polite that he had no trouble flirting with the girls.

One day, Gomez asked Nichols to accompany him to the Radisson Hotel in downtown L.A., where he said he had a business matter to attend to. James agreed and waited in the Radisson's lobby while Robert went upstairs. "After I sat down, a doorman came over and asked me to leave because I was disturbing the guests," James recalled. "I didn't understand how I was disturbing anybody. But I'm black, so I guess he thought I was a thief. Just then, Robert jumps off the elevator, and he really chews this doorman out, tells the guy I'm here on business, not a thief, you can't talk to my friend like that. He even asked to see the doorman's manager. I was impressed. I didn't realize that a person so young could have such say-so, such power right then and there. I felt like Robert had stood up for me. I was very proud of that. I never forgot that."

Only one month into their friendship, James invited Robert to the Nicholses' family home in Carson—almost as a prospective bride would bring home her fiancé—and introduced him to his parents. "Sam and Rose were nice folks," Gomez remembered. "I started spending time there. We'd go to James's parents' house after work, drink some coffee, then go cruising. We double-dated a couple of times. James introduced me to his boyhood friend Steve Finnie. It was an easy, friendly time. A good time to plan my life."

When James revealed that his goal was to become an L.A. cop, Robert responded with his own career plans. "Gonna become a professional gambler," he said. "All the gamblers will know my

15

name, from Larry Flynt in L.A. to Steve Wynn in Las Vegas to Donald Trump in Atlantic City." Gomez had never been to Vegas or Atlantic City.

"Robert had a lot of these huge plans, so I didn't know whether he was serious or not," Nichols recalled. "But I knew enough to tell him, 'You want to gamble, you have to get someone with cash to back you, at least when you start.' And that's when Robert lays the bomb on me. He says: 'No problem. Listen to this. I was adopted at age six by a man named John Bowers, who's this big Christian guy who tries to help ghetto kids who are likely to get into trouble.' He told me Bowers was a prominent white businessman, that he worked for the Gruma Corporation, running the engineering division of Mission Foods in Irving, Texas. He said Bowers was well educated, spoke ten languages, and was a well-rooted person with government contracts that he probably earned when he was affiliated with the CIA. He said Bowers had gone to Ohio State University, had played minor league baseball, and was a shrewd businessman worth millions. Who knew if it was true, you know? But I was intrigued. I was listening."

A few days passed. Then it occurred to Nichols to ask, "Why would your dad want to back you in a career of gambling?"

Gomez had a ready answer: "He *wouldn't*," he said. "In fact, he's pissed off at me, because I'm a recovering alcoholic, have substance-abuse problems. But I'm his heir, right? Sole heir to his estate. Me. *Get it?*"

There was a long pause. Nichols couldn't imagine anyone in his right mind bequeathing millions of dollars to pudgy Robert Gomez, king of the crossword puzzles. What's more, he wondered what had happened to Gomez's biological father, the man who instructed the barber to shave Robert's big ol' pumpkin head.

But James Randall Nichols didn't wonder about it too long. And he didn't wonder about it too hard.

3

ROOMMATES ON KEMP AVENUE

Now nineteen, James Nichols had served his year of "tough love," had supported himself and performed maturely without complaint. But he resented spending his minimum-wage income on an apartment. That was no way for a young man to earn a BMW M3.

In December 1994, he thus asked his parents if he could move back into his boyhood room, the room with the Porsche and Lamborghini posters taped to the wall. Sam and Rose agreed, but house rules stipulated that James would again be attending Christ Christian Home Missionary Baptist Church three to five times weekly. James consented. Then he asked another favor. He wondered if Robert Gomez could move in, as well. Before Sam and Rose could reply, James reminded them of a maxim they'd pummeled into him as a youth: "You told me a thousand times that our family will take in a stranger, because you never know if you're entertaining an angel."

Rose doubted that Robert was an angel. She asked, "Is Mr. Gomez reputable?"

Her son replied, "I'll let him speak for himself."

"And then here comes Robert," Rose remembered. "So I

asked him, was he willing to cooperate with the rules of our home, and he said, 'Yes, ma'am.' I said, 'First of all, we *do* go to church here. And second, we do *not* drink alcohol on these premises or abuse substances. And I asked if he was willing to abide. Again he said, 'Yes, ma'am.' "

James Nichols and Robert Gomez became roommates. They would go on to share the little room on Kemp Avenue, in Carson, for nearly two years. It was a tight squeeze, and right away it became tighter. That's because the boys did an odd thing. They filled the room with a computer, a fax, answering machines, filing cabinets, and a double-decker desk. It looked more like an insurance-salesman's office than a bedroom. What it looked like, in fact, was that they'd gone into business together.

Fifty-seven years earlier, Rose Nichols had been born in Jackson, Mississippi, and she still had family there. Now her hair was gray, her skin was as light as her son's, and she had a receding chin. From some angles, she looked almost Asian. She was soft-spoken but iron-willed, sometimes defiant. She weighed two hundred pounds, was physically strong and imposing, and ran a tight ship. "She took a dim view of adolescent shenanigans, of what she called 'the nonsense' in her home," recalled a Kemp Avenue neighbor. "If one of the kids crossed the line, you'd hear the explosion all the way down the street."

But it wasn't long before some nonsense erupted anyway.

James reported to his mother that he'd received a "creepy" phone call. He explained that a man named Vince McNeil had called, and that this man purported to be a corporate attorney for Gruma Corporation, which owned Mission Foods in Irving, Texas. The man told him that Robert Gomez "had serious problems with authority, that he had a dependency problem with alcohol, that, all in all, he was just a problem child who needed guidance." What's more, James reported that this McNeil character "had an automated voice box, like a person who'd had cancer surgery would have." James had never heard such a thing, and it made his skin crawl. McNeil called a few more times. If Rose answered, he'd ask abruptly for James. On at least one occasion, a second lawyer called. He said his name was Shawn Houston, from New York City. "The attorneys promised to put me [James] ahead on a list for the apprenticeship program that Gruma Corporation was starting for mechanical engineering," he told his mother. "And they promised me a company car and said I'd be paid handsomely."

Rose was suspicious. Her son had just turned nineteen and had no degree in anything, certainly not mechanical engineering. She asked James what, exactly, he'd have to do to be "paid handsomely." James wasn't sure. He said he'd find out.

A few weeks passed, then John Bowers called. *The* John Bowers. The eccentric but "well rooted" figure Gomez claimed was his millionaire adoptive father. Bowers reiterated what attorneys McNeil and Houston had said, that chubby little Robert had problems with authority and was an undisciplined delinquent. "He asked me to spend twenty-four hours a day with his son," James told his mother.

"What did you tell him?" Rose asked.

James replied, "I told him he was out of his mind. But then he said, 'Well, *I'm* not going to be the one who pays the piper.' He said I had no choice, my options were all gone now and that I'd have to watch over Robert because, as he put it, 'Robert would rather trust a nigger than his own father.'"

Rose did not like the sound of this Bowers person, not one bit. The man was obviously crude and insensitive. On the other hand, this was her son's business. James had completed his year of tough love, and it was now both parents' intention to treat him as an adult. She asked James if he believed Bowers was telling the truth. James said he didn't know.

Next thing she knew, James explained that he had actually met the man.

He told her he'd driven over to Virginia Country Club, in Long Beach, at the behest of Robert. Robert was there in the pro shop, strutting around telling club members he was a lobbyist, even though he had only the barest notion of what a lobbyist did. "Then Robert said to me, 'Hey, just be cool, don't be nervous, John will take care of everything for you, and I'll be waiting outside.' Sure enough, in walks a man in golf attire. About five feet six, Caucasian, 240 pounds, sunburned, kind of balding up top with hair plugs like a fuzzy muskrat on his head."

Rose asked what Bowers had said.

"He wanted to know if I'd taken his offer," James replied. "I told him I wouldn't accept any extra pay because Robert was my friend and had pretty much been there for me, supportwise. Then Bowers asked if I'd see to it that Robert didn't drink too heavily, get into any cars and drive, get himself arrested, end up OD'ing or something. And if I did that, he'd bump me ahead on the apprenticeship program."

Rose thought this story was peculiar, but she didn't say anything.

Robert showed up at the Kemp Avenue house later that night. He and James retired to their little bedroom-turned-office. Robert said to James: "This is way better than working as a security guard. *You're on your way.*"

What James Nichols did next was write a letter to John Bowers. For some reason, he put no date on this letter, and it was handwritten. In part, it read:

Dear Mr. Bowers:

If you still will hire me, I am both honored and privileged. If you will allow me to work for you without the extra benefits, that would make me feel a lot better. Robert and I go out very often and we always have a great time. He has been there for me so many times, I can't count them all. That is why I refuse the extra pay, out of respect for my dear friend. Robert has not seen . . . this acknowledgment. I appreciate this opportunity, and I hope to see you when you come back from your business trip.

Yours truly, James R. Nichols

James showed the letter to Rose, who wondered what Bowers's mailing address might be. James told her what Robert had said, that Bowers had homes in New York, New Jersey, and California. In fact, James and Robert had already driven to Bowers's California residence in Palos Verdes Estates. "The house was white stucco," he told his mother, "and had a big huge gate, and there was an X in the street in front of it." He said they didn't ring the doorbell because Robert had already been expelled from the home for unspecified misdeeds. The boys merely observed the premises from the outside, then drove away.

Instead of mailing the letter, James handed it to Robert.

Rose wasn't entirely persuaded that Bowers and the lawyers were legit. On the other hand, James and Robert had already related so many intricate details, details that were almost too bizarre to be invented. An automated voice box? Hair plugs? An X on the street? Who would make up stuff like that?

And that's when the tale turned even more bizarre.

On a sunny day in January 1995, a black Lincoln Town Car pulled up in front of the Kemp Avenue house at one P.M. Robert told James: "Get inside and do whatever the chauffeur tells you to do. Bowers is putting you through a test, a test of loyalty, in which you're to help transport gold bullion and some jewelry belonging to him."

James climbed into the back seat. "The driver was Samoan or Hawaiian, very short, weighing maybe 350 pounds," he later told his mom. "Inside the car was a Heckler and Koch MP5 submachine gun, I guess for anyone trying to rob us. We drove straight to Temecula, near Palm Springs, the desert area. We pulled into a nice house, sort of like a ranch. I stayed in the back seat, because that had been my assignment. Some people approached from behind. The trunk opened, there was a rustle, then it shut, and the people walked away. Then we left, drove two and a half hours straight back to Carson. When I got home, I was told I'd passed the test. My understanding was, basically, they wanted to know if I'd ask the chauffeur to stop and open the trunk. You know, to take a look."

Sam and Rose were incredulous. This was more like a made-for-TV movie than anything that could be happening to their quiet nineteen-year-old son. James knew that his straight-arrow mother wasn't thrilled with the prospect of inky-black Lincolns and submachine guns and gold bullion. This was Carson, California, not Hollywood.

And that's when the Bowers saga went eerily quiet. The boys turned their attention to their church duties, and the peculiar movements of Robert's adoptive father were left to simmer and stew.

4

ADVICE FROM THE PULPIT

Ugly iron bars cover the windows of Christ Christian Home Missionary Baptist Church. That's because it's on Compton Boulevard in crime-ridden Compton. The building is coated in mustard-colored stucco, although there are irregular white bands down low, where gang graffiti has been repeatedly painted over. The church's motto is "One big family in spirit." Deacon Sam Nichols's name is displayed prominently on the façade, carved in a marble inlay. The church stands beside a nameless take-out joint boasting the "best BBQ in Compton," where a colossal chopped-pork sandwich costs $3.25. Customers commonly drive twenty miles to patronize the place, but only during the hours of daylight.

Robert Gomez wasn't big on organized religion, but he took special interest in tagging along with James, who was, per his parents' crystal-clear instructions, again a fixture at the church where he'd been baptized thirteen years earlier. The boys seemed inseparable, often huddling in private conversations, and Gomez displayed obvious affection for James. As a result, his sudden appearance at the Nicholses' church didn't raise any eyebrows.

The three hundred congregants knew James as the solemn,

polite boy who helped the infirm ladies get out of their cars. They knew Robert only as the roly-poly kid who was quick to brighten your day with a story about how he'd just met his TV hero, Jay Leno, and how he and Jay had talked about cars for fifty minutes. Whether it was true almost didn't matter. It was fun to listen to Robert spin tales. He was welcomed into the fold as James's pal.

A feature of Christ Christian Home Missionary Baptist Church is a pulpit reserved not for the Reverend Houston Buggs but for veteran church members who have special announcements. Usually, folks told of bake sales or asked for prayer for "backsliders" or pleaded for financial relief on behalf of a sick or dying church member. Any announcement was okay, as long as it was important or affected the church. Robert Gomez seemed inordinately fascinated by this second pulpit, which the regulars called "the discipleship."

For the first ten months of 1995, right up to James's twentieth birthday, the Bowers business was mentioned only rarely. All that transpired was an occasional call from attorney Shawn Houston or Vince McNeil. Then a third attorney began to call. His name was Howard Gaines, purportedly Houston's boss. James said little to his family about Howard Gaines, except to claim he'd actually met the man once, in the Wilshire District. "He was six feet tall, silvery-white hair, slim to medium build, about 180 to 190 pounds," he reported. James was a stickler about estimating weights, a skill he expected he'd need when he joined the LAPD. "Mr. Gaines told me that he was John Bowers's closest friend, that he'd helped him through a bankruptcy and had been Bowers's attorney for over twenty years. He asked if I was taking care of Robert. I told him I was doing my best."

Then, on October 23, three days prior to James's birthday, the whole Bowers saga went back on the boil. That's the day the phone rang at the Kemp Avenue house, and Sam Nichols answered. The caller identified himself as attorney Shawn Houston, and this time he didn't immediately ask to speak to James. Instead, he told Sam that John Bowers was seriously ill, that he'd had a heart attack. Houston added, "Your son may have to go to New York City, fly there with Robert." Sam wasn't keen on paying for an expensive cross-country ticket. Houston replied, "I assure you the company will be paying for it."

A minor panic erupted in the Nichols household. Robert started crying, although he ceased in ninety seconds. James appeared anxious—he'd never traveled that far from home before, didn't even have anything like a bag of toiletries for such a trip. Rose ran out to Kmart to buy her son a flight bag, deodorant, toothpaste, a shaving kit. Robert made airline reservations, then said he had to go out to make additional arrangements. In the meantime, Houston called again. This time, the attorney said: "I'm deeply sorry to tell you this, but Mr. John Bowers has passed away. James will not be needed. But we will still be needing Robert."

Robert returned to Kemp Avenue at eleven P.M. He burst into tears as he walked through the door, before anyone had said a word to him. "I tried to console him as best I could," James recalled. "Then he went over to my mother and spoke with her."

The next day, James drove Robert to Los Angeles International Airport to catch his cross-country flight. Robert seemed composed, even excited. He flew to the Big City, all right. But it wasn't to New York City. Instead, Robert Gomez flew to Atlantic City.

One week after John Bowers's death, twenty-year-old Robert Gomez was back in L.A. As usual, he and James went to church together. That's when he surprised the elders at Christ Christian Home Missionary Baptist Church by climbing into the discipleship pulpit. James knew he was going to do it, but no one else did.

Only half the congregation even knew Robert's name. Most knew him only by Rose's generous description as "a new member of the Nichols family."

In front of the audience, Robert wasn't shy. He asked the congregants, "Pray for me, because my father has just died, and I expect to undergo a lot of turmoil with my father's business." His eyes welled up with tears at least twice, but he was able to continue. Robert further confessed that he was "inexperienced with matters such as wills, beneficiaries, probates, and trust funds," and that he was "a recovering alcoholic, substance-dependent, and in need of the Lord's blessing." He even tossed in one of James's favorite expressions: "I am not afraid of what's in front of me, but I am very afraid of what I cannot see."

As an orator, Robert Gomez was a natural. He had flair, an immense smile, a strong voice, and he waved his arms dramatically as he spoke. He sounded a little like the Reverend Houston Buggs, in fact. The congregation was charmed. They put him on what they called "watch care" and prayed for his health, for his well-being, for his success in the business travails ahead. When Robert sat down, he turned to James and smiled. He said, "I'm not sure that ol' Buggs was too thrilled with that," and James agreed. After all, Robert was not officially a church member. His appearance in the discipleship pulpit was borderline inappropriate. But various congregants patted him on the back, fussed over him, promised to support him in his hour of need. Robert basked in the attention, then, as services continued, began working on a crossword puzzle.

Rose was confused. She'd never seen Robert abuse alcohol or drugs, nor had she known him to attend a single AA meeting. She had never heard him so much as casually mention liquor in even the subtlest context. No one had. Not her husband, not anyone in the whole congregation. On the other hand,

Robert remained an enigma. Nobody knew a thing about his mother, who supposedly lived in Bell, or about his earlier life with his brother and two sisters. Apart from James, Robert apparently had no friends at all, yet he was one of the happiest, most affable kids Rose had ever met, with bright prospects and funny stories and an engaging laugh and a white-hot ambition for fame.

After the sermon, a friend close to the Nichols family, who lived in nearby Rancho Dominguez, remembered telling her husband that Robert Gomez "sure didn't sound like a Hispanic kid from the barrio," that he sounded "more like a talk-show host." Her husband replied, "You talk to *James* recently?" When she asked what he meant, he explained, "If you only knew him from phone conversations, you'd swear he was a white stock-broker."

When Robert returned to the Kemp Avenue house, he sought out Rose. "He told me at first he was the sole heir to his father's estate," she recalled. "Then later he said he and *James* and Howard Gaines were the recipients of his dad's estate." For Rose, this was a shocker. Her son would be inheriting money? "But there were stipulations, apparently, that Robert and James might have to go to college." Rose liked the sound of that and asked James if he'd given thought to any particular school. He admitted he had, somehow sidestepping his lifelong ambition to become an L.A. cop. He told her that Hollywood Community College sounded quite appealing.

James, however, did not send away for course descriptions or entrance requirements. Instead, he drove over to Kinko's and had letterhead printed up. Each page bore the address of his family's happy home on Kemp Avenue. At the top appeared the inscription "James R. Nichols Private Investing." He liked the sound of that. So he had Kinko's print up a second batch. That one said, "Nichols Investments and Securities." That sounded even better.

Throughout 1996, attorneys Shawn Houston, Howard Gaines, and Vince McNeil never showed themselves but continued to phone at random intervals, often at odd hours. James would speak to them. He reported no major developments, only that they were continuing to inquire about Robert. How was he doing in the wake of John Bowers's death? Was he drinking or abusing drugs? The attorneys reminded James that an executor of Bowers's estate would soon need to be appointed, and that it would be quite a big deal.

Robert and James sat down with Rose. Robert wasn't his usual clownish, glib self. He said: "I have a lot on my shoulders. My father died still having contracts with people. The board at Gruma Corporation might try to force me out because I'm so young and inexperienced." It looked like he might cry. Rose asked if Bowers had left a will. Robert was quick to assure her that he had and that it was a whopper, with so many stipulations and covenants and tax dodges that all three lawyers would have their hands full for at least a year, maybe longer. After all, the estate was valued at $411 million, and property was scattered from New York to Los Angeles. Robert turned to Rose and asked, "Would you mind serving as the executrix?"

Rose squirmed. Robert certainly appeared to need help, but all of this was overwhelming. She didn't really know what the executor of a will did. She wondered if she would answer to Gruma Corporation, to Mission Foods, to the three attorneys, or to Robert Gomez. She had never heard the phrase "letters testamentary," had never taken any law or accounting courses. She asked her son what he thought of the idea.

James replied, "I don't know anything about it"—a funny thing to say, because James had become as much a conduit of

Bowers information as Robert. Yet Rose knew from his tone that he was discouraging her.

Rose declined, but it was tempting. Over and over, she'd catch herself getting caught up in this Bowers saga, which she'd now heard about for more than two years. It was somehow thrilling and a little scary, all this talk of corporate empires and powerful businessmen who were wheeling and dealing in the shadows. But she was too old for this, still had a household to run, still had teenage children who required a firm hand, still had a church that relied on her, even after four decades of faithful service.

Robert abandoned the topic for a while. So did James. They worked grudgingly at their minimum-wage jobs. Then an unexpected thing happened. About a month before Christmas in 1997, James stood at Christ Christian Home Missionary Baptist Church and said, in his most solemn and sincere Barry White basso profundo, "I'd like to introduce you to the heir of the Bowers estate."

The congregants looked at one another. Bowers? Who the heck was Bowers?

That's when Robert Gomez again climbed into the discipleship pulpit. The Reverend Houston Buggs frowned, but before he could do anything about it, Robert was speaking. "Around holiday time is gift-giving time," he said, "and I love to help people who are less blessed, less fortunate than me. I've been advised by my late father's estate attorneys that we should give away some things—some toys, some cash. And, you know, there were automobiles in his estate that we want to give to certain members of the congregation. They're like runabout cars, but there are also some executive cars and some vans."

Rose was bewildered. Give away some cars? To whom? Robert didn't have two pennies to rub together, and now he's giving away inherited automobiles? Rose considered herself "a witness to the congregation." As such, she was obliged to make a record of the church's promises to its members or to the community. She began writing down what Robert was saying.

"And these gifts from the estate go especially to the less fortunate, to single parents, for instance," Robert continued. "Mr. John Bowers, my father, was a hard and shrewd businessman, but he was a Christian, too. That's why he helped me. And it was his intention, always, that items from his estate go to Christian men and women who need help in their lives, just like I did, who want some sort of miracle to demonstrate that God is watching and that He cares. A miracle in your life, now and then, reminds all of us to remain faithful to His teachings."

Robert was beginning to preach. The Reverend Houston Buggs shifted from foot to foot. Weeks earlier, Buggs had tactfully reminded Gomez that it was inappropriate for a nonmember to address the congregation. Now here he was, bald-headed Robert, a boy who was raised a Catholic and worked on his word jumbles during the sermon, suggesting to Buggs's flock what God specifically intended by His miracles.

Gomez knew he was skating on thin ice. He later told James, "I thought Buggs was gonna turn off my microphone."

Rose continued to take notes and occasionally glance at her son, who looked a little nervous himself.

And that's when Gomez concluded his little speech with an oratorical hand grenade. He said: "And those of us working for the estate also pledge a monetary gift to the Reverend Houston Buggs. When the estate is closed, we intend to donate $100,000."

Rose dropped her pen.

The church echoed with gasps and cries of "Praise the Lord!" and "Hallelujah!" The Reverend Buggs had trouble restoring order. He gave Gomez a black look, like a slap across the face—a funny reaction from a man who'd just been promised $100,000. Gomez sat down, again soaking up the attention. Everyone was smiling at him and flashing the thumbs-up. He smiled and waved back.

After church let out, James and Robert disappeared like a shot, so the congregants swarmed Rose, whom they knew far better than Robert anyhow. Rose had not been known to utter a falsehood in four decades. "What kind of cars?" church members asked her. "Who, exactly, qualifies for a miracle? When will the cars be delivered? Are they in good condition? Can you get leather seats?" One church member later described the scene in the parking lot as "a kind of small riot."

Rose explained that she didn't know more than about three details of the Bowers estate, despite having heard Robert and James talk about it, on and off, for nearly thirty-seven months.

"This has been coming for *three years* and you didn't say anything?" asked a friend named Dorothy Bell.

Until that day, Rose hadn't heard a single word uttered about any cars in the estate. But she promised to sit down with Robert and find out what she could.

More than a few families within Christ Christian Home Missionary Baptist Church were represented by four generations— great-grandchildren were running around in Sunday school. Virtually everyone was on a first-name basis. They knew one another's phone numbers, too, and weren't afraid to call in moments of crisis or celebration. This development was the latter. That night, the phone lines sizzled. Church members called friends and relatives, some of them halfway across the country, to describe the vehicular miracle apparently about to befall them.

"That's when the Nichols family began adoring me," Gomez recalled. "I mean, I'm the long-lost son or something. They couldn't get enough of me."

Dorothy Bell's husband told her that the whole thing sounded like a crock. No one gave away cars, he pointed out.

Dorothy disagreed. "I don't think that two teenage boys have the patience or maturity to think up a story that takes three years to enact," she replied. Her husband thought back to when he was nineteen. She was right.

Not long after Robert Gomez's "I Give You Riches" speech from the pulpit—on another Sunday morning, in fact—he sat down with Rose to answer her questions. "He said there were sixteen vehicles, personal vehicles of his father's estate," she recalled. "They were intended for myself, my siblings, and the church family. Robert said, 'All we're asking is that each person pay for the tax and licensing of each vehicle.' That ranged from $1,000 to $1,100, depending on the car."

Gomez went on to explain that the three estate lawyers would be happy to flush these automobiles out of the John Bowers estate, that they represented a huge tax liability and were a pain in the neck to dispose of. The lawyers were busy with the meat and potatoes of the $411 million estate and didn't have time to flog the penny-ante stuff, didn't want IRS agents suggesting the automobiles might inflate the estate's taxable value. Rose didn't know anything about taxable values and wasn't sure Robert did, either.

"I know you declined to be the executrix," Robert continued, "but would you act as a representative of my father's estate in the selling of these sixteen cars alone?"

Rose was a deaconess at Christ Christian Home Missionary Baptist Church, and one of her duties was to teach newcomers that "there is goodness in everyone, and you should reach out to people to help them when they ask for help." It had been her daily mantra for forty years. Robert's complaints about alcohol dependency worked on those beliefs. When he asked directly for assistance— not for his alcoholism, but for "administrative duties pertaining to the Bowers estate"—Rose rushed to his rescue.

From the pocket of his khaki pants, Robert withdrew a hand-written list of the sixteen available autos. It was a scrawled mess, almost illegible. There was no description to speak of. There were no vehicle identification numbers (VINs), no engine or transmission types, no exterior or interior colors. The cars were simply listed as "1997 Toyota Camry ($1,100), 1996 Dodge pickup truck ($1,000), 1997 Ford Windstar van ($1,100), 1996 Dodge Aries sedan ($1,000)," and so forth. It was peculiar that a 1996 Dodge Aries was being offered for sale—1989 had been that model's last year of production. Exactly no one noticed.

Robert handed the list to Rose. He told her that the cars would be delivered "in just a matter of months, late fall, or by the end of the year [1997]." No matter what, he warned, "It won't be until the estate clears probate, whenever that is."

"He said the cars could go to my siblings, to church members, but not to my children," Rose recalled. She didn't waste any time. Rose phoned nine of her brothers and sisters, as well as three church members, but only after receiving permission from the Reverend Houston Buggs. She considered it a matter of protocol. Rose's sister Gladys Milligan, who lived in Carson only a block away, immediately bought a car for $1,000. Another sister, Johnnie Meyers, signed on for two. A fellow church member told Rose, "I cannot afford it, but I need a car, and will you speak with three of my daughters?" Rose did. The daughters quickly amassed $1,100 for their impoverished mother, then signed her up for a 1996 Lincoln Town Car. The woman was ecstatic.

Within forty-eight hours, Rose's phone was ringing off the hook. Some of the callers demanded in-depth descriptions of the cars—which Rose didn't have—only to be scared off by the demand for payment up front. Some of the callers were total strangers, folks who'd heard about the deal through distant relatives who belonged to the church. One was from Nevada, another from

Mississippi. To the strangers, Rose would always say: "You do not know me, and I do not know you. So pray about it. And then if you feel that God wants you to have a car, call me back."

One such caller, apparently a fast prayer, called back in ten minutes.

In one case, Rose was faced with collecting money from an out-of-stater. She knew nothing about the buyer and asked James what to do. He was adamant about how to proceed. "From here on out," he instructed, "get a postal money order or a cashier's check for every car, nothing else." He said the three lawyers had already warned that personal checks would just bog down the estate as it inched its way through probate. Buyers were to remit their cashier's checks to Rosetta Nichols. Then a close friend of the Nichols family showed up at the front door, declaring, "I want to buy one of the miracle cars." The woman paid in cash.

That's when Rose began writing out receipts. She began keeping meticulous records of who bought what, when, and for how much. The boys hadn't told her to do that. She just knew it was proper in the face of so much incoming money. In a week, she had sold all sixteen cars. She cashed the checks and handed a sum just shy of $17,000 to Robert. Her son told her, "The money will be held in a noninterest-bearing escrow account, where all liquidated items from the estate are automatically funneled." Robert personally thanked Rose for keeping careful records, telling her that the lawyers would be impressed.

A couple of weeks passed, then Robert arranged another sit-down. He had shocking news, he said, and he wanted Rose to hear it first. "There are more cars," he revealed. "There is a corporate will involved in this situation. The cars aren't just John Bowers's personal cars. There are also cars that employees of Mission Foods were driving that are now also part of the package.

They're all late-model cars, around ten thousand miles, really well maintained, like brand-new."

"There are more than the sixteen I just sold?" Rose asked.

"Yes," said Robert.

"How many more?"

"Hundreds," he said. "Hundreds."

In a flash, Rose grasped what this meant. If she were selling hundreds of cars, she'd be dealing with vast sums of money, and vast sums of money inevitably led to vast disputes. People were people. Money often separated them.

Gomez sensed her resistance. He said, "I want you to understand something about these cars, and I can't say this often enough or emphasize it strongly enough. Anybody who buys a car, if he later gets cold feet and wants out, then that person gets a full refund immediately, *no questions asked*." He paused to let that sink in. "These cars are intended for Christians who want a miracle in their life, and if they can't wait for the miracle to happen, well, we'll give that miracle to someone more deserving." As before, these newly unearthed cars were to be delivered at the end of the year, or whenever probate was completed.

Robert added that if Rose continued to sell cars, she would now be handing the proceeds not to him but to her son, and that if a buyer should require a refund, at any time and for any reason, then she should acquire the cash for that refund from James. "It's improper for the heir of the estate to be handling funds himself," Robert explained. "And, of course, I can *never* be perceived as selling cars myself. The lawyers would go nuts. It would be a disaster."

That was a relief to Rose. She felt far more comfortable directing the proceeds to her son than to someone who'd recently confessed to having been kicked out of his own home for alcoholism, a kid with weird tattoos on his arms. But she still had reservations. What about the earlier buyers who'd demanded more details than she could supply? "I'll need more information, VINs and such, because I don't know what to tell these people," Rose said.

"Tell them *nothing*," Robert blurted. He seemed almost personally offended that buyers would be so nosy. "The judge in this case, Judge Jack Lomeli, has put a gag order on everything pertaining to the estate," he explained. "The judge was having the same problem—you know, strangers calling with a million dumb questions—and it was hindering the process, and he had to yell at the attorneys about it."

A gag order? Wasn't the purpose of probate to bring matters to light?

Rose thought about it. She had no burning desire to become a car salesman, but it was a thrilling experience to bequeath these miracle cars to persons she loved and to needy members of the church, folks who'd never owned anything but ten-year-old rust-riddled clunkers. It made them so happy. What's more, the first batch of cars had practically sold themselves. It wasn't as if she'd had to arrange test-drives or financing, and strong-arm sales tactics certainly hadn't been necessary. Moreover, her phone was still ringing. Buyers were still calling even after the first sixteen cars had been snapped up. Half of them wanted to buy a second or third car.

Rose said she'd do it, but she warned that she was inexperienced and that she was merely a volunteer. She might quit if the work became burdensome. Robert eagerly supplied a new list of cars. This list was a lot longer, and the variety had improved. She noticed some of the prices had risen, too. The $1,000 cars included Jeep Cherokees, Ford Tauruses, Honda Accords, and Buick Park Avenues. The $2,000 cars included Jaguar sedans, Mercedes-Benz E320s, Buick Rivieras, and Lincoln Continentals. The latter had been driven by fat-cat executives of Gruma Corporation, Robert said. They were very snazzy.

Sales didn't so much continue as explode. Every time she picked up her phone, Rose heard the same question: "Do you have any cars left?" She set up a small office in her bedroom, where she filed her sales records and receipts. What this meant was that car-sales proceeds flowed into the Kemp Avenue bedroom/office of Rose Nichols and then traveled fifteen feet to the Kemp Avenue bedroom/office of James Nichols.

It was a quick and efficient transfer. Donald Trump would have been impressed.

This time is wasn't Rose who was surprised. This time it was the boys.

Buyers weren't interested in reserving one or two cars. They were interested in reserving five, six, a *dozen*. Sometimes they were buying for friends and relatives. Sometimes they were buying cars they hoped to resell at a profit.

Elijah Buggs, the brother of the Reverend Houston Buggs, was seventy years old when he first heard about Gomez's little speech from the pulpit. Elijah had toiled thirty-five years in the engineering shop of McDonnell Douglas, then had retired to a tiny beige stucco house in Long Beach, where he lived reclusively with his wife, Rubye, amid an armada of seventies-era smoked mirrors and Levitz furniture. Like his brother Houston, Elijah was known as a gentle man, soft-spoken, modest, and uneasy in the company of strangers.

"Rose Nichols was like a secretary in the church," Elijah said. "My brother, Houston, depended on her. So when she began to sell cars, I didn't need to ask anybody if the seller was legitimate. I invested right off the bat. I bought two Jaguars at $2,000 apiece, one Lincoln Town Car for $2,000, and one truck with a boat attached for the same amount. That's what it said on the list. 'One truck with a boat attached.' So that was $8,000. But then my friends began asking, 'Can you get a car for me, too?' So I said, 'Get your money together, I'll see what I can do.' So that second investment included Town Cars, Cherokees, Accords, a Caddy, an Expedition, and—don't laugh at this—an eighteen-wheeler. Rose couldn't tell me if it was a trailer or a tractor or both. Just an eighteen-wheeler. And that investment came to $30,000. I gave the money to Rose, at her house. James said the cars would be delivered in December of '97. But that date came and went, and then they said it had been postponed to March of '98. So, I waited."

Gladys Milligan was Rose Nichols's sister and lived only a block from Kemp Avenue. She had a round face and an endearing grin. Like Elijah Buggs, Gladys came back for seconds, and she didn't stint. In total, she bought $30,800 worth of cars. She was at Rose's house often and on one occasion ran into Robert Gomez. There was a car on the list she particularly desired, a $2,000 car. "Well," Robert told her, "you could give the money directly to me, but I can only take cash, because I don't have a driver's license, so I can't cash checks."

A little later, Gladys got a phone call at home from an attorney saying he was Shawn Houston. "He said to me, 'You know, we're gonna need a little extra money to pay for the cars you ordered.'" Gladys stiffened. She said: "No, a deal is a deal, and if extra money is required, then I want out. I want a refund for the whole works." The man on the phone suddenly reversed course. "No, no, don't do that," he said. "We'll leave it like it is."

Rose had begun to refer to the cars alternately as "the blessings" or "the miracle cars." In short order, Dorothy Bell, forty-four, a friend of the Nichols family's for fifteen years, called to inquire. She had known James for eight years and enjoyed listening to him play the drums in church. "I watched him grow up," she said. "So I trusted him, and I trusted any person he would introduce as his friend. I got some cash together, and so did some of my friends, and we put in around $20,000 for Expeditions, Camrys, all different kinds. On two occasions, I gave cash directly to James. He said he was like the assistant to Robert, but he was in control of car delivery."

Rose loved and trusted Dorothy Bell. And Dorothy was so enthusiastic about the "blessings" that Rose had an idea. She asked Dorothy if she'd like to become a "Miracle Cars team captain." That title, she said, would empower Dorothy to sell cars, either in conjunction with Rose, from the little Kemp Avenue office, or from her own home. Dorothy jumped at the chance. She began selling cars right away.

Two months later, Dorothy Bell's phone rang at eleven P.M. It was Robert. He said, "Hey, I was wondering if you sold any cars today. If so, can I drive over right now and pick up the cash?" He didn't mention a dollar amount, if he had one in mind. Dorothy reminded him that her conduit for checks and money orders was Rose Nichols, and team captains—of which there were now several —reported only to Rose. Robert seemed disappointed but did not pursue the matter, and Dorothy went back to sleep.

Even with all her newfound help, Rose's phone rang almost continuously. Each day, she'd stop answering it at four P.M. to complete paperwork and catch her breath. She cashed the incoming checks and money orders, then handed the money to James, who handed it to Robert. Sales were booming. Whenever Rose sold all the cars on one list, James or Robert would deliver another.

In December of 1997, Robert quit attending Christ Christian Home Missionary Baptist Church. "It became too unpleasant," he explained. "People there thought I was a millionaire or something. They were always trying to borrow money from me, asking for things, telling me their problems. Anyway, Reverend Buggs told me to stop coming, that he didn't want me. I said: 'Hey, man, talk to James about this estate stuff, not me. He's the one who brought it up. I don't need your church. I'm not a member. I'm Catholic, remember? I'm outta here.' When I told James, he just said, 'Don't worry about it, just go with the flow.' "

After his conversation with Buggs, Robert drove back to Kemp Avenue and explained everything to Rose. She hoped that Robert hadn't done something to offend the reverend. But she knew in her heart that Robert was a fish out of water in that church anyway.

Robert had one more piece of news to deliver. "I've reconciled with my mother, who's moving back to Bogotá, Colombia," he said. "So before she goes, I'm moving back home. Thanks for putting up with me, I know I've been a nuisance." Then he flashed his big goofy bald-headed smile and his eyes welled with tears.

But Robert didn't move back home. He moved into a hotel.

James had some news himself. At the end of 1997, he told his mother he'd abandoned the idea of attending Hollywood Community College and was instead again conditioning himself for the LAPD. What's more, he added, he couldn't stand all the hustle and bustle of the Kemp Avenue house. The phones and the doorbell were driving him crazy and he needed some rest. So James moved out, too. Also to a hotel.

James still showed up every morning to work in his little bedroom office, and he was conscientious about helping his mother process incoming orders. But Rose needed even more help, so she began recruiting more Miracle Car team captains, most from her church. They all agreed to meet regularly at a hotel in Compton to discuss sales. At those meetings, James and Robert usually attended, acting like cheerleaders. Rose did not question why Robert wasn't in Bogotá, helping his mother.

"The boys would tell us to be patient, that they were finding more and more things in the Bowers estate, and that's why car delivery was taking so long," remembered Dorothy Bell. "They said the cars were being registered and smog-tested. James told me, 'I'm paying a lot of money for storage of the estate vehicles.' And, during one of those meetings, James walked up to me and said: 'I've just been over to look at the cars. I have the perfect car picked out for you, Dottie.' When I told my husband, he's like, 'You're *sure* you believe all this?' I said: 'Come on, think about it for a sec. If you were going to run a scam, who'd hire his mother as the general sales manager?' He said, 'Well, yeah, you've got a point.' "

5

THE GAMBLING LIFE

By the spring of 1998, Robert Gomez wasn't at just any hotel. He was comfortably ensconced at the Crystal Park Hotel in Compton, which had the benefit of being attached to the Crystal Park Casino. He was working only a few hours per week as a security guard, earning as little as $700 per month. "I was taking my security-guard paycheck in there to try to turn it into $2,000," he said. "I wanted to be a gambler, but I was still learning."

He worked hard at it. When he could manage it, his regimen was to awake at five P.M., eat "breakfast," and be inside the casino by eight P.M. Then he'd gamble until five A.M., eat "dinner," watch the morning news on TV, and crawl into bed by eight A.M. "Eventually, I started doing pretty good, winning more than I was losing. So I said to myself, Why work at a real job when I can do this? And when I really *did* have $2,000 in my pocket, I thought, Wow, I'm a wealthy man, I've arrived!"

One night in May, Robert strolled into the Dragon Room of the Bicycle Casino in Bell Gardens. "I was playing poker with this little old lady, and I beat her bad. I was trying to soothe her, make her feel better, so I told her I was just lucky. She said: 'Yes, you *are* lucky. You're lucky like Buddha. You *look* like Buddha, too.' We both laughed. My shaved head, my big stomach. I liked that name, being into karma and all. After that, when I met people who'd ask my name, I'd tell them, 'Buddha.' It really stuck."

A Bicycle Casino employee named Robert Turner, a thirty-six-year veteran of gaming houses nationwide, remembered meeting Gomez: "He told me he had an uncle who'd come into a large amount of money from winnings in Las Vegas, and his uncle wanted him to take the money and gamble in California, to make some profits. Right away, that didn't make sense to me. No gambler would choose California over Vegas. When you're in California, you have to pay collection fees to the casino."

Gomez didn't seem to show great talent at the conventional poker games, but he quickly proved adept at an Asian version called "pai gow." In pai gow poker, the card rankings are familiar, but seven cards are dealt. A player's five-card hand is called the back hand, and his two-card hand is called the front hand. Those two hands are compared with the dealer's. If both of the player's hands beat both of the dealer's, it's a winner. If only one hand beats another, it's a tie. That's why the casinos like the game so much—every tie initiates another round of play, and every round of play produces a "collection"—a fee that the casino charges to cover the dealer's salary and to maintain the premises. Gomez would play so many hands, so quickly, and for so much money that a casino could sometimes take thousands from him in collection fees alone. *Day after day.*

California card parlors are unique in that they can't bank games. The casino provides a dealer, but customers don't wager against the "house." The house makes its money by charging a small fee for every bet. Customers actually gamble against a lone third-party banker who is invited to the table, generally seated in the first seat. He wears a badge, carries a license, and represents someone else's financial interests. The biggest third-party banker in California is called Network M. Such outfits make money because they play the sober statistics—they hit when they're supposed to hit and stand when they're supposed to stand. Customers, on the other hand, drink alcohol, distract one another, and play hunches. As a result, the third-party bankers possess at least a 1 to 2 percent advantage. It's usually just a matter of outlasting every player who comes along.

Gomez, though, actually *was* more skillful than the average player. He reckoned that his flair for pai gow was a consequence of doing so many crossword puzzles and word jumbles. "If you rearrange the letters in a word, I can usually see how to reconstruct it right away," he said. "It was the same with the cards. I'd glance at a hand, and my mind would instantly see the cards' value and what order they should be in."

Turner had never seen anyone like Robert Gomez. For one thing, he was so incredibly quick to set his hands that the dealers often couldn't keep up, and he'd sometimes play three, four, five hands simultaneously. "What was strange," said Turner, "was that he'd be talking to you in a calm, professional manner one minute, and the next he'd be yelling. Sometimes spitting. And his method of gambling made no sense to me. He had what's known as a 'big heart,' the term for a guy who places a hundred-dollar bet and, when he wins, automatically takes that two hundred dollars and bets it again, and so on, and so on. But even gamblers with big hearts know when to walk away. Not Gomez. He'd play with such large amounts, and in such a careless and nonsensical manner, that I immediately knew two things. First, he wasn't a professional. Second, he was playing with someone else's money."

If there was one thing the third-party bankers adored, it was a reckless gambler. They followed Gomez like a gaggle of groupies. They urged him to call before he gambled, and they'd meet him at whatever casino he fancied. "They'd lay on food and drinks and concert tickets and be ready to suck up to him," Turner remembered. "Then the guy wouldn't show. Or he'd show up hours later and walk in laughing. He'd make everybody wait. You could tell he loved it, because it made him feel in control."

One night that spring, Gomez walked into the Bicycle Casino and used cash to purchase $20,000 worth of chips. The cage manager handed over the chips, then asked for his address. Gomez balked. "My address?" he asked. "What for?"

"Gotta file a CTR," responded the cage manager.

"A what?"

"A cash-transaction report. It goes to the IRS. We have to file it for any cash transaction over $10,000 during a twenty-four-hour period."

Robert gave the manager his mother's address in Bell, even though he wasn't living there. When asked his occupation, he replied, "Computer technician," then corrected himself, saying, "Retail sales." He had a poleaxed expression on his face. The IRS? That didn't sound good. That sounded like trouble.

Robert thought about it, then came up with a plan. He immediately cut up his credit cards. He closed his bank accounts. He threw away his remaining blank checks. He opened player accounts at the casinos—if you kept some money there, the casinos would act like a bank and would even cash checks. What's more, the casinos offered safe-deposit boxes, which Robert now selected as his "official bank." He didn't have to worry about a house or a condo in his name—he was living in a hotel. He resolved that, whenever he purchased anything henceforth, it would be with cash. And if an item came with a warranty that required a name or address, he wrote down the Kemp Avenue address and Rose Nichols's phone number. Robert wanted his name to disappear from all documents. Shortly thereafter, in fact, he was shopping in a store that sold posters of celebrity athletes. After he made his purchase, the clerk, Pauline Oliva, asked for Robert's particulars so she could put him on a mailing list. Robert replied, "James R. Nichols, Kemp Avenue, Carson." It surprised the tar out of Oliva, whose best friend, by coincidence, was dating a guy named James R. Nichols. She *knew* James. James was black, not brown.

Robert didn't care. He had officially begun his career as a professional gambler. He was remaking himself as *Buddha,* not pudgy little Robert "Bobby" Gomez. He didn't need that persona any longer, didn't need a label drawing attention to his modest Mexican heritage. He had a steady income, he had a profession, and he didn't need to share a cramped bedroom with *anybody* anymore. Buddha was now in charge. Buddha liked to sound like a businessman. Buddha liked *living large.* That month in the hotel, Buddha racked up a $1,200 bill. Not for the room, but for movies alone.

As 1998 began, car sales were booming. It seemed as though every member of Christ Christian Home Missionary Baptist Church who wanted a car had already purchased one. And now members of other churches in L.A. were buying. A Baptist churchgoer as far away as Chicago was buying. There seemed no end to it. The nation's reverends and pastors apparently subscribed to some sort of underground intelligence network that kept them all in touch.

Rose was cashing money orders and cashier's checks like crazy. She handed the cash to James or Robert, whoever was the first to drop by. Although she kept meticulous records of who had purchased what, Rose never asked Robert or her son for a receipt when they accepted money. And the sums were wondrous. It wasn't unusual for her to hand James $30,000 toward the end of the week, after the mail had begun to pile up.

Rose studied her ledgers. She had sold three hundred cars. Then she added up the proceeds. It was close to *one million dollars.* Never in her wildest dreams had she imagined that a black girl from Jackson, Mississippi, would one day handle $1 million in cash. Yet she had. The money had passed right through her own hands and was now, well, somewhere. Robert said it was going to a noninterest-bearing account at Chase Manhattan Bank. She had no reason to doubt him.

Unfortunately, the March 1998 date for delivery of the cars came and went. Several buyers were getting antsy. Robert explained that the lawyers were still finding property John Bowers had owned and "were handling Mr. Bowers's breach of contracts upon his death." It was a mess. Even Probate Judge Jack Lomeli, he said, was becoming testy. There had been occasional blowups in court. What's more, probate had been hugely delayed when proceedings were bodily moved from a court in New York City to a court in Santa Monica. So many lawyers were involved that Robert said it resembled a bar association convention.

One buyer who was becoming impatient was the Reverend Houston Buggs's brother, Elijah. He attended one of the team captains' meetings in Compton. "Robert was there," he remembered, "and he said June 15 was the new target date. He said some of the out-of-state people were already getting their cars—some in Florida, in fact. So I actually began to worry about it, because I'd ordered so many cars, how was I gonna get them all home? I asked whether I should rent a van or something to take a bunch of drivers to get my cars. They said, 'You know, that's a good idea, 'cause if you don't collect them, there's a forty-five-dollar-per-day storage fee.' Then James told me he'd already gone to court to complain about the delays and had been so outspoken that he'd been held in contempt, that he got a ten-thousand-dollar fine from the judge. He told me I could have my money back, no problem, but if I dropped out now, I couldn't come back later and reinvest at the original rates."

Buggs's wife, Rubye, met Robert Gomez that day. She told her husband, "He sure doesn't *look* like a millionaire."

To placate buyers, Robert Gomez rented a small helicopter. He installed Rose's brother-in-law in one of the two passenger seats, and they flew over the San Fernando Valley. At one point, Robert looked down at a lot filled with automobiles. He blurted: "Those are the estate cars! Some of them, anyway." Elijah Buggs asked for the same helicopter ride. He wanted to see this miracle with his own eyes. But Robert replied, "Maybe later," and the airborne stunt was never repeated.

The June delivery date came and went. Buggs hung on, however. He felt better after James told him: "Your cars are in a Beverly Hills lot, and it's right next to a Department of Motor Vehicles office. If you'll stay patient, we'll pay the registration fees ourselves, to make up for the delays." Buggs knew it would save him a lot of money. He agreed to wait.

But other buyers were less submissive. One, in fact, really blew his stack. He went looking for Gomez and found him in the Bicycle Casino, in Bell Gardens. "He says to me, 'I want my ten thousand dollars back,' " Gomez recalled. "I said, 'Look, man, you gotta talk to Rose and James, not me.' Then he threatened me. So we got into this big fight, shoving and yelling. I got into trouble with the casino for that, creating a scene. But I was worth about ninety-five hundred dollars then, and I sure didn't have ten grand to give to this jerk. He went back to James and got his money, not a problem. But I was pissed, because James had told him where to find me. It wasn't very businesslike. We had words over that."

By September 1998, "Million Dollar Rose" was nearly spent. She was working ten-hour days, then cooking and cleaning and trying to maintain the household. She wanted out. That's when

Robert showed up one afternoon with a manila folder tucked under one arm. He sat down and declared, "I want James to be the executor of my will." Then he displayed the "Last Will and Testament of Robert Gomez."

It was an exceedingly odd document. For starters, it was handwritten, which seemed inappropriate for the heir to a $411 million estate, a man in touch with New York lawyers almost daily. Robert had written his biological father's name as Fidel Gomez and his mother's as Mercedes Medina. Then he wrote his own full name as Robert Bowers Gomez. If he'd been adopted, his name should have read, Robert Gomez Bowers. But perhaps it didn't matter—there was nothing in the will to indicate he was adopted anyway. Asked to list the location of the will, Robert had written, "Shawn Houston, attorney at law, New York." And he had stipulated that the occupation of his multimillionaire adoptive father was "longshoreman." Then he had written, "I, Robert Gomez, declare James Nichols as executor of my estate and that he alone, with both my godmothers, Rosetta Nichols and Benita Petty [a close friend of the Nichols family], execute my estate." He went on to decree that 75 percent of his property and assets be left in control of his executor, James, and two godmothers, and that various members of Christ Christian Home Missionary Baptist Church "be offered an amount of living expenses for the remainder of their lives." Beyond that, he wrote, "All promises to [the church] shall be honored in full." These promises included cash and cars, but the details were only to be found in "a cash box in Chase Manhattan Bank, New York, New York." Robert Gomez signed his own will and listed his address as Kemp Avenue, Carson, California.

The document was drawn on an E-Z Legal Form—the sort of form available at bookstores and office-supply outlets for $1.99.

James signed the will, but recalled that Robert seemed

dispirited that day. James described him as "being in one of his shambles" about having to contemplate his own death. "Of course, Robert was *always* having one of those tear-jerking moments," he said, "whether it was his mother sick with brain cancer, or his feelings had been hurt because people were using him because he was rich, or he missed his father." When Robert was in one of his shambles, he'd talk even faster than usual. Words would gush a mile a minute, topics would come and go at breakneck speed, and there'd be pernicious accusations followed by saccharine self-pity followed by colorful cursing followed by tears. But it would all blow over in five minutes.

James was now executor. Robert said: "Congratulations, you're on your way. I can't do it without you. Before you know it, you'll get what you deserve financially." James described his job duties as "handling all the refunds, making sure all the records were straight, and explaining every detail of the estate to whoever inquired." It was also his job "to give accurate figures of all sales and bank accounts [of which there were then none] for Robert to forward to Howard Gaines and Shawn Houston." Left unstated was the most important duty of all: James was in charge of selling cars.

Robert let it be known that he had been in discussion with attorneys Gaines and Houston, who had agreed to pay James $5,000 per month for his trouble. He was to pay himself that salary directly out of car-sales proceeds. James was now a professional executor. He went to a men's clothing store and bought several custom-cut dark sport coats, long-sleeved dress shirts—mostly black—and a variety of tailored slacks that fit his muscled frame to perfection. He also bought a box of Cohiba Coronas that he installed in a small humidor. Wearing his tortoiseshell Foster Grants, he resembled a cultured and worldly celebrity. He looked like a million bucks.

Although the boys now possessed a will for Robert Gomez,

what they did not possess was a will for John Bowers. It didn't seem to matter. James and Robert both went on to use the E-Z Legal Form, with its less-than-highfalutin legal language, in their representations of what was contained in the Bowers will. The two wills became one.

Not one single soul ever objected.

6

NATIONAL FINDERS

In November of 1998, Robert flew to Las Vegas to try his luck at a few new casinos. Vegas didn't seem as much fun as the California card parlors, however. For one thing, the Nevada dealers didn't smile when he announced his nickname, didn't seem to know he was a pro, didn't treat him like a VIP. Robert played halfheartedly for a day. Then he cheered himself up by walking over to Signature Lincoln Mercury on East Sahara Avenue, where he purchased a Lincoln Town Car. The salesman asked how he wanted to finance the vehicle. Robert wasn't sure. He reached into his pockets and said, "Well, for starters, I've got $23,300 on me." He climbed into his new car and drove home to L.A.

Robert had enjoyed his helicopter ride over the San Fernando Valley. On weekends, he began hiring a helicopter to fly him to Catalina Island. He said island life helped him relax, and, in any event, he wasn't fond of the casinos on Saturdays, because they tended to fill with rubes and sodbusters and tourists laying down two-dollar bets. The gamblers called such riffraff the "stationary targets."

All was not perfect in paradise, however. Although Rose Nichols had stopped selling cars, some of her buyers—especially in the church—were now calling to ask for refunds. Many were impoverished and couldn't lay out two or three grand for six months, much less a whole year. Household emergencies had arisen. Both James and Robert had become tardy about supplying refund checks. Robert explained, "The trustees of the estate only give permission from time to time to release money." Refunds that had previously taken ten days now took forty-five. It put Rose in an embarrassing spot. These were the people she most respected in life. She had sold cars that hadn't been delivered when promised, and now she felt responsible for making things right. Some of the gossipy women in the church had even begun wondering aloud if Rose might be running some sort of scam. Apart from her kids, no thing in Rose's life was more important than her church. As a result, she and her husband took out a $59,000 home equity loan on the Kemp Avenue property. On the same day the bank released the funds, Rose distributed it—every last nickel—to buyers clamoring for refunds.

Although James was supposedly the executor of a large estate, was selling cars and had ready access to cash, he did nothing to assist his mother in her hour of financial need. Instead, Robert showed up. "I've talked to Shawn Houston," he told Rose, "but we can't repay you until the estate closes." He didn't know when that would be. Not soon, anyway.

Rose said she would wait, but she felt miserable. She'd sold $1 million worth of cars and didn't have a penny to show for it. Now her house was in hock. She was beginning to go sour on the whole Miracle Cars adventure. What she needed was a minor miracle herself. And that's exactly what arrived.

At six A.M., the phone rang, waking Rose in her bedroom. The caller was a woman who said: "You don't know me, but I overheard a conversation with your niece, Peggy Bracey, about purchasing a 1998 Grand Cherokee. And I'm calling to see if you have any more cars. I'd like to buy a Jaguar." Rose was initially depressed. It was just another buyer, and she had definitely retired as a car salesman. On the other hand, this caller was especially kind, complimenting Rose "for helping God's people," and she explained how she'd already shared the news of the Miracle Cars with her pastor in Memphis, Tennessee. The woman sounded like a mover and shaker within her community. Forceful, businesslike, and devout.

Rose promised to ask Robert Gomez if there were any more Jaguars. The caller said that she'd settle for a 1998 Cadillac STS. Rose let her know that it might take a while, that she was soon flying halfway across the country to take care of a sister dying with cancer.

"Where is your sister?" the caller asked.

"Jackson, Mississippi," Rose replied.

"I'll meet you there," she said.

Robert Gomez heard about Rose's sick sister. Before Rose left, he called to say, "Tell her that I have a Mercedes E320 for her as a gift."

The Mercedes-Benz hadn't arrived in Mississippi by the time Rose made the trip. But the caller had. When Rose set foot in Jackson, she was warmly greeted by Gwendolyn Marie Baker.

Gwendolyn Baker was a light-skinned African American with thin eyebrows and reddish hair that she usually pulled back tightly against her head. Her almond-shaped face—smooth and wrinkle-free—was complemented by almond-shaped glasses. Her lips were usually painted bright red, and she was fond of elegant suits that appeared to have been purchased on Fifth Avenue. Other than a cut-glass ring as big as a fifty-cent piece on her right hand, she looked like a buttoned-down professional, like a banker. In 1997 and 1998, in fact, she had worked as an office manager for Primerica Financial Services, where she earned a paltry $18,000 annually. Baker knew she was worth far more.

Divorced and with two grown daughters, Baker was forty-eight years old when she met Rose Nichols. The two hit it off immediately. Baker possessed a powerful sense of who she was. She'd had only a year of college but was among the most worldly women Rose had ever met. Baker was working on a novel called *Days on the Porch,* had written a play that was to be performed in San Francisco, and was a towering figure within her nondenominational Temple of Blessings Church in Memphis. She was a mature woman who was *done* being a housewife and was ready for a challenge. When Baker walked into a room, people stopped what they were doing and looked up. She radiated power and confidence, and it wasn't a put-on.

Gwen Baker told Rose Nichols that she knew dozens, maybe hundreds of faithful Memphis churchgoers who'd leap at the chance to buy "the blessings." Rose was personally sick of that whole topic, but she encouraged Baker to sell if she wished. She explained the process—money orders or cashier's checks only, give everyone a receipt, and funnel the proceeds to the executor of the estate, who happened to be her own son in Los Angeles.

Baker agreed. Excited, she drove back to Memphis and phoned James, who'd already heard quite a bit about Baker from his mother. The woman sounded promising. James faxed a list of cars to Memphis, and Baker immediately lined up buyer after buyer, many of them at Primerica. She caused such a stir there, in fact, that her boss threatened to sack her if she didn't knock it off. But it didn't slow her down. Within weeks, she stuffed a pouch with car-sales proceeds and sent it by FedEx to James.

It definitely got James's attention. Like his mother, he wasn't fond of talking to buyers on the phone. They asked the same questions about VINs, about options, about colors. They wanted to know everything about John Bowers and rich little Robert Gomez, and they asked whether they could send some of the money now and some of it later. On top of that, the buyers were quickly spooked, and then they demanded refunds, which was tedious and involved endless trips to the post office for money orders. Even worse, the majority of buyers—so far, at least—lived within ten miles of the Kemp Avenue house, and they were not shy about showing up at the front door to register complaints. Already, one of them had started a fight with Robert in the Bicycle Casino.

James was nothing if not practical. It occurred to him right away that moving the entire sales operation twenty-one hundred miles from L.A. might be wise. There would be fresh buyers in the Midwest, and this Baker woman had more church contacts than he could muster in a lifetime. What's more, she was the office manager at what was essentially a bank. Who knew more about the ins and outs of efficient money handling? Forget about "Miracle Cars team captains." What James had in mind was hiring a few "National Finders," honest-to-God professionals who would sell cars and maintain their own efficient offices. It would allow James to concentrate on corralling cash, not buyers.

James didn't know it yet, but in all of America there likely didn't exist a Miracle Cars salesperson as spectacularly qualified as Gwen Baker.

James urged Baker to fly to California, and at the end of 1998, that's what she did. Rose met her at the airport, with a surprise guest at her side—the lone heir to John Bowers's estate, the man himself, Robert Gomez. Robert had never before met Gwen Baker, yet he planted a big wet kiss on her cheek, then slapped his hands on his hips and shook with laughter. In short order, Baker was introduced to the executor of the estate in his little office on Kemp Avenue—whether he was the executor of the Bowers estate or the Gomez estate was never made perfectly clear—and she attended Christ Christian Home Missionary Baptist Church with the Nichols family. The church ladies *loved* Gwen Baker. To them, she resembled a black Martha Stewart, the epitome of good taste, elegance, and distaff strength.

James explained to Baker that he had briefly worked for John Bowers before the millionaire businessman's death, acting as a chaperone for Robert, who was an alcohol abuser, undisciplined and dissolute. James recounted once getting a phone call from Bowers, who asked him to fly to Miami to retrieve wayward Robert, who was on some sort of gin-fueled bender. James further explained that, strictly speaking, he reported to the estate's board of directors, who had petitioned the court to impose a gag order that prevented him from divulging many more details. He couldn't even show her a copy of the gag order—there was, in effect, a gag order on the gag order. They both laughed at that.

Most important, James gave her a list of cars for sale, and it was a doozy. The selection had again improved. Now there were Porsches, Bentleys, Rolls-Royces, and an array of Kenworth and Freightliner eighteen-wheelers. There were still $1,000 Tauruses and Accords to be had, but the premium cars had risen in price to $4,000. "These were corporate cars that had belonged to the companies that Bowers owned," Robert explained. Baker did not ask why salesmen at Mission Foods—whose principal product was corn tortillas—would be driving Rolls-Royces, Acura NSXs, and Porsche cabriolets.

Robert told Baker that his natural father was dead and that his mother was recovering from brain surgery in Bogotá. He told her that the estate cars would first arrive at the port of Long Beach, then would be transported to private lots. One of those lots was in Redlands, California. Baker didn't know where that was. On the sly, Robert added, "By the way, I've overcome my drinking problem. It's okay now for me to have one drink." Baker congratulated him, and they did have drinks together. Robert liked Baileys Irish Cream on the rocks. It didn't seem to affect him. He certainly didn't appear to be drunk.

By the time she left California, Baker had been shown no gag order, no will for Bowers, no will for Gomez, no court documents indicating which probate court was administering the estate, and no court order appointing James the executor of any estate, near or far. But Robert hinted that if all of this worked out as planned, he'd have a word with the board of directors and insist that Baker be paid an appropriate salary, and it would be more than $18,000.

She flew back to Memphis. Gwen Baker was now a "National Finder." She immediately said adios to her job at Primerica.

As 1999 got rolling, so did Gwen Baker. She followed Rose Nichols's lead by selling first to the parishioners in her own Memphis church. Unlike Rose, however, she wasn't afraid to branch out, contacting any reverend or pastor who would listen to her story. One such clergyman was Leo Holt, a cadaverously thin black man, well over six feet tall, who for fifteen years had been the pastor of Grace Christian Fellowship Church on Holmes Road. At first, Holt was suspicious of the Miracle Cars. He asked for VINs. Robert Gomez called him from California and said, "That's the problem with you Christians, no faith." Pastor Holt was peeved by that remark, but Baker comforted him. She explained that Robert was a bit of a mess, that he had "a liver condition because he drank so much earlier in his life," and that he was given to undisciplined outbursts. Baker added, "Mr. Gomez will fly in later on his private jet if the doctors will allow it."

Pastor Holt trusted Gwen Baker. He went ahead and purchased a Mercedes, a Rolls-Royce, some Hondas, and an eighteen-wheeler. Then he told his congregation about "the blessings." At the time, his church claimed some twelve hundred members. That's when Baker's phone began ringing in earnest.

In her various representations of John Bowers's $411 million estate, Baker referred to both Nichols and Gomez as her "godsons." It was a term of endearment that implied she'd known the boys all their lives, when, in fact, she'd known them for only months. On the phone, Baker was smart, cheerful, confident, and aggressive. She felt most comfortable selling cars to devout blue-collar Christians, but she wasn't afraid to sell to white-collar non-believers. Even rich ones.

David K. Harp was a gray-bearded attorney from Arkansas, and his son, David L. Harp, was a used-car dealer. The younger Harp had a friend who'd worked with Baker, and the friend had mentioned the Miracle Cars. Harp liked the sound of those cars. He talked to Baker five times, then checked into her background. Sure enough, she'd been employed at Primerica, just as she'd claimed. Sure enough, she was an object of adoration within the religious community in Memphis. Harp asked his attorney father for a loan so that he could invest heavily. Harp the elder said, "Hold on, I want to check this out myself." He drove to Memphis. When he arrived, Baker said, "I'm just about to go to a church function. Why don't you tag along?" On the way, she showed Harp a "package" of cars totaling $157,000. Harp declined, saying it was far beyond his budget.

"Then she took me to a little church way out in the country," he recalled, "and they had some lady from Chicago there who could see things in the future and was telling fortunes. She looked at me and said, 'I foresee you getting a lot of money.' I just laughed, because I thought she was gonna say, 'I foresee you getting screwed!' But I listened, then I took Baker to dinner so I could ask more questions. There was a pro basketball player there, someone else she was sort of wooing. One of the things

Baker told me was that if I telephoned the heir, he'd back out, that he was selling these cars on the Q.T., and if I queered the deal, he'd sell cars to nobody. It was all hush-hush, she said, only for certain people."

Harp fretted over the deal. The whole setup looked a little flaky. But his son felt that their questions had been satisfactorily answered. He purchased $40,000 worth of cars. It was a break-through. If Gwen Baker could sell cars to a successful white attorney and to his professional car-dealer son, both of whom had cross-examined her in multiple face-to-face encounters, she could sell cars to God, the Son, and the Holy Ghost. She called James in L.A. to let him know he'd be receiving another FedEx package full of cash. He said, "I'll come pick it up myself."

In April of 1999, James flew to Memphis, but he did not arrive empty-handed. He and Robert had drawn up a contract they wanted Baker to sign. She read it and was seduced almost immedi-ately. "I was to receive 18 percent of whatever I could sell, to be paid upon release of the estate," she remembered. "Plus they would pay 43.5 percent of any home of my choosing, and I would also receive some free cars." Those cars included a 1999 Lincoln Navigator, eight 1998 GMC Suburbans, a 1998 Mercedes-Benz 500SEL, and a 1997 Lamborghini Diablo. The contract had been handwritten, so Baker typed it up herself. Then she and James drove to First South Bank in Memphis to have their signatures notarized.

Before James flew home with a packet of cash bulging inside his camel-hair sport coat, he had one more piece of news for Gwen Baker. Robert had gone to the estate's board of directors, he claimed, and the directors had granted permission to pay her a salary. She asked how much. James replied, "What they suggested was $30,000." Baker was satisfied—at least it was more than she'd ever earned at Primerica. Then James added, "No, no. Not $30,000 annually. Thirty thousand *a month*."

Baker about fell out of her chair. These cars truly were a miracle. So were these two boys, her godsons, especially handsome and polite James, a clean-cut youngster who represented all the best qualities of American youth.

James explained that she now bore new responsibilities. He wanted her to open a dedicated sales office. He told her he'd seen his own mother nearly drown in paperwork, and now he knew how to avoid such drudgery. He suggested she hire an employee to answer the phones and another to log sales, issue receipts, cash checks, and make refunds. That would free Baker herself "to sell everywhere in the country *except* California"—James and Robert's back yard—"and *except* Mississippi"—Rose's relatives' back yard. Before sending Miracle Cars proceeds to California, Baker was to deduct her $30,000-per-month salary, as well as office expenses, then make a note of those deductions to either of her godsons. After that, James promised the accountants would take care of everything, including her huge lump-sum 18-percent-commission payout as soon as the estate cleared probate.

Gwen Baker had never felt more motivated in her life. She did what James instructed, hiring her own daughter, Angela Arnold, and her best friend, fifty-nine-year-old Margaret Martin, to work in an office five minutes from her Memphis home. From now on, every buyer got his own file folder, and Baker created professional-looking "inventory call sheets" that enumerated the particulars of each transaction. With these control sheets in hand, she flew to California in late April of 1999, and, with Rose's help, assembled a master list of every car that had been sold to date. Furthermore, she drew up a one-page contract that all purchasers would henceforth be obliged to sign. Among other things, the contract stated that the buyer could request a refund at any time but that it would take sixteen business days to process, and that all cars "will be in excellent working order upon delivery, with an average of 10,000 miles." A final paragraph stated:

"Estate Representative & Executor of the Estate declare that they have the approval from Arbitration Judge Jack Lomeli, the estate, the board of directors of the estate, and the heir of the estate to make this offer." It was a document that would likely have troubled a lawyer, but it greatly comforted more than a few skeptical investors.

Starting in the summer of 1999, James began flying to Memphis to pick up bags of cash. He would later recall making identical trips "between six and seven times." The packages contained as little as $50,000 and as much as $200,000. James liked staying at Baker's home, extending his visit whenever he could. She had an appealing back-yard pool, where he found he could relax and exercise at the same time. And Baker's daughter, Angela Arnold, was James's age. Angela had a hypnotic, childlike voice and was extremely attractive. James started taking her to the movies and to restaurants and to the mall. "He was so polite, interested in all topics, a soft-spoken gentleman," she recalled. "He sometimes told me he'd get so exhausted back in L.A., because he'd be up all night at the rail yards, where they were getting ready to load cars for delivery. I liked James very much."

Robert, on the other hand, never traveled to Memphis. "We were told he had to get special permission to leave California," Angela remembered. "But he would call at all hours, sometimes about the cars, sometimes just to talk about anything that popped into his head. Robert often told me, 'You should move to California.' He asked me to send a picture of myself, so I did. He said he viewed me as a sister." It was not a baseless claim. Back in L.A., Robert was sometimes accompanying Baker's other grown daughter, Kimberly Baker, on social outings—once, most memorably, to tour the *Queen Mary* in Long Beach. The Baker daughters and the California godsons were really hitting it off.

During the early summer of 1999, during one of his trips to Memphis, James attended Pastor Leo Holt's church. His purpose was to thank Holt's congregation for "helping out with the estate and purchasing vehicles." He was so overcome by gratitude that he took a page from the "scripture according to Gomez," suddenly standing before the congregation and promising a cash donation of $100,000. The parishioners were stupefied. James reported his spontaneous act of largess to Robert—more than a little worried that Robert would explode. Instead, Gomez calmly replied, "You know what? Give $50,000 to Baker's church, too."

It was an inspired move, an action born of genius. Anyone who was giving away money couldn't be dishonest. Baker had to install extra phones in her office. "The ringing never stopped, hundreds and hundreds of buyers," remembered Angela Arnold. "Sometimes we'd have fifty messages in a day. And when my mother got calls from people who were skeptical, she'd say, 'Well, I *know* the cars exist.' She was never suspicious. She's a strong person. If she told you something, it was real." Baker began referring to her three-woman company as the "Auto Emporium." She ran the outfit conscientiously. She had become the businesswoman she'd always wanted to be, and the folks at Primerica who had paid her so poorly were now eating her dust, jealous of her sudden success.

Upon hearing of Nichols's unexpected promises of cash, parishioners "screamed and shouted and danced," recalled Pastor Holt. "You know, James impressed me. He was so knowledgeable. He had a good business mind. He gave a hundred-dollar bill to each of ten [high-school] graduates at our church, then spoke with them—gave them some advice about life." So smitten was Pastor Holt that he increased his personal Miracle Cars investment to $50,000. He hoped James would visit Memphis often.

And always, at unpredictable intervals, James or Robert would call Baker's Auto Emporium and say, "Well, it looks like we found more cars." The boys were now offering year-2000 automobiles "from John Bowers's collection of company cars being refreshed and replaced."

Not one soul ever wondered how year-2000 vehicles could have wound up in the estate of a man who died in 1995. That too was apparently a miracle. That too went unquestioned.

7

IRONING OUT THE WRINKLES

Throughout 1999, Robert Gomez was spreading the wealth around L.A. He was now known as Buddha at five casinos: the Crystal Park in Compton, the Bicycle Casino in Bell Gardens, the Hollywood Park in Inglewood, the Club Caribe in Cudahy, and the Hustler in Gardena. He was really putting in the hours. He was welcomed at the door, valets rushed to park his car, hors d'oeuvres and drinks were served, and secret calls were made to third-party bankers.

Robert would occasionally take time out of his busy schedule to meet with antsy buyers at a ballroom he and James rented in the Crystal Park Hotel. On one such occasion, Elijah Buggs showed up, impatient for his cars. "There was free food and drinks," Buggs recalled. "Then they postponed the delivery date again. But James reassured everyone, said we could get our money back. I talked to Robert briefly. He told me, 'I'm a big investor in the stock market, and here's a tip—*General Electric*.' I guess I didn't look too cheered up. So he added: 'Stop worrying. If this estate-cars thing was a swindle, the con men would already have taken the money and run. The money would be gone.' I thought about it, and I had to agree with him."

It was a risky ploy, however. Robert was gambling colossal sums within minutes of the original buyers' homes and businesses. Word began to spread that the lone heir to Bowers's estate was a flamboyant spender, a "backslider" who wasn't attending church and wasn't of the highest moral character. Robert assured his detractors that Miracle Car proceeds were, indeed, being funneled to an escrow account at Chase Manhattan Bank and that he was gambling merely with funds regularly wired to him by a former friend of John Bowers's, a shady character named Sam Pellegrino from Miami. Whenever Gomez mentioned Pellegrino, he'd laugh and wink, implying mob connections. It sounded farfetched, but few of Robert's Baptist interrogators wished to pursue a topic so seamy. Maybe it was better not to poke into Mr. Gomez's affairs.

In April 1999, Buddha became extrafamous at the Hollywood Park Casino. Bypassing the safe-deposit boxes on his way out one night, Robert decided to visit his mother, who was purportedly recovering from brain surgery in Bogotá but was instead perfectly healthy in Bell. When Gomez pulled into her driveway, he was approached from behind by a man who stuck a gun between his shoulder blades. The man said, "I just want the cash." Gomez handed over his wallet and car keys. The man said, "You're not listening, are you?" That's when Robert fished out a roll of bills four inches thick—$45,000 worth of folding money, held together with a red rubber band. The incident, known as a follow-home robbery, was fairly common among high-stakes gamblers. But Robert was still learning.

He reveled in the excitement of the subsequent police investigation. The cops showed him videotapes of customers leaving the casino, and he was able to identify the gunman within hours. The holdup had been scary for a moment, but now Robert was all smiles, quick to tell the story to James, to the dealers, and to fellow gamblers. He made himself out to be a folk hero who'd survived a depraved assault.

But the casino employees knew he was hardly an exemplar of Christian probity when, only days later, in the midst of a losing streak, Robert got into a heated exchange with the Hollywood Park's floor manager. As a security guard arrived, Gomez was screaming, "Leave me alone, you fucking asshole! I'm trying to win some money, and you keep fucking with me!" Everyone in the room stopped to watch. As Gomez walked to the cage— where chips are purchased or cashed out—he continued to curse. The security guard called the police. "Go ahead, call it in, you fucking asshole," Robert bellowed. "You won't do shit to me!" The guard stayed calm but informed Gomez that he might "get rolled up"—the gaming term for "excluded." Gomez didn't care. If he were ejected, he knew it wouldn't be for long.

Over the course of the next month, Gomez estimated he won close to $500,000 gambling. "We threw a huge party," he later said. "Booze, strippers, the works. James came. We had a ball. It was nice to see him relax, sure. He's a guy who worries, you know. He's a very uptight person."

As 1999 wore on, Robert became more and more savvy about the ins and outs of casino life. For one thing, he was finally finding ways around the infernal cash-transaction reports, or CTRs, that were sent to the IRS. Holding a check that James had given him, he'd enter a casino and convert the whole thing to chips. Because no cash was involved, no CTR was generated. When he was done gambling with the chips, he'd exchange them for no more than $10,000 in cash, then leave the casino with the remaining chips in his pocket. Because the California card parlors all honored one another's chips, Gomez could drive down the street and cash in another $10,000 worth. With five casinos to choose from, he could convert $50,000 into cash daily, $1.5 million monthly.

That was the *usual* way to beat the system. But there were other, less time-intensive methods to circumvent the CTRs. High-stakes gamblers are often surrounded by sycophants known as "shoe shiners," usually gambling-addicted losers looking for a handout. Gomez would gather his shoe shiners in the parking lot and hand each a pile of chips. "Exchange these for cash, and keep a hundred dollars for yourself," he'd instruct. The shoe shiners could walk right back inside or drive down the street, and if they were so clumsy as to trigger a CTR in their own names, it was their problem, not Robert's.

In the morning, if Robert found his pants stuffed with as much as $50,000 in large bills, well, that was easily solved, too. He'd drive to Kemp Avenue and tell James, "Wire that to my player's account tomorrow." There was no government oversight of wire transfers, thus no CTRs.

And there was a third way to avoid CTRs, perhaps the easiest of all. It required only that the casinos knew and trusted you. Robert would sometimes walk to the cage and say: "Here's a check for $30,000. Verify that it's good, but don't cash it—just hold it for me." He'd then gamble all night, return to the cage in the morning, and buy his check back. Rarely would the casino have made a copy of the check, and there'd be no record of the transaction.

Before he'd caught on to these slick evasions, however, Robert had made more than a few mistakes. For instance, he'd exchange chips for $10,000 in cash from one cage manager, wait for a shift change, then cash out another $10,000 with the manager's replacement. It seemed clever enough, and sometimes it worked. But what he didn't know was that the cage managers already had his name and address and kept "multiple transaction logs," or MTLs. The clerks didn't have to tell him when they filed a CTR. Sometimes the dealers would silently witness a shoe-shiner transaction, report it, and, *voilà,* another CTR. This was especially likely among casino employees Robert had abused. In his presence they'd smile, fetch drinks, laugh at his jokes. But as soon as he turned his back, they'd squeal. In fact, some of the casinos had started dedicating an autonomous gaming-table camera to video-tape Gomez alone, because of the amount of attention he attracted and the sums he wagered. The tapes led to a few more CTRs.

Buddha was paying the price for making sure everyone knew his name.

Robert reported his CTR woes to James. James didn't have much advice to offer. But, in his Nichols Investments & Securities letters to buyers requesting big refunds, James thereafter warned, "Also be aware if I should have to refund you any amount over $10,000 within a 24-hour period, U.S. Treasury Law, Title 31, states, any [such] transaction must be reported to the IRS." Elijah Buggs got the letter. So did Rose's friend Dorothy Bell.

In 1999 alone, big bad Buddha, the self-proclaimed "king of pai gow poker," triggered sixty-two cash-transaction reports. The total came to roughly $900,000—money that someone at the IRS would presumably know about, if anybody took the time to look.

Funny thing was, when Robert filed his tax return, he claimed only $4,062 in taxable income. But that was better than James, who didn't file any return at all.

James Nichols was swamped. Cash was cascading in, refunds were flowing out. About 46 percent of the Miracle Cars proceeds was being converted almost immediately into refunds for impatient buyers. Twenty-four percent was being split between Gwen Baker and James to pay salaries and operate the Memphis and L.A. offices. And the rest—some 30 percent—was consigned to Robert's various casino accounts. Robert seemed to win more than he lost, but it was hard to tell. Once the money was converted into poker chips, it was no longer on anybody's books. Maybe he was pulling all of it out in cash, or maybe he was losing all of it at the tables, or maybe it was a combination of the two. No one knew.

When James sent out business letters, he started getting them notarized at an outfit called Mail Boxes Etc. The notary there could do no more than attest that the signature on the documents was genuinely James's. But many of the recipients assumed that the official-looking seal ensured the truthfulness of the messages themselves. James grew fond of one notary in particular. Her name was Juliet L. Lozano, a short Latino woman in her twenties, who, in a blue-jeans skirt and tight black sweater, cut quite a striking figure. He began dating her. She never asked what James did for a living. He never revealed that he was simultaneously dating a woman named Kimberly Suzanne Hall. But Lozano was his personal notary when James sent out a batch of letters containing good news. He told buyers:

> The out-of-state delivery destination for the state of Louisiana will be New Orleans; for the state of Mississippi, the central distribution will be Biloxi; for Tennessee, vehicles will be in Nashville; and for California, distribution will begin from the port of Los Angeles and the San Fernando Valley area. No exceptions will be made.

This news buoyed the spirits of impatient buyers. It sounded as if the day they'd been waiting for were finally drawing near. But others, especially those at Christ Christian Home Missionary Baptist Church, had heard it all before. Some of them had been waiting for cars for twenty-four months. There were low rumblings of discontent, murmurings of dissatisfaction. Robert Gomez's minor dustup with the Reverend Houston Buggs in December 1997, as well as his unsavory gambling habits, had soured relations further. Stories were circulating that Gomez was some sort of flimflam man.

James was disturbed, and he leapt into action. He mailed letters to his most influential local investors. The meat of the text read:

It has been brought to my attention . . . that my dear friend Robert Gomez has been accused of scamming and defrauding the cities of Compton, Long Beach, and surrounding cities. This is an outrageous lie and totally false. Mr. Gomez is outraged at this "gossiping and slandering." He, along with his team of legal advisers, are going to be filing slander suits against those who have lied and slandered his name.

I would like to make something clear to you: Mr. Gomez has not conducted any business on behalf of selling any vehicles or collecting financial resources . . . nor has he benefited financially from the sales of any vehicles. Mr. Gomez has had failing health for some time and needs support, not false accusations or slanderous lies.

Mr. Gomez is nothing more than a business entrepreneur and a very well-resourced man. I ask that he not be contacted any further . . . until he can recuperate. Doctors do not expect a full recovery for an indefinite period of time.

With great sincerity,
James R. Nichols

Unlike his earlier letter-writing campaigns, this one had immediate consequences. Dorothy Bell and Elijah Buggs were steaming mad.

"I invited him to sue me," remembered Buggs. "*Begged* him to. I was so angry that I drove over to the Kemp Avenue house. Robert was there. Robert apologized and said the letter should never have been written." Elijah's brother, the Reverend Houston

Buggs, was devastated. He assumed he was about to be sued for slander by a previously beloved member of the best-known family in his church. He was cut to the quick, and, unlike Gomez, the reverend's health actually *was* failing. He felt weak and had recently fallen off a ladder. Then he was diagnosed with colon cancer that looked terminal. As he became sicker, the Reverend Buggs began to wonder if he had somehow countenanced a fraud that played out in his own church, right under his nose. It ate him up inside. Had he helped introduce evil into the Lord's modest house in Compton? He couldn't sleep.

"Robert drove me over to see Houston in his sickbed," recalled Elijah Buggs. "Robert apologized for the letter. I think Houston understood, but he couldn't talk at that point. Robert bought him an expensive recliner."

James was a little unhinged, too, but it wasn't a result of the reverend's deteriorating health. When buyers called, about half of them would ask, "Have you *seen* the cars with your own two eyes?" James hadn't and was quick to say so. He'd go on to explain about the gag order, but a lot of buyers didn't even know what a gag order was. James complained to Robert, who said, "Well, looks like I'm going to have to defy the attorneys and show you the location of the cars!"

"We went onto the 710 Freeway to Long Beach and exited at Anaheim Boulevard," James later related. "It led to, like, a pier. It's enclosed with two gates. There are containers and cranes for off-loading tankers, big ships. I saw hundreds of cars there, and Robert said they were estate cars. He waved at everybody as we passed by and everything." It was never made clear why cars formerly driven by employees of Mission Foods in Irving, Texas, would be shipped *by sea* to reach L.A. On the other hand, no one asked.

James continued to fly to Memphis to pick up packets of cash.

Then he received a fax from a company in Whitby, Ontario, Canada. With regard to estate-car sales, the writer asserted, "We can put together *any amount* of money required." "Any" and "amount" were underscored. It suddenly dawned on James that he was in charge of a multimillion-dollar operation that didn't even have a bank account. Up until then, the proceeds—minus James's salary and Gwen Baker's salary—had simply been dumped into Robert's various player accounts. In September 1999, James drove to nearby Lakewood and opened a business account at the First Bank & Trust. To simplify his life, he added Baker as a cosigner. She could forward proceeds directly to the bank, desposit them, and withdraw what she needed for office supplies or travel expenses. It would save a lot of running around.

Baker flew to Los Angeles to help set up the account. While she was there, James drove her to the Long Beach pier to show her the fenced-in lot. It was still chockablock with shiny cars that looked surprisingly new. It was a great relief to Baker, whose buyers—just like James's—had been asking whether she'd seen the cars.

Well, now she had.

Back in Memphis, the scarecrow-tall-and-thin Pastor Holt, at Grace Christian Fellowship Church, was reviewing blueprints. His church was expanding. He could really use the $100,000 that James Nichols had promised earlier. He called Gwen Baker, who called her godsons in L.A. The boys said it would be okay to release a quarter of what they'd promised, $25,000.

Pastor Holt was thrilled. It truly *was* a miracle. He called a woman in Missouri who'd occasionally spoken to his congregation. He described the two wonderful boys and "the blessings" being offered at rock-bottom prices, then explained that he'd purchased quite a few cars himself. He told the woman that this *couldn't* be a con. Heck, the boys had just handed back five-eighths of Holt's personal investment. *As a gift.*

The woman on the phone was Corinne Marie Conway, and she wanted to hear more. Pastor Holt didn't know much more, so he gave her Gwen Baker's number. When Conway called, the two women talked like long-lost friends. In their social and religious beliefs, Baker and Conway were identical twins who'd miraculously found each other late in life. Both were keen to succeed in business.

Conway, originally from Pensacola, Florida, was in her late fifties. She was a tall black woman who was fond of expensive dark suits with sequins and gaudy cut-glass earrings. She had a brilliant, bigger-than-life Joe E. Brown smile. She was assertive and physically imposing, made to look taller by hair piled atop her head like a stovepipe hat. For twelve years, she'd been living in bucolic Higginsville, Missouri, on the rolling plains fifty miles east of Kansas City. She had a B.A. in psychology and considered herself a counselor. But the 4,600 residents of Higginsville knew her as the cocky but well-spoken founder and president of an organization she unabashedly called the Virtuous Women's International Ministries. It wasn't exactly a church. More like a nondenominational women's group that met regularly to sort through life's many difficulties. "The Virtuous Women's mission," Conway explained, "was to train and to empower and to support women in their purposes in realizing their potential." No one knew exactly what that meant, but the local women liked the get-togethers, and it certainly wasn't doing any harm.

Like Baker, Conway was less interested in buying cars than selling them. Baker said she'd talk to her godsons to see if that was okay. James and Robert loved the idea. It meant they now had a second "National Finder," and they wouldn't have to spend much time training her, because Conway was to report directly to Baker, the car-selling queen.

Gomez called Conway to supply the background info she'd need—that the Bowers estate was worth $411 million and might contain "as many as 4,000 cars," a figure even Baker hadn't yet heard. He then explained the rules—cashier's checks or money orders only, and proceeds had to be forwarded directly to Baker in Memphis, who, in turn, would funnel them to the estate's executor in Los Angeles. Gomez then promised $100,000 to Conway's Virtuous Women's International Ministries, payable as soon as the estate cleared probate. It was the same promise that had been made to Pastor Holt, and Holt had already realized a healthy chunk of it.

Conway was ecstatic, but she wasn't offered a salary, as Baker had been. She was living in a dilapidated trailer. What's more, the Virtuous Women needed money *now*. Conway contemplated her position and came up with a solution. Without telling the other three players, she decided to charge a $50 "finder's fee" for every car she sold. Buyers would simply have to make out two cashier's checks: one to Baker for the price of the car, and one to Conway for the fee. "It covers administrative work, the paperwork, the phone calls," she explained to buyers. In truth, there *was* a lot of office work involved, and the long-distance bills were enormous.

Conway applied body and soul to this new challenge. In little Higginsville, she was known as a devout and trustworthy Christian, and now she was also a car-selling whirlwind who brought to the task the same indefatigable energy and optimism that Baker had applied. The ladies in Conway's Virtuous Women's International Ministries immediately bought cars. But like Baker, Conway was eager to branch out. By the end of 1999, she had approached her personal banker to buy cars. She had approached the mayor of Higginsville to buy cars. She had even approached the chief of police.

The lone voice of caution, Chief Cindy Schroer replied, "Corinne, you need to be careful with this."

With Gwen Baker as a National Finder in Memphis and Corinne Conway as a National Finder outside Kansas City, the two boys in L.A. had assembled—almost by divine intervention —the sort of sales team that CEOs across America would kill for. Baker and Conway weren't just power hitters. They were the Maris and Mantle of Miracle Cars sales.

8

AN AVALANCHE OF CASH

In October 1999, James received his initial statement from First Bank & Trust, and he got a taste of what strong-willed women can do. In one month, Gwen Baker and Corinne Conway had forwarded deposits totaling $393,451. The women were raking in almost $20,000 every single business day. James showed the statement to Robert, who slapped his thighs. He said, "We're a real company now, and real companies have company cars."

The boys drove to Cerritos Ford and took a few test-drives, with James at the wheel. Robert fell in love with a huge seven-passenger Excursion that cost $44,195. James didn't care for the truck—said it was too big, guzzled gas, and rode so stiffly that business colleagues would complain. In truth, they had only one business colleague who ever actually visited, Gwen Baker. But Robert insisted, explaining he was to be the vehicle's principal driver anyway. James wrote a check for the whole amount, using his new First Bank & Trust checkbook. Then he asked if Robert wanted the truck in his name. Robert rolled his eyes and made a farting sound. "What do you think?" he said. James filled in his parents' Kemp Avenue address.

Two weeks passed, then Robert called. "Meet me at Cerritos Ford," he told James. "I *hate* this truck."

The boys repeated a series of test-drives. This time they bought a zoomy $29,045 Mustang convertible whose back seat was so small that Robert couldn't sit in it. But they did receive some trade-in money, which they deposited immediately in a player's account at the Bicycle Club Casino.

Life was good. James surprised his parents by moving in with twenty-three-year-old Kimberly Hall, a short woman with long fingernails and subtle blond highlights in her lustrous brown hair. They had met at a video store. Kimberly liked James because he was solemn, polite, soft-spoken, and dedicated to learning the intricacies of business and high finance. James told her he was the executor of a sizable estate and that he didn't make much money now but might soon. It made sense to Kimberly. She knew that James worked eight hours daily, wore beautiful sport coats, but otherwise flaunted no obvious trappings of wealth. James was then taking home $5,000 per month in salary. It wouldn't make him a millionaire, but it was a fine wage for a twenty-four-year-old man with no college degree.

Kimberly had known James's friend Robert since 1998. She considered him a "goof." Gomez had once told her that his rich father's mansion, complete with heliport, had been featured on a TV show called *Sightings* because it was haunted. "Robert's mouth moved all the time, either talking or chewing," she recalled, "and you had to assume half of what he said was made up. But he could make you laugh, and he was an optimist about life, really upbeat. He was lovably irresponsible. It was hard to stay mad at him."

Kimberly knew that James adored fast cars. They'd sometimes attend car shows, driving James's aging GMC Typhoon—a vehicle he called the "Black Mob"—or any number of BMW

3-series demonstrator models, which he was fond of testing at the time. "I liked to try out brakes and suspensions to the max," he explained, "and I'd scare Kimberly so bad her eyeballs would pop out." In fact, James seemed to unwind by driving fast, which Robert could provoke at the drop of a hat. He'd swivel in the passenger seat and shout: "Oh, my God, that black Buick back there is *following* us! I just *know* it's one of John Bowers's guys. They want to kill me because I won't go to rehab!" In response, James would mash the throttle. Kimberly was not amused by such immature displays. On the other hand, her mother trusted James sufficiently that she had sent him $4,000 to reserve a couple of Miracle Cars.

James steadily obtained cashier's checks from his new First Bank & Trust account in Lakewood. The checks were made out to any of five casinos, whichever Robert stipulated, usually for around $35,000. Once a week, James delivered those checks to Robert, rain or shine. And in his spare time, he was writing more letters, inadvertently stirring up trouble. He wrote Dorothy Bell that there was "no near end in sight for delivery of vehicles" and that he was so mad about it that he was considering "filing a breach-of-contract suit against the estate" in which he planned to ask for "punitive damages for mental stress relief."

She asked for her money back.

In another letter, James assured a suspicious buyer that Nichols Securities was "in compliance and bonded with all state and federal laws when it comes to handling other individuals' finances," and at the bottom of that document he added, "cc: John Bowers Estate of London, Paris & New York City." Apparently, Bowers had a few continental contacts.

There nonetheless remained scores of buyers James could not stonewall. Those buyers were writing their own letters, in fact, and they revealed various tales of woe:

Dear James:
I Johnnie Johnson hereby is requesting my $2000 back
From the car that i have bought From you that i have not
receive.

A buyer named Laurence Poche wrote:

Dear Mr. Nichols:
I had purchased one of the cars that you were selling almost 2
years ago, because my car was falling apart. Now the time has
come, that my car's Transmission is going out. Regretfully to
say, I need to get my $1000 back. I really appreciated being
apart of this blessing. JESUS LOVES YOU AND SO DO I.

That was the problem with the small-time players, James
thought. They weren't into this thing for the long haul.

Back in Missouri, Corinne Conway was experiencing no such
difficulties. She'd just landed a whale of an investor named Matt
Jones. Jones was a young Seattle businessman who shaved his
head and wore handsome brown suits. He was a University of
Washington graduate so accomplished at football that he'd played
for pro practice squads. Now he was producing interactive video
and computer software and was a raging success.

Jones wanted to buy cars but was suspicious. He hired a private detective to interview Baker and Conway. The detective said
he couldn't vouch for everything the women were asserting, but,
he added, "They had all the right answers." Moreover, Baker had
confirmed she'd seen the cars in the flesh. Jones persuaded a law-
enforcement friend to run background checks on the women.
Both were squeaky clean. Still a little nervous, Jones had his
attorney draw up legal contracts. Baker became a little miffed.
"Matt, are you losing faith?" she asked. But she didn't hesitate to

sign the contracts. As a result, Matt Jones and a cadre of Seattle businessmen forwarded $223,250 to Corinne Conway to reserve eighty-eight automobiles, among them five "Porche Carrea's," as Conway inelegantly listed them on a receipt from her "Faith Car Club" offices in Higginsville, Missouri.

Jones didn't mind the misspellings. He just wanted his cars. "Let me know the timetable for vehicle pickup," he admonished Conway. "I need to let my boss know what days I'll need off." Then he added, "I am giving you an extra $2,000 because you have been so good to my family and me, and you deserve it." Such gratuities weren't uncommon from investors who were grateful for a taste of "the blessings."

So much money was rolling in that James wondered if it wouldn't be prudent to invest at least a chunk of it in bonds. His letterhead, after all, said "James R. Nichols, Private Investing & Securities." In truth, James didn't know much about bonds. By coincidence, however, Gwen Baker had just been chatting with a bond trader named Jim Dugan, whom she'd encountered through a Miracle Cars buyer. When James called Dugan, the man spoke so persuasively and with such eloquence that James quickly wired $105,000 as an investment.

A spell passed, then a two-inch-thick FedEx envelope arrived. Unfortunately, the bonds inside didn't make much sense. Some were expired, and there seemed to be copies of copies stacked atop one another. James shipped everything right back, waited, and heard nothing. Exasperated, he picked up the phone and left a message for Dugan to call pronto. Instead, James received a letter from Dugan's wife. She politely pointed out that her husband couldn't talk to James right now, because he was in upstate New York. He wasn't on vacation, either. He was in prison.

James Nichols was livid, just beside himself with fury. He had just learned what it felt like to be conned.

* * *

Because he was a freelance writer for gambling magazines, Max Shapiro was a frequent denizen of California's card parlors. He began hearing stories about a potbellied, six-foot-two kid with a bald head and a hair-trigger temper. "When I first met Buddha, he was convinced that dealers were the sole reason for whatever misfortune befell him," Shapiro recalled. "He'd start with the f-word and escalate from there. He told me, 'At the table, I'm a demon—I just can't stand losing. When you're playing $20,000 a hand, you have to give a damn and take some responsibility. I don't believe it when a dealer says he has no control over the cards. He shuffles. He cuts. He absolutely *does* have control.'"

Buddha maintained a treasure chest of barbs and insults. One of his favorites was to offer dealers "a free ride to Hawaii on my private jet, without gas." He often told Shapiro, "I'm very popular, although maybe not in a good way." Gomez claimed that 90 percent of the dealers were accustomed to his behavior and let it roll off their backs. He added, "They know if they just stay cool and don't react, they'll get tossed a hundred-dollar toke [tip] at the end of their shift."

Shapiro wasn't put off by Gomez's antics. The boy seemed bright and witty, if given to dramatic mood swings and colorful reconstructions of the truth. He was always good for a quote or two. Shapiro asked Gomez the source of his wealth. "Buddha told me his parents came from South America and were heavily invested in commercial real estate, worth maybe $70 million," he said. Gomez nearly cried when he told Shapiro, "I'm closer to my mother than my father, who was quite authoritarian and didn't hesitate to administer beatings. I was a rebellious teenager, and my father was very cruel." Shapiro had no reason to doubt that Gomez's parents had been wealthy. He'd already observed

Buddha dropping $150,000 in a single night. "Any normal player would have slashed his wrists, but to him it was just chump change. He told me his biggest win was $849,000 and his biggest loss was $620,000. He said he recycled most of his winnings, but some of the gravy was siphoned into investments—industrial real estate, car washes, discos. He was quite a guy."

At the time, Patricia LeBlanc was a third-party banker who worked in the Bicycle Club, or the "Bike," as the regulars called it. She'd been in the gaming biz for twenty-seven years. "At pai gow poker, Buddha's skill level was *very* high, excellent," she recalled. "He was quick to read the hands. We lost money to him—$500,000 in a six-month period, our biggest loss."

The third-party bankers played the statistics, sans emotion, and they weren't accustomed to losing, especially to a pudgy boy who played wildly and superstitiously. Gomez would create a scene any time someone stood behind him. "You're disrupting my *energy!*" he'd bellow. He was superstitious about standing in lines, which he felt eroded his karma. Whenever Buddha was in the house, security guards would hover nervously nearby, hoping he'd remain calm, hoping no one would provoke him.

At the end of 1999, Gomez took a brief break from gambling. That's because the Reverend Houston Buggs, seventy-three, had succumbed to colon cancer. It was the last straw for the reverend's brother, Elijah. "I believed that this car business hastened his death," he said. "I couldn't take it anymore. I asked for my money back, and the refund came from a woman in Tennessee. I remember wondering how she was involved."

As the funeral approached, James and Robert felt as if a small black cloud had parked above their heads. Church members were grumbling, gossip was building, and the boys were being given the cold shoulder. James felt that a PR stratagem was in order.

"At my brother's burial, a peculiar thing happened," Elijah

Buggs remembered. "When the casket was opened, the first two people to stand and approach were Robert and James. They began fumbling around inside the casket. I was told they put a ring on Houston's finger. It was supposedly an heirloom that had passed down through Robert Gomez's family. They said it was worth thousands."

"It was James's idea," Robert later griped. "He went out and bought a $50,000 ring. He wanted me to pay for half. I said: 'No *way*. Buggs scolded me, just about kicked me out of his church.' I told him it was crazy to bury a guy with a $50,000 ring, but he did it anyway. When I first saw it, I said: 'Wow, that looks fake! It looks like a cubic zirconia. It's worth *half* what you paid.' James really got mad at that, pissed-off big time, and he began to sulk."

At the wake, James's disposition darkened further when Elijah Buggs asked, "Why didn't you just give that money to Mrs. Buggs? She really needs it."

Robert hustled over to act as a peacemaker. He told Buggs, "We'll cover the cost of the whole funeral, pay it to Mrs. Buggs."

"But they never did," said Elijah. "I remember at the funeral James was with a lady nobody knew. Much later, I saw a picture of Gwen Baker. I think that's who it was."

When Baker flew home, there was more bad news. The two David Harps—father and son—wanted their money back. All forty grand of it. Harp Senior, the attorney, had been trying to locate a probate court handling Bowers's estate in New York or California. He had struck out. He called James to get the phone number of one of the three never-seen estate attorneys—McNeil, Houston, or Gaines. James supplied a number, but when Harp dialed it, the man on the line essentially went mute. "All he'd say was, 'I'm not working on that matter,'" Harp remembered, "and he sounded sort of annoyed, like he'd had other guys asking the same questions." Harp called James back, who comforted him with the news that the very cars he'd ordered, upon release from probate, would promptly be shipped to a rail yard in Tunica, Mississippi. There would be no delay, James assured.

David Harp Jr. called Tunica. "'Guess what?'" he told his father. "'There aren't any rail yards there.' And that's when my dad says, 'David, drive to Memphis, and get your money back right this minute.' So I did, and Gwen Baker was real polite, didn't act like this was a big deal or anything. But she handed me an envelope, and when I peeked inside, there was my $40,000. *In cash.* Maybe I've watched too many movies, but I really thought, Oh, my God, these people are setting me up for a robbery as soon as I reach the end of the street. I got in my car and called my father. He was like, 'Roll up the windows, lock the doors, and drive *straight* home. Do not stop. Not for anything. Not for *nobody.*'"

Elijah Buggs had bugged out. Now the Harps had bailed, too.

At Christ Christian Home Missionary Baptist Church, the dearly departed Reverend Buggs was replaced by the Reverend George Denton, who himself had invested $2,000 in one of the blessings—a pickup truck. Denton didn't want to say anything bad about Robert Gomez, but he recalled hearing the boy promise "homes, a horse, and fireworks" to various mourners at the funeral. That's all the reverend needed in the church right now. More fireworks.

9

LET THE CELEBRATIONS BEGIN

R ay Sutherland was a slim but rugged all-American kind
of guy, with a teenage son and a wife named Jill. He was
tanned and looked like he might be a farmer but was
instead the principal of the middle school in Higginsville, Missouri.
When he strolled down Main Street, he couldn't take two steps
without someone's child shouting, "Hey, Mr. Sutherland, how ya
doin'?" There were no brush-offs, no quick hellos. He stopped to
talk to every student who beckoned. "Y'all have wrestling practice
today?" he'd ask, or, "Is your mom gettin' over her flu?"

Sutherland's sixteen-year-old son had been befriended by
Corinne Conway, who'd sit and talk to the boy during weekend
lunches at a Mexican restaurant on the road leading into town.
Sometimes he'd travel with Conway into nearby Kansas City to
buy Bibles. "We liked Corinne so much, because she built up my
son, told him how much he could accomplish in life," Sutherland
recalled. "She was an optimistic person, forceful, a commanding
presence with a real energy about her, real charisma. She and her
husband Wilbur walked the walk, you know? I once asked
Wilbur, 'Which parts of the Bible do you believe?' And he told
me, 'Sir, I tend to eat the whole loaf—all or nothing.' "

Sutherland's son eventually begged his father to buy a couple of Miracle Cars. His idea was to sell them for a profit, which he would then use for college tuition.

Jill Sutherland called Conway's bank and spoke to the vice president. "I said, 'We're thinking about these Miracle Cars, do you have any advice?' He told me he didn't think it was wise. He said, 'If it sounds too good to be true. . . .' But I had this little part of me that was saying, Corinne wouldn't trick me. It was based on faith. She's not a person who'd use her religious convictions in a scam." The Sutherlands talked about it, then bought a Ford Expedition and a Toyota Camry. They paid $2,000 for the cars, plus $50 apiece to cover finder's fees.

"I never worried about it," said Jill, "but as time went on, the delivery dates kept getting pushed back. And then Corinne got this kind of superior attitude that was unlike her. And the next thing I know, she's traveling all over the world—the East Coast one day, California the next, even South Africa. She started wearing beautiful suits, and she'd talk a lot about her office, how expensively it had been redecorated. Got a little full of herself."

As a matter of fact, Corinne Conway *had* recently journeyed to South Africa, where she attended the "Fifth Annual Believers' Conference." While there, she was introduced to a local pastor named Sam Fidelis, to whom she mentioned the Miracle Cars. Pastor Fidelis pointed out that his church "ministered to many villages in the higher regions, where cars can't go but Jeeps and that kind of vehicle can." He wanted something with four-wheel drive.

Conway placed an overseas call to Gwen Baker back in Memphis. Baker didn't hesitate. "Yes, I'll donate several Jeeps and Lincoln Navigators for his ministry," she promised. "Tell him, 'No charge, it's my pleasure.'"

So elated was Pastor Fidelis that he purchased a handsome

framed portrait of Nelson Mandela, which he asked Conway to present to Baker upon her return to the United States. A token of his appreciation.

Conway followed through. On January 12, 2000, in homey Higginsville, she sponsored a glitzy reception in honor of Gwendolyn Marie Baker, and it was a very big deal. There was special music, delicious food, and guest speakers, including the mayor. The *Higginsville Advance* dispatched two reporters.

"Gwendolyn Baker was honored for her active role in the Miracle Car Club," wrote reporter Stephanie Spalding. "The cars, part of a large inherited estate, range from Mercedes to F-150 trucks and Hondas. Baker, the author of *Days on the Porch,* a poetic drama about a Southern friendship, was recognized for her charitable work. From Zimbabwe, an impressive bust [actually, a photograph] of Nelson Mandela was sent to Baker, in appreciation for her help."

During this festive soiree, Baker expended more than a little effort promoting her book and even conducted an impromptu writing seminar, which wowed the Virtuous Women. Many attendees walked away with the mistaken impression that the so-called Mandela Award had been a gift from Nelson Mandela himself. Afterward, everyone walked to Higginsville's historic Davis Theatre for a private showing of the movie *The Omega Code.*

Would-be buyers who'd previously been dubious soon saw the big story in the *Advance,* which clearly laid out where the Miracle Cars had come from. It had a legitimizing effect, and local sales rocketed. One such buyer was Fran Schwarzer, a blond small-town girl who, along with her husband, had restored the Davis Theatre, one of the most impressive structures in town. "Corinne had created this *happening* here," Schwarzer said, "and she'd seen my husband's ugly fishing truck. She said, 'Fran, you really *must* buy that man a new one—come see me later.' I wanted to believe, but I was suspicious. Then I saw all the people in town who'd already purchased. I wanted to be a part of the miracle. I was just hoping there really were people out there who would do good. So I purchased a 1998 Ford F-150 and a 1998 Ford Windstar van as the theater's pickup and supply vehicle. It came to $2,500. I used the profits we'd made from our first year with the theater. It was our first cash to the good, every cent. It just felt like, if Corinne is doing it, then it's a sign from above to go ahead."

When Schwarzer received the receipt for her cars, she told Conway: "You and Gwen are mighty women of God. Your life is a testament to what life should be like with the Lord."

Schwarzer's investment was small, but there'd been a far larger fish in the audience at the reception. He was from Fleetwood, Kansas, and was a professional car dealer, operating a company called ABA Leasing. He was soon to become the general manager of a Lincoln Mercury dealership, in fact. His name was Randy Lamb, whose rugged face and lantern jaw made him look like a forty-year-old version of actor James Garner. At the gala, he'd bonded with Baker, who offered him a small acting role in a play she was writing that was to feature a professional actor from a popular TV sitcom. Lamb knew the ins and outs of selling automobiles, knew the value of these late-model vehicles, and knew how to auction or lease them in volume.

Lamb gathered all his cash. Then he borrowed from his mom. Then he borrowed against his house. He purchased 121 cars. Later on, when Gwen Baker finished adding the sums, she noticed that Lamb's investment replaced the lost Harp investment more than five times over. Randy Lamb had handed her $218,500.

By March 2000, Gwen Baker and Corinne Conway seemed playfully locked in some sort of Saleswoman of the Year competition. In one twenty-nine-day blitz, the duo deluged the First Bank &

Trust with cashier's checks and money orders that amounted to *$602,900*—about $30,000 per business day. It meant that Robert Gomez, in the casinos, was becoming even more flamboyant. He branched out, occasionally making sports bets with bookies, although his knowledge of pro sports was derived mostly from *Monday Night Football.*

"The casinos liked me so much right then," Gomez recalled, "that I had four tickets to every Lakers game. I had a box for anything at the Staples Center. Casinos and third-party bankers were giving me watches up the wazoo, oh, sure. I really got into jewelry then—ruby rings and titanium men's bracelets, Georg Jensen silver stuff. Very beautiful. I didn't wear it often, but I got an appreciation for the finer handmade stuff, which I previously knew zip about."

Anna Sagato, a cage manager at the Bike, remembered that her casino "opted to extend Buddha a $100,000 line of credit." Another employee there, Jack Rosenfeldt, worked as a "proposition player"—the gaming equivalent of a pro tennis instructor, paid by the hour to teach and stimulate customers to wager. "Buddha told me that James Nichols was backing him," Rosenfeldt remembered. "I once saw him win $360,000 in a three-hour game of pai gow poker. The most I saw him lose was $100,000."

Gomez ordered a replacement license-plate frame. It still said, "Buddha, King of Pai Gow Poker," but now it was gold-plated, like Larry Flynt's wheelchair. Gomez was occupying complimentary hotel rooms at the Crystal Park for months on end. All he had to do was flash a special badge, and he was in. When he posed for the photo ID, he cocked his head onto his shoulder, mugging for the camera, a cockamamie grin on his face. He looked like John Candy.

Crystal Park employee Ralph Nunley claimed that Gomez became so skilled and so fast that "he'd often play at a table where eight players could sit, and he'd play seven hands plus his own." That meant he was setting fifty-six cards per hand. Even so, the dealers and third-party bankers sometimes had difficulty keeping up. It was occasionally tricky to verify if a given hand was a winner or a loser or a tie. But if anyone questioned Buddha, or asked to look again, he was likely to become enraged. Like a child, he'd then petulantly mix all the cards so his claim couldn't be verified, or he'd throw the whole lot on the floor. The dealers usually said nothing. It wasn't their money anyhow.

"He'd bring in, like, five cashier's checks for $20,000 apiece," recalled Nunley. "James Nichols was the remitter, although one wire for $70,000 came from Gwen Baker. Buddha was the biggest volume player we had." Crystal Park execs intimated to Nunley that Buddha had so far brought in $3 million but had apparently pocketed as little as $200,000 of it in cash. "Of the chips he took away, no one knew what happened to them. He could have lost them, taken them to other casinos to gamble with, or cashed them elsewhere. It was impossible to tell."

On March 22, 2000, Gomez was swimming in so much money that he lent $7,000 to the former owner of the Crystal Park Casino, Rouben Kandilian. Kandilian was a hard-core gambler who promised to teach Gomez the tricks of the trade. Robert would eventually go on to lend him another $166,000, then hire a downtown attorney to get it back. "It wasn't long before my lawyer called to say that Rouben was filing for bankruptcy," Gomez later complained. "I said to him, 'Oh, great. Guess I'll go play cards.' "

A much-revered poker celebrity named Barbara Enright—who'd often been featured in gambling magazines and on TV shows—said, "Buddha didn't need Kandilian because he already *knew* the tricks of the trade." Enright spoke with a unique, breathy voice, a little like Billy Bob Thornton in *Slingblade*. She played seven-card stud with Gomez on occasion. "He'd play $20,000 to $80,000 per hand," she said. "And he'd curse when he lost. He'd call women dealers every awful name—'cunt' was his favorite. It got him kicked out a lot." Enright had seen brash young players come and go. She felt Buddha was reckless, a candidate for premature flameout.

Robert certainly remained reckless about cash-transaction reports. One night at the Crystal Park that spring he inexplicably cashed out $97,200, triggering a CTR. Four days later, he handed the cage manager $77,000 in chips and said, "I'll take half of it home." That $38,500 in pocket change triggered another CTR.

And Gomez continued to draw attention whenever he was losing. At two o'clock one morning in March, at the Hollywood Park Casino, he began cursing at a dealer for the weak hand she'd dealt him, calling her a "bitch" and a "monkey." To emphasize his displeasure, he threw a $2,500 stack of chips at her. One of the ever-lurking security guards rushed to the scene. Gomez said to him, "Fuck you, I'm not talking to anyone, and I'm not paying back the money." Telling a casino that you won't pay what you owe is like spitting at a heavyweight prize fighter. Robert was excluded—escorted out the front doors and into the dark parking lot. But the ban was temporary. As usual.

James Nichols had occasionally witnessed such blowups. "It would just make me ill, actually sick," he said. "So many times I'd say, 'Robert, it's time to shut your mouth. Let's go.' But he wouldn't. There were guys in some of those casinos who would have beaten him up, really hurt him. And the security guards actually ended up protecting him from that so many times. I wondered if they should've just let nature taken its course, helped him learn a lesson about his mouth."

"You worry too much," Robert would say whenever James talked like that. "You're always fretting about something." And it was true, but James had reason to worry. He once explained to Robert that, at any given moment, the two of them owed close to $1 million in estate-car refunds across the nation. "That's what got under his skin, kept him awake at night, sure," Robert reckoned. "He was as jumpy as a little bunny. So one time I took him to Arnie Morton's steakhouse in Burbank. All the waiters there knew me, called me *Mister* Gomez. We had filet mignon. They'd always save a double serving of chocolate mousse for me—with extra chocolate. So here I am spending $300 on dinner, but James was still fidgety, like somebody's gonna jump out of the bushes or something. I said, 'James, my man, I shoulda taken you to der Wienerschnitzel.' "

Ricky Siglar is an intimidating physical specimen—six foot seven, 315 pounds, with a chest as expansive and unyielding as a Mack truck's grille. He played pro football with the Carolina Panthers, the San Francisco 49ers, and the Kansas City Chiefs. When he retired, he and his statuesque wife, Janice, bought a home in Overland Park, Kansas, where they heard about the Miracle Cars from a friend in church. The story Ricky heard—slightly skewed—was that Robert Gomez's father owned a trucking company, plus a few casinos, and had been involved in a big way with Donald Trump.

The ex-football player didn't give two hoots about Donald Trump, but he'd long wanted to start a trucking company. When he saw there were Freightliners for sale—listed on the sales sheets as "18 whlr, cab, trlr, sleeper, sunroof, $2500 ea"—he and Janice viewed it as a great opportunity. They tested the water by initially purchasing six trucks, forwarding a cashier's check to Corinne Conway in nearby Higginsville.

"We were told the price was just to offset taxes that the estate would eventually face," Janice recalled. "Otherwise, the trucks would have been free." The list of vehicles now included Honda Interceptor motorcycles, SeaRay boats, and SeaDoo watercraft. "Gwen Baker told us she'd seen the cars in an indoor facility, some with less than ten thousand miles, and that she'd peeked inside one of the Freightliners, which really had low miles and looked new." What the Siglars also learned—inadvertently—was that Baker, unlike Conway, wasn't charging finder's fees.

Ricky was annoyed and called Baker to see if he could get a refund for the finder's fees he'd already shelled out. Baker phoned Robert Gomez, and they worked out the problem amicably during a three-way conversation. "Gomez said he was sorry I'd been overcharged," Siglar recalled. "He said the probate judge knew about the fees, and if it didn't get fixed, they were gonna have to give everyone their money back. But what Gomez said he could do was sell me five Cadillacs for a dollar apiece, and that would make up for it." Sure enough, Baker soon fired off an invoice for $5. There was no mention of what model Cadillacs these might be, and the Siglars didn't ask.

"Robert told us he loved the NFL and knew everything about pro football," recalled Janice Siglar. "And he said he knew a man who owned a casino in Las Vegas who wanted to purchase *all* the estate cars—every single one. But Robert had told him, 'No, I won't allow it, because I want Christian people to be blessed nationwide.' "

It wasn't long before the Siglars were planning a California vacation. They called Gwen Baker to say, "When we're in L.A., we want to take your godson to dinner."

Baker replied, "Which one?"

"I didn't know she had two," said Janice later. "But then she says, 'Oh, it doesn't matter. Robert can't meet with clients—the gag order and all—and James is out of town working on another estate.' "

The Siglars never met James or Robert, but it didn't slow them down. They went on to invest $180,000.

What was more important—at least to the boys in L.A.—was that the Siglars were friends of Neil and Shari Smith. Neil, thirty-six, had played for the Denver Broncos, the San Diego Chargers, and the Kansas City Chiefs. He'd been a defensive end and was physically Ricky's equal. When he retired, Neil bought a Kansas City restaurant called Copeland's of New Orleans. Like Siglar, he was vigilant about watching for unique investments.

"We love the Lord, believe in the Lord and His many miracles," said Shari Smith. "Gwen Baker was so soft-spoken, but true to her beliefs, to the miracle of these cars, of people being blessed. When she came to Kansas City, we all worshiped together, prayed together, sat down and ate together."

Just like the Siglars, the Smiths spoke briefly to Robert Gomez in a three-way phone call, although this time he was introduced as Robert *Bowers*. "As we talked, I noticed that Robert referred to her as '*Miss* Baker,' " Neil Smith remembered, "which I thought was kind of funny, if this was his own godmother he was talking to." But it didn't scare him off.

Neil and Shari Smith went on to buy 150 cars worth $522,900.

It marked the single biggest investment to date. More important, Gwen Baker and her "godsons" now had a pair of nationally respected professional Christian athletes who'd joined the Miracle Cars team—together enriching it to the tune of $703,000—and these powerfully built men weren't shy about saying so. It was the sort of endorsement most corporations only dreamt of. Baker felt a little like a sneaker-company exec who had just signed Michael Jordan and Tiger Woods. Except, in this case, the athletes were paying *her*.

10

COAST-TO-COAST PENETRATION

Corinne Conway was flying all over the country speaking to various congregations. Her themes centered on leadership, character, and integrity. She was popular among female congregants, who were eager to learn how a black woman from an essentially all-white farm village in Missouri had hit the big time. "If I can make it, *you* can make it," Conway promised, and listeners were hungry for details.

Conway gave one such sermon to the Heath Mission School of Theology in Philadelphia. In the audience sat a thirty-two-year-old doe-eyed woman named Kim Krawizcki, from Lancaster, Pennsylvania. Kim was svelte and trim, with long brown hair, full lips, and a slight overbite. With her immense brown eyes, she could have worked as a model for Ann Taylor, from whom she bought her clothes.

Krawizcki had been working for a mortgage company and was a single mother. She felt burned out. When she heard about the Miracle Cars, she envisioned a new life for herself and her ten-year-old daughter. Krawizcki was deeply religious—was raised Catholic but now considered herself a "full gospel Pentecostal"—and had a strong business background. Even an executive headhunter could not have located a better estate-cars salesperson.

Corinne Conway, Gwen Baker, Robert Gomez, and James Nichols were all thrilled to welcome Krawizcki on board as their third "National Finder." They'd previously had no one selling to East Coast buyers. Now they had sales reps coast to coast, giving them "national penetration." By March 2000, Krawizcki had set up a small office that held four staffers. She had letterhead printed that reflected the new business's name: Global Financial. Then she set her mind to selling Miracle Cars.

It wasn't difficult. Her boyfriend, Lionel—himself a Philadelphia pastor—bought cars, starting with a Bentley. And Pastor John Alexander, a teacher at another school of theology, began purchasing cars as if he had a quota to fill. With the word now spreading throughout three fresh congregations, all that was left to do was answer the phones. "They'd ring from seven in the morning to eleven at night," she recalled.

Krawizcki was a quick study. She knew Conway was copping a commission on every sale. But $50 per car? That sounded like peanuts. The overhead in Philadelphia was greater than the overhead in little Higginsville. Krawizcki had in mind a juicier cut. For every car she sold, she began asking buyers to make out *three* cashier's checks. The first was for $2,000, the price of the car. The second was for $1,000, a "broker's fee" earmarked for Conway's Virtuous Women's ministry. And the third was for $5,000, Krawizcki's personal finder's fee. She had just raised the stakes. The price of a luxury Miracle Car had risen to $8,000, sometimes $10,000.

It may have seemed odd that she was pocketing a finder's fee two and a half times the price of the car, but exactly no one complained. "It's because buyers were still getting a great deal," she rationalized. "I mean, on the open market, these Mercedes-Benzes and such were worth $40,000 or $50,000, and I'm selling them for eight or ten grand, you know? It was still a miracle, still a blessing." Like Baker and Conway, Krawizcki kept flawless records. On each receipt she accurately logged where, when, and to whom every single dollar had been forwarded. She understood that the funds first flowed to Higginsville, then to Memphis, then to Los Angeles. But after that, the path got murky.

Krawizcki had ambition and spunk. She interviewed shipping companies to find out how to truck the cars from L.A. to her East Coast buyers. "We had two movers ready to roll," she recalled. "My plan was that cars would eventually be trucked to seven or eight different drop locations. Buyers would have to pay [an extra] $500 per car, but it would be way cheaper than flying to L.A., then driving back home."

Krawizcki, whose mother had recently died, formed a loving relationship with Conway. "If I were about to travel," she remembered, "Corinne would call and say, 'Honey, look for some new shoes for me, and pick up some perfume, too, okay?' And I would. She became like a second mother. I was thinking about getting married at the time, and if I did, Corinne was going to be sitting right there with my dad, as a stand-in mother."

Krawizcki spent $50,000 of her finder's fees as a down payment on a home but otherwise lived a simple life. She was drawn to pricey clothes but was never better dressed than the real-estate women down the street. She regularly donated generous sums to charity, per the teachings of her church. And when buyers complained or got cold feet, their refunds became Krawizcki's number-one priority. Her clients loved her, especially the men. She was cute, with a thousand-watt smile. It was like buying cars from Geena Davis.

Which is why it wasn't long before Kimberly Krawizcki had sold 400 Miracle Cars. She'd raised $2 million—not in car-sales proceeds but in *commissions and fees alone.*

11

A CIVIL ACTION

Back on Kemp Avenue in blue-collar Carson, James Nichols was swamped with requests for refunds. In turning them around, he wasn't as efficient as his three female finders. Some buyers were patient about their refunds. But others would call almost daily to complain. Some wrote letters. And a few found their own solution.

A handful of impatient buyers over in San Bernardino County had simply *resold* their Miracle Cars—had done so, in fact, at quite a tidy profit. Those secondary buyers were now waiting for cars, and when the delivery dates passed, they didn't know to complain to James Nichols—hadn't even heard that man's name. Instead, they demanded refunds from the first buyers. This would not have represented a problem if the initial buyers hadn't already spent the proceeds. Now there were no cars, no refunds, no known delivery dates, and no one to complain to. Except the police.

Kenneth Ayers was a gray-haired detective with the San Bernardino County DA's office. He was in his mid-fifties, with a small potbelly and the sort of stressed-out facial features of an accountant in April. When Ayers first got a complaint from a man named Lonnie Wall, he couldn't fathom who was doing what to whom. The complainant wasn't alleging a crime. He simply wanted his money back for some cars that hadn't yet been delivered. And it wasn't a huge amount—less than $20,000. Ayers looked into it. It sounded as if the initial seller was Rose Nichols and the initial buyer had been a woman named Geneva Buckley. Talking to Buckley didn't clarify matters, so the detective called the Nichols family on Kemp Avenue. An answering machine picked up. The voice said: "You have reached James Nichols. I will not be in my office due to an out-of-state business trip. Leave a message. If you are trying to get hold of Robert Gomez, you may reach him at his New York penthouse. Thank you."

Detective Ayers identified himself and asked Nichols to call back.

In truth, Robert Gomez wasn't in any penthouse. In fact, he was standing right there in the little office-cum-bedroom on Kemp Avenue, and he didn't like the sound of this. A detective asking about estate-car sales? Robert didn't mention the call to James, who actually was out of town. What he did instead was pick up the phone the next time Detective Ayers called. When Ayers asked, "Is this Mr. Nichols?" Robert Gomez answered, "You bet."

Gomez then staged an extemporaneous impersonation so extraordinary that it could have landed him the opening guest slot on Jay Leno's *Tonight Show,* his favorite.

Pretending to be James, Robert told Ayers: "I'm in the entertainment industry and I have to stay clean, so there's no nonsense here. This man's estate is worth $330 million, this Gomez fellow. The estate cars exist, and I'm not trying to rip anybody off. Anybody who wants a refund can have one. My mother, Rose, was selling these cars to her relatives, you know? All my dear relatives. Does that sound like a con?"

Ayers replied, "No, it doesn't, James."

The conversation was lengthy. Throughout, Robert remained confident, poised, and at ease assuming Nichols's persona, referring to myriad of his "mother's" daily Christian habits. It was the kind of stuff that only a son would know. Ayers harbored no doubt that he was talking to James.

But the detective soon called back. Gomez again intercepted the call. This time he told Ayers: "I'm almost thirty years old, and I don't even have a parking ticket. So I obviously wouldn't be involved in something like a car-selling scheme. I own a $340,000 house, so don't worry, I'm not going anywhere. I certainly have no interest in defrauding anyone of money."

Ayers said, "What do you do for a living, James?"

Robert answered: "Well, I'm a production manager. I just worked on the movie *Titanic*. I work with the union directly. I get the manpower together for them. We go in there and build a set."

Ayers told "James" that all he wanted to see was a receipt showing that Lonnie Wall had been refunded what he was owed. It would have been simple for Gomez to have supplied the refund himself. He may well have had $20,000 in his pocket. Instead, he replied: "I assure you that those people can have refunds or already have refunds. I have a deathly ill aunt [Rose's sister in Jackson, Mississippi], so I couldn't get to faxing the receipts. To be honest, had I known these people were like this [reselling cars for a profit], I'd never have done business with them. Honestly, Geneva Buckley is involved in other illegal things." Then Gomez gave Detective Ayers a piece of advice. He said, "You know, the heir, this Mr. Gomez, he has nothing to do with all this. It stops with me. It never went beyond me."

Somewhat confused and a trifle suspicious of anyone who used the phrase "to be honest" so often, Ayers again said he'd nose around and call back. And when he did, Gomez became James Nichols for a third time. "Are you aware of the criminal records of some of these people?" Robert asked the detective. "One woman has a signature just like Geneva Buckley's. I think they may be trying something. She keeps mentioning Robert Gomez in this. I don't know why. Mr. Gomez is a businessman, an entrepreneur, a humongous big shot. He's a multimillionaire who deals with Trump and Helmsley, you know. So I don't know why she keeps throwing him in there. Gomez has nothing to do with it. Has anybody else mentioned that to you?"

Ayers almost didn't have a chance to answer. All he knew was that this Nichols character was a mile-a-minute talker, was adept at deflecting questions, was agile at changing topics, and was quick to accuse his accusers. What he sounded like was a spoiled L.A. yuppie, possibly with a nose full of cocaine, but definitely not a con man.

Rather than solving the problem—that is, paying Lonnie Wall—Gomez had been more intrigued by flummoxing a professional investigator. It was fun being an actor, and Gomez realized he was good at it. In the short term, he had turned Ayers away. But in the long term, he'd made a mistake. James and Rose Nichols would now be named in a civil suit filed by Lonnie Wall. And it didn't take long.

When James returned to his Kemp Avenue office, Gomez marched in looking huffy and hurt. He threw a handful of court documents at the bedroom window. "Can you *believe* it?" he screamed. "This son of a bitch is *suing* us!" As James picked up the documents, Robert calmly added, "I've got somebody that's pretty good at this. You need a personal attorney." James wasn't certain what was going on, but the two boys climbed into Robert's Lincoln Town Car and drove to the Torrance offices of Ronald Wasserman, attorney at law.

In May 2000, James Nichols was called to Municipal Court in Los Angeles to face a suit alleging fraud. He pulled out his trusty

First Bank & Trust checkbook and wrote a check for $18,000. To his surprise, everybody involved with the suit smiled and shook hands. Problem solved. The case was settled.

Robert and James had just dodged a bullet that rightly should have deflated the giant hot-air balloon that was the Miracle Cars operation itself. No investigator or representative of the court had asked to see documents proving James was the executor of any estate. No one asked to speak to Probate Judge Jack Lomeli or attorneys Shawn Houston, Howard Gaines, or Vince McNeil. No one asked to see the wills for John Bowers or Robert Gomez. No one asked to see where the estate cars were being stored.

Any other man would have gone home, wiped his brow, and said, "Thank you, Jesus—*that was close.*" But not James Nichols. James drove home and forwarded a new list of cars to Corinne Conway. And Robert Gomez zipped over to the Hustler to see if Big Larry was in the house.

12

AWARDS AND HONORS

The glittery reception for Gwen Baker had been such a success—and had spurred so many Miracle Cars sales—that Corinne Conway planned another. Only this time, the reception would be *really* big, held not in little Higginsville but in downtown Kansas City, at the swanky Doubletree Hotel. She called it the Millennium Conference International Women's Summit. In a promotional flier, Conway had written: "The Wealth that God has taken from the gentiles . . . is now available to advance His kingdom. I wish above all things that thou mayest prosper."

During the Higginsville reception, the woman being honored had been Gwen Baker, on whom Conway had bestowed the "Mandela Award." This time, the honoree was to be, well, Gwen Baker *again,* only now she'd be receiving the "2000 Excel Award." The explanation for this was not crystal clear. All that Conway said was, "Gwen has shown leadership—together we've touched nations."

Two hundred women signed up for the conference. Many were Miracle Cars buyers. Baker was called to the stage—she wore a black gown with sequins—and spoke extemporaneously for fifteen minutes. It was a speech she gave often, and its text returned frequently to "the blessings." Baker began by mentioning that James Nichols, her godson and executor of the estate, could not attend because his father was sick. "But he appreciates your patience," Baker claimed. "He is working diligently around the clock. Sometimes he gets only two hours of sleep. People just don't understand the dilemma my godsons have been under for years now, trying to work through this probate thing, with an estate so large. It's a real task. But we appreciate everyone who placed trust in us, and I *guarantee* you will not be sorry. But I would also like to tell you that no matter what the attorneys or the IRS says, everything is done not to man's time but to God's time. God has a time when He is going to open His hands and release these assets to you. God has an agenda. Just because you don't know what it is, it doesn't mean He won't perform or stand by His word. God wants to deliver. You can miss the Promised Land by being impatient, by being disobedient, by grumbling and complaining. Pray for patience. I appreciate you from the deepest part of my heart, because I know it's not easy to turn over your hard-earned money and not know me so well. I told every buyer to pray and ask God first, and once God has put His stamp of approval on something, just forget about it. Forget about it and just wait. Because if God has approved it for you, you don't need anything from me. I'm just walking this earth trying to do what I'm supposed to do. But He's the one who brought us here and wants to bless you more and more abundantly. If something is wrong, you question God about it. We all want to live that abundant life. If God gives you a word, don't call anybody on the phone to ask him to reveal more. God is an awesome god. God is an almighty god. God is a wonderful god. He's merciful. He's patient. I thank you for having faith and purchasing the cars. It's going to be a wonderful, wonderful miracle when they come. Corinne Conway has moved these cars all over, into Africa even. God told me He wants me to take advantage of the opportunity. No more questions asked. Just do it. Whatever He says, just do it. I thank Corinne Conway for being a driving force. If she says she's going to do something, she will. She's a workaholic. That's why God loves her. He knows she's gonna get that job done."

Baker was working up to a crescendo, and the audience was right with her. That's when she shouted, "God wants you to prosper, *God wants you to roll!*" The conventioneers went wild. As if on cue, Baker's preternaturally beautiful twenty-four-year-old daughter, Angela—looking truly angelic—then joined her mother on stage. Baker concluded, "Well, I could go on and on. I'm a writer, you know," and she laughed heartily.

It was a speech Baker had delivered in restaurants, at coffee klatches, during three-way phone conversations, and occasionally from the pulpit. It had the effect of making impatient Miracle Cars buyers feel guilty for harping about their investments, which, they now realized, were in God's hands, not Baker's or Conway's.

When Conway eventually handed Baker her Excel Award—a baseball-size chunk of glass cut to resemble a single colossal diamond—Baker joked, "Now *that's* a ring I'd like to see on this hand right here."

Baker appeared ready to give a second speech—God apparently wanted *her* to roll, too—but Conway somewhat impatiently grabbed the microphone. She had a few words of her own. "I want every person in this room who is a recipient of the blessings to stand," Conway ordered. Approximately half the women leapt to their feet. "God will do what He needs to do for those who have purchased and are waiting patiently," she assured in a booming voice. "Now let us pray for James and Robert and James's father, and we're gonna pray for the attorneys and for the judges, because

God is using them. I believe God is waiting for us to get into just *one* good courtroom. Then we can change things, with God's help." She then grabbed two apprentice preachers to stand beside her in the positions that James and Robert would have taken if they'd been present. She looked skyward, as if in supplication, and implored, "God, we want you to *release* this estate!" It was as if she were casting out the devil.

The audience cheered and whistled and stamped their feet.

But the fireworks weren't over. Ex-NFL stars Ricky Siglar and Neil Smith were on hand. Huge and handsome, the athletes thrilled the women. Conway wanted to honor the burly men for their faith. Not their religious faith but their faith in the Miracle Cars. As a token of her appreciation, she had ordered custom-made red blazers for the men. One was size 50, the other was a 46 long, and on each breast pocket was embroidered the slogan "Miracles in Motion Car Club." Conway let it be known that if other husbands invested as generously as Siglar and Smith, they'd be getting tony red blazers, too. When Neil Smith first tried on his jacket, the women hooted excitedly, as if he were a male stripper.

Robert Gomez was to have received a blazer as well, and his wasn't appreciably smaller than Smith's. At the last minute, however, the heir to the Bowers estate had called to cancel, saying that attorneys Houston, Gaines, and McNeil didn't want him so far afield "without a bodyguard." Conway mailed the jacket to him, which he never once wore and couldn't find later when asked.

"I was disappointed that the godsons didn't attend," recalled Neil Smith's wife, Shari. "They were supposed to discuss delivery dates. They said they had to keep Mr. Gomez in a 'safe haven.'"

East Coast finder Kim Krawizcki shared a table with the two smiling football celebs. "Some of the conference sounded more like a sales rally than a convention to empower women," she later grumbled. She didn't feel it was appropriate. "Corinne's husband,

Wilbur, was there as a guest speaker, but it was clear that Corinne ran *that* particular show. Not that I'd ever say that to her face."

The crimson blazers had been handmade by a Kansas City seamstress named Thelma Carnes, whose drawn and weathered face reflected the hardscrabble life she'd led. Carnes had worked for decades and had nothing new or fancy to show for it, so she bought eight Miracle Cars. She paid Conway $11,500 for the autos and $400 in finder's fees. "At that big Doubletree conference, one of the door prizes was a Cadillac STS," Carnes recalled. "They said it was a Miracle Car they were giving away. And it was funny, because my brother-in-law actually won it. He waited and waited, but you know what? It never came."

Gwen Baker flew home to Memphis and positioned her Excel Award next to her Mandela Award.

Corinne Conway drove home to Higginsville. She knew it was nice to receive awards, but it was nicer to receive cash. She didn't have to wait long.

A devout Christian named Robert Fluellen called. He was a member of New Covenant Church in Grove City, Ohio, and he'd heard about the Miracle Cars through a Midwestern minister. By profession, Fluellen was a loan officer for Comerica. As such, he understood the fiscal ins and outs of raising funds. In fact, he'd already met with a handful of New Covenant members, and they'd all come to a decision. He called Conway simply to warn her that he'd be forwarding a tidy little sum. It turned out to be $140,000.

And the hits just kept on coming.

Greg Ross was a graduate of Kansas State University with a degree in journalism. He wrote ads and brochures for car dealerships for a spell, earned a car broker's license in 1995, then started a company in California called Market Place Motors. Ross, forty,

began locating luxury cars for buyers too busy to do it themselves
—for execs at Warner Brothers, for instance.

"I had a car-salesman friend in Kansas City," Ross explained.
"Knew him for twenty years, just this hard-core businessman, the
most buttoned-down guy I know. And he tells me, 'You know,
Greg, these big Chiefs players out here are into this.' So I got a list
of cars from Corinne Conway, just this handwritten list with no
VINs. I wanted the VINs real bad, because I know how to read
them. You can get engine type, transmission type, body style, two
doors, four doors, date of manufacture, everything. But it was
always this gag order, a Judge Lomeli, who was already mad at
outsiders poking into the estate's affairs, they said. Anyway, on
October 30, 2000, I did it. I purchased everything Conway had
sent on the list. I had my bank wire $120,000. It was for twenty
1998 Mercedes-Benz SL500s at $5,000 apiece, ten 1998 Honda
Accords at $1,000 apiece, and ten 1998 Toyota Camrys at $1,000
apiece. Then I sent a check personally to Conway for $2,000 for
her finder's fees. I got back a generic receipt, the kind you buy at
a dime store. But I work with banks a lot, so it wasn't hard for me
to track where my money went. It wound up in an account at
First Bank & Trust in Lakewood, belonging to James R. Nichols.
I said, 'Well, that makes sense.' I'd heard his name mentioned as
the executor. And whenever I'd get cold feet, I'd call, and they'd
say: 'Listen, guys are *lined up* to buy these cars. You'll get your
$120,000 back in a cashier's check in ten days, no questions asked.'
After that, I'd have this daily discussion with myself. I'd say,
'Well, I'll just keep monitoring this. I'm not a kid, not emotion-
ally attached to these cars. I can bail at any time.' I'd con myself
into waiting a little longer."

Every time a big investor like Robert Fluellen or Greg Ross
signed, fifty smaller one- or two-car investors followed suit. The
smaller fish proceeded on the assumption that college-educated

businessmen—men who'd accumulated wealth by pushing the levers and buttons of high finance—could not be duped. The smaller fish were about to learn a lesson. Sharks don't worry much about size.

Gwen Baker, Corinne Conway, and Kim Krawizcki remained aggressive saleswomen—Miracle Cars cheerleaders who carried order books instead of pompons—but their enthusiasm was no longer essential. The cars were selling themselves. When James Nichols examined his First Bank & Trust statement on May 14, 2000, it again left him reeling. The ledger showed he was in control of $500,234. Not bad for a former security guard who worked nights. It seemed almost too easy.

Robert Gomez must have thought so, too, because he started getting lazy. It was becoming annoying to meet James all the time, either at the Kemp Avenue house or in a parking lot, to collect his weekly cashier's checks, many of which were now in the $50,000 range. The casinos all knew Gomez, and the casinos also knew that the checks remitted by James Nichols were always good. Robert decided to "borrow" a book of blank First Bank & Trust checks— swiped them out of the Kemp Avenue office, for which he still held a key. If he got into hot action at two or three in the morning, well, no sense in waking James. He'd just write his own checks—dozens of them, ranging from $20,000 to $50,000—and forge Nichols's signature. At first, he took pains to replicate James's subdued cursive. But when he realized the cage managers were hardly bothering to look, he reverted to his own loopy devil-may-care scrawl. On one check, he began to sign his own name—thus, James's name appeared to start with an "R"—and on another he forgot to include any signature at all. Nobody complained, mostly because Robert would repurchase the forged checks in a matter of hours, well before they could be presented to the bank, using whatever funds he'd won that night. And if he'd lost, then he'd merely have to open one of his safe-deposit boxes and make up the difference with the loot stashed therein. But he didn't often lose.

"I considered Buddha among the top one to five percent of gamblers in California," recalled Gerald Jackway, then the general manager of the Club Caribe Casino. "But I told him I couldn't honor a forged check." Gomez didn't like that. He stomped away in a huff. "Then all of a sudden a man calls me on the phone, says he's James Nichols," Jackway continued. "He tells me, 'Cash it anyway or face losing Mr. Gomez's business.' Like it was an order." Jackway was peeved by such threats. He'd already observed Gomez and his pal Rouben Kandilian hobnobbing and living it up. "Kandilian owed the casino a great deal of money," Jackway said, "and I noticed the two of them with stacks of cash wrapped in the 10K labels—perhaps $100,000 in total." Jackway wondered what was going on. He hoped the two gamblers would pay up and get out.

The director of loss prevention for one of the third-party bankers asked Buddha how much he'd won that year. "Don't know for sure," Robert replied. "Maybe $10 million," although that was surely a gross exaggeration. Nevertheless, the company persuaded one of the casinos to videotape Gomez, "to see if he was winning in a clean game." They switched cards often and focused a second camera on the dealer, in case it was a two-man swindle. The investigation's conclusion? "Mr. Gomez is an extremely fast player, quick to understand the house weight, knowledgeable of the games. He's among the top three players in California. While we were watching, *nobody* was cheating."

Not in the casinos, anyway.

Gwen Baker, Corinne Conway, and Kim Krawizcki had become three peas in a particularly profitable pod. But when you got down to brass tacks, they remained little more than ambitious businesswomen selling automobiles out of a dead man's estate. Corinne Conway thought of herself as God's instrument here on earth, and His intention was surely that she act as a superior power, a *force majeure.*

To that end, Conway enrolled the group in Friends International Christian University (FICU), in Merced, California. It was not accredited by any agency recognized by the U.S. Secretary of Education, but it did have the benefit of offering all manner of degrees. An undergraduate degree cost as little as $3,900. An M.B.A. or a D.D. (doctor of divinity) cost somewhat more. Entry requirements were not rigorous. FICU applicants had to check a box beside one of the following three statements:

1. **I am a member of the body of Christ.**
2. **Please contact me about becoming a member of the body of Christ.**
3. **I just prayed the prayer of salvation and became a member of the body of Christ.**

By the beginning of June 2000, the Three Musketeers had qualified for doctor of divinity degrees. It was another miracle. The trio traveled to their graduation ceremony, held in a Los Angeles hotel ballroom. Estate executor James Nichols even showed up, although he looked inexplicably glum.

At the time, Nichols and Conway had yet to meet face-to-face. Before he'd even had an opportunity to encounter her, James buttonholed Baker. "When Corinne comes over," he instructed, "just tell her my name is Sam. I don't want to be bothered with all the car questions tonight. I'm worn out with that."

Baker felt bad about lying to her friend but did as James had asked. "Sam" and Corinne Conway then chatted amicably for twenty minutes. Nichols told her, "I'm in the military, which is why I speak and stand like I do." Then he added, "Gwen Baker and my mom went to school together." Conway got up to use the bathroom, and when she returned to the table, "Sam" was gone.

It was a peculiar and seemingly unnecessary exchange, and it didn't make sense to Baker. Nichols later explained, "I'm not a big fan of Conway's." What irked him was her insistence on charging finder's fees. If refunds had to be paid, buyers forfeited those fees, and more than a few had given James an earful on the subject. On the other hand, he needed to respect Conway's feelings. He couldn't ride roughshod over her astonishing moneymaking techniques. The woman sold cars like nobody's business. She was a walking, talking profit center generating a monthly cash flow that a small Wal-Mart would envy.

After their graduation from Friends International Christian University, the three women asked to be introduced as Dr. Baker, Dr. Conway, and Dr. Krawizcki. And their names would subsequently appear with that honorific on all letterhead and business correspondence. It had a nice ring to it. A doctor was a professional whose intentions went unquestioned. A doctor was put on this earth to *help* folks.

"You *deserve* to be a doctor," Conway assured Baker, "because of all the work you're doing for Third World countries"—a reference to the free SUVs she'd promised to Pastor Fidelis in Zimbabwe. This was working out so well, in fact, that Baker wrote a letter to Friends International asking whether she could swap $50,000 worth of Miracle Cars for "tuition fees" toward an M.B.A.

Conway flew back to Higginsville and started looking for the sort of building that would do justice to her burgeoning Virtuous Women's International Ministries. Before the summer of 2000 concluded, she found a place she liked at 409 West Nineteenth Street—a white wooden structure set atop a hill, with a spacious walk-out basement. When the sun shone down upon it, the edifice seemed to glow. She wrote a check for $106,500 and proudly posted the virgin-white Virtuous Women's sign out front. Not only was Conway now a doctor, but she also owned a structure that really *looked* like a church. Plus, it helped her to acquire a handy little perk she felt she might be needing in the near future—*tax-exempt* status.

By June 2000, James Nichols didn't have a half-million dollars in his account anymore. Now he had $617,350. A man with such resources didn't need to be tooling around southern California in an aging GMC Typhoon truck. James had always adored M3s, the 240-horsepower top-of-the-line 3-series from BMW's revered hot-rod division. It was, in truth, the perfect performance car for an L.A. businessman—agile in traffic, universally admired by the *Car and Driver*–reading cognoscenti, but surprisingly low-profile in its styling. Only insiders knew it was a special car.

James drove to Santa Monica and bought a $34,210 M3. He used cash to pay for half that sum. It was everything he'd hoped for—a bullet with a back seat, a sleeper that shocked the bejabbers out of lowriders who challenged him at stoplights. He knew how to modify the suspension and brakes, and he added a supercharger for an extra fifty horses. Kimberly Hall liked riding with him, too, at least until he went into Mario Andretti mode.

Within months, James was driving his sparkling M3 on the freeway when the front suspension "collapsed," as he put it. "It fell and split the tire, and I pretty much went skidding all over the place." James asked his attorney to look into whether a manufacturer's defect was to blame, but nothing ever came of it. The car was totaled and sold for salvage.

"So then Robert came over," James later recounted. "He said, 'Hey, man, you wrecked your car. Here, go get another, sure.

Whatever you want, good buddy.' " Robert forked over a wad of cash he said was derived from an incoming wire transfer from mob friends in Atlantic City, maybe Miami. James was relieved. In fact, he *did* have his eye on another M3 at a dealership in Norwalk. But before he purchased it, he bought a Chrysler LHS sedan for his mother. Maybe it was wise to ensure she was happy before he showed up in another flashy German coupe. Which, as it happened, he also totaled.

It was the start of quite a car collection. In L.A., however, a handsome young man wearing a designer sport coat and seated behind the wheel of a shiny BMW was not a sight that aroused even the slightest suspicion. It drew a few looks on Kemp Avenue, however.

Robert Gomez, conversely, was drawing monumental attention. On July 12, he sauntered into a closed portion of Hollywood Park Casino to smoke a cigarette. Three employees asked him to move elsewhere. He steadfastly refused, calling them "bitches" and "whores" at a volume that put an end to all nearby gambling. The police were summoned, and Buddha was "rolled up"— barred again. But in little more than a month, the casino sent a memo to its employees stating, "Mr. Gomez's actions off the table have never been disruptive"—that is, he'd previously been a perfect monster while gambling but never while smoking—and he was to be welcomed back. "Mr. Gomez attracts a great deal of business to the casino," a second memo explained, "and we will attempt, one more time, to accommodate him."

It was much the same elsewhere. At the Crystal Park Casino, Gomez once became incensed about not being able to cash a check. He declared that owner Leo Chu's wife was a "slut." Chu banned him, then relented. Not much later, after losing three consecutive hands, Gomez warned a dealer, "Speed it up." When she didn't, he added, "I take it you didn't get fucked the right way by your boyfriend last night." That was followed by several racial epithets, and when the dealer began to cry, Robert insisted she be "removed for incompetence." She was grateful to be out of the line of fire.

Perhaps a little nervous that he might be fouling his own nest, Gomez drove to the Normandie Casino in Gardena—a casino he'd previously called "a pigpen for first-timers and food-stampers"—where his mouth almost immediately landed him in hot water. The general manager said: "I didn't take his shit. He was a foulmouthed little bastard. I tossed him out for accosting a waitress." It was the only casino to which Buddha never returned.

Robert tried to smooth over the matter by purchasing round-trip air fare for the waitress to visit her homeland—Vietnam. "The casinos would sometimes get pissed at me, sure," Gomez explained, "but you could tell they didn't mean it," and he was right.

But when he had to lie low, he repaired to his suite at the Crystal Park Hotel, where the employees had nicknamed him "Bobby Code Blue." "Code Blue" was the password for complimentary status, which Gomez used for just about everything. In fact, he'd even swung a Code Blue for James, who could stay either for free or for as little as $25 a night. For nearly fifty days, James did exactly that, and when he faced a $1,032 charge for movies and telephone calls, the hotel offered him a $617 "guest refund" to ensure he wasn't too troubled by the incidentals.

Robert certainly wasn't troubled by incidentals. One of his gambling cronies watched him empty a small in-room safe. "He withdrew cash totaling between $50,000 and $80,000," the man claimed, "plus two racks of $5,000 chips and five racks of $1,000 chips."

Across town, by coincidence, "Dr." Kim Krawizcki was in a hotel, too—the Embassy Suites in Arcadia. In August of 2000, she'd flown cross-country on her own initiative after hearing Nichols's reassurance that cars were almost ready to be shipped. "I wanted to be the first person there," she said, bringing with her an assistant named Lori. "I had my shipping packets all ready to go, so when people got their cars, there'd be a nice little thank-you letter inside from Global Financial, my company. I was running a first-class shop."

Expecting someone to call momentarily to reveal the location of the cars, Krawizcki sat by the phone in her room for *thirty consecutive days*. "See, I wasn't supposed to call James Nichols, and I was told that Dr. Baker was just about having a nervous breakdown with all the business pressure," she remembered. "So the only person I could call was Dr. Conway. Over and over I'd ask, 'Did you hear where the cars are?' And she'd say, 'Well, no, *I* haven't, honey, but I'm sure *God* has.' " Conway couldn't field too many of Krawizcki's calls, however, because mid-month she flew to Jerusalem to attend the "Third World Leaders Association for the World Leadership Summit," where she hoped to be received as one of the world leaders.

In September 2000, Robert Gomez jetted to Vegas, where he again had a lousy time. Among other disappointments, he lost $55,200 at Caesars Palace and triggered a CTR. Once back in L.A., he drove to the Kemp Avenue house to pick up a cashier's check, then accidentally left his much-depleted wallet there. Rose Nichols didn't know whose it was, so she opened it. Inside was a business card that read "Robert Gomez, Federal Bureau of Investigation."

At first, Rose wondered if the boy really *was* an FBI agent. It would explain his weird comings and goings, why he was up all night, why he seemed to be living in a hotel. Becoming nervous, she told James, "I'd feel better if you got Robert's key to the house. Maybe he shouldn't come around here so often."

James insisted that she was overreacting. Everyone knew Robert occasionally lived out these colorful fantasies—a dying mother in Bogotá, death threats from mobsters shadowing in black Buicks—but they always proved baseless and harmless. Rose disagreed. There was something "not quite right" about pot-bellied Robert, the class clown. She didn't understand why he was hilariously funny one minute and hurling legal documents the next. She was beginning to think the boy had emotional troubles, maybe even multiple personalities.

James shrugged it off but secretly knew what she was talking about. On a previous trip to Vegas, he had accompanied Robert, who suddenly announced he was flying home. "I told him I'd return the next day," James recalled. "So Robert flies alone back to L.A., drives to my mother's house, and says to her, 'Where the heck is James? He'll be late for our meeting.' *Meeting?* He just left me in Las Vegas. Then he goes into our office and begins shredding documents. He could be mentally pretty 'out there' at times, and when he got like that, you didn't want to be around him."

Robert had no interest in explaining his puzzling movements. Instead, he hired a helicopter to fly all 275 pounds of him to Catalina Island for the weekend. As he skimmed one thousand feet above the Pacific, he whipped out a pencil. He had graduated to his first *New York Times* crossword. It was a toughie, but he was determined. "I'm Buddha, the king of pai gow poker," he bragged to the uninterested pilot upon landing. "No reason I can't also be Buddha, king of puzzles."

13

ENTERTAINING THE TROOPS

On October 26, 2000, James Nichols turned twenty-five. Robert Gomez gave him a corny birthday card and signed it "Buddha" with a stylized smiley face that had "$" icons for eyes. There was also a little gift stuffed inside: $50,000. The next day, James wrote a check to IC Enterprises—the corporate name for Crystal Park Casino—for three times that amount. James sometimes couldn't tolerate Robert's moods, but he was a generous kid who had a knack for making people forgive his faults.

A few days passed, then the boys came up with an idea. Corporations sometimes rewarded valued employees with weekend junkets. Off-site motivational outings. Why not reward a few of the Miracle Cars investors? Better yet, why not reward the investors who'd been asking Gwen Baker what a guy had to do to become a finder?

"Right away, I recommended Vegas," Gomez remembered, "but it was mostly because Larry Flynt was gonna be there at some sort of porn convention, and I knew he'd be gambling." Still, it made sense. Robert knew the town, which offered all the entertainment anybody could handle. He went ahead and set everything up and instructed Baker to invite whoever would most appreciate a three-day all-expenses-paid extravaganza in the desert.

Seven folks signed on, fewer than the boys had hoped. On the other hand, this was a bit of a dry run. They expected larger soirees in the future. When the invitees landed, Baker introduced Robert as the heir to the estate, the Big Guy himself. The investors were impressed, among them a devout Baptist bishop who wasn't at all sure he should even *be* in Original Sin City. But everyone liked Robert, who was funny and affable and a Vegas tour guide extraordinaire.

Baker warned the group, "Robert won't be able to discuss the details of the estate—he's not allowed to do that." The attendees were disappointed. They wanted to know when their cars would arrive, and they wanted to discuss contractual details of becoming regional finders.

The group stayed in the Aladdin Hotel, where Robert commandeered the executive suite, sharing it with Baker's daughter, who was on hand to help her mother. The investors enjoyed two expensive stage shows, a magic show, and a Whitney Houston concert. In addition, they all ventured out to Hoover Dam as unapologetic tourists. They ate at pricey restaurants, where they whooped and hollered and generally had a bang-up time, and at night they wandered in and out of the neon glow and gawked at the gamblers and freaks strutting along the sidewalks.

"Gwen Baker said she'd give us $10,000 advance commissions if we became [regional] finders," recalled Melvin Hackett, an investor from Memphis who drove trucks on weekdays and was an evangelist on weekends. "Plus, we'd get a 15 percent commission and two free cars. I kept expecting a business meeting to set all this up, but that didn't happen. Baker *did* say she'd seen the cars. And I asked Mr. Gomez about his tattoos. He told me, 'I got drunk one night and just did it.' He bought me a coat and some cologne. And he bought outfits for the women. He paid cash for everything—for the rooms, the shows, the gifts, the dinners. Had a roll two inches thick. I heard from Gwen that when Mr. Gomez wasn't with us, he was gambling with someone. But, hey, it's Vegas, why not? Mr. Gomez later told me there'd be another meeting, and it would be in Hawaii. Because he was the son of a millionaire, he said they'd use the company jet. I thought that was odd, because I noticed earlier he'd flown in on Delta."

"I know Melvin was a little stunned when he saw me doling out the Ben Franklins," countered Robert. "I said to him, 'Melvin, my man, it's no big deal. Cash is king. It's what I do. You just use cash in this business and nothing else.' He liked that." And Robert liked playing the role of the big shot, the sugar daddy from trendy L.A.

Before Melvin Hackett departed Las Vegas, Baker gave him the $10,000 she'd promised. He was delighted.

"That weekend, Robert acted like this rich orphan boy," remembered Baker's daughter Angela. "And he'd call my mother at all hours, wake her in the night to talk about all sorts of crazy things." In truth, Robert had acted like the heir to a $411 million estate—generous, happy, eccentric, unwilling to discuss vulgar business matters. He boasted to the group that he didn't trust banks and was tempted to convert all of his accumulated wealth into diamonds. The investors felt as if they were traveling with Donald Trump.

What the investors didn't know was that the moment Gomez arrived home in Los Angeles, he e-mailed James to complain bitterly about having to shell out $12,500 in pocket money just to wine and dine the rubes. He expected to be compensated. It made James angry. "Here's this big fatso rolling in the dough that other people earned for him," he said, "and he doesn't seem to understand that, as a company, we have expenses."

But nobody got too upset. Robert's speech about investments had caused Gwen Baker to wonder if she should convert some of her holdings, too. When she arrived back home in Memphis, she purchased two lots in the Cole Farms subdivision worth $89,800.

By the end of 2000, Robert had scored 318 free nights in the Crystal Park Hotel, this despite credit records stating he had "no bank, no employment record, bad credit, bad conduct, [but was] a good action player—*lots* of collection." In truth, Robert was getting sick of living in a hotel. For one thing, he slept all day, and the cleaning staff kept trying to make up his room in the morning. The maids never got accustomed to his nuclear tirades.

Robert began watching *Monday Night Football* with gambling buddies he'd invite up to his room. One of those buddies was Richie "Fingers" Sklar, who was likewise living in the hotel.

Fingers was forty-four, was perpetually clad in tennis whites, and had a habit of running his hands through his blond hair, front to back. He was the Kato Kaelin of the California casinos. Fingers was famous for three things. First, he was pals with innumerable local "makers"—insiders' slang for bookmakers. Second, he told everyone who'd listen that he annually "missed the cut from the PGA senior tour by one lousy stroke." Third, he had done a term in federal prison for fixing horse races.

"I guess I fixed about three hundred harness races," he boasted, "three hundred quarter-horse races, and over four hundred thoroughbred races." He claimed to have won millions before he was arrested, but the sums were never verified. "I won 90 percent of the fixed harness races, mostly at Los Alamitos," he estimated. "But I took a beating, because the idiot drivers I paid took the money and bet it through the windows themselves, lowering the odds and killing the price."

Fingers and Gomez initially met at a pai gow table, where

Robert was drawing attention with his $5,000 bets. "I was stunned by how fast he could sum up the value of a hand," Fingers recalled. "I remember that Robert turned around and asked me to shake the dice cup for him. I told him, 'No, thanks.' He comes back with, *'No one* tells me no.' So I explained, 'If I shake the cup and you win, you'll expect more. And if I shake the cup and you lose, you'll blame me.' "

Robert was impressed by that answer. It indicated Fingers was a backroom guy, a player who'd been around the block a time or two. Robert started handing his new pal $2,000 pots to gamble with. In return, Fingers promised to pay back half of his winnings and to watch for dirty dealers. "With Robert's rapid style of play," he explained, "dealers sometimes lifted a hundred bucks here and there, and Robert wouldn't detect it. So I'd sit with him at the tables. I caught a lot of mistakes. You know, Robert would commonly bet $5,000 a spot, and with six spots on a table he was in for $30,000, so it was important. In twenty-five years of being around casinos and seeing whales, I'd never seen anyone bet with such speed and accuracy. His play became flawless. And he was very lucky. I once saw him win seventeen times in a row. Nobody, and I mean *nobody,* is ever that lucky."

Robert asked Fingers to introduce him to sports bookies who would cater to his unique demands. Robert insisted, for instance, that he be allowed to place his bets with the front-line bookies only, not the underlings who answered the phones. Plus, he wanted to settle up the day after any bet was placed. That was unusual. Bets were universally settled on Monday or Tuesday only. Further, Robert demanded that he be allowed to pay his debts not in cash but in casino chips.

At first, the bookies told him to take a hike. Who'd this pudgy boy think he was? They ran a background check and learned that Gomez hadn't grown up a trust-fund baby in Beverly

Hills, as he'd claimed. Fingers wasn't surprised. "They told me he was just some dumb Mexican kid who grew up poor in Bell," he recalled, laughing. The bookies worried that the kid might be a cop or an informant. In response, Fingers insisted they come watch Robert gamble. "After that, they knew from the amounts he was betting that he *couldn't* be with law enforcement. Nobody undercover would risk losing so much."

Robert began wagering anywhere from $15,000 to $30,000 on football games. When he lost, it was Fingers's job to deliver bag after bag of casino chips to the bookies. Fingers tried to coach his friend on the nuts and bolts of football—star players, defensive formations, why penalties were called—but, as he put it, "Robert always seemed too dumb to really understand." In return for handling Robert's bets, the bookies were paying Fingers 15 percent under the table *but only if Robert lost*. It was an unholy arrangement that no one ever divulged to Robert.

In no time at all, one of the bookies presented Robert with an antique five-hundred-dollar bill for his birthday. Robert was ecstatic. The bookies were beginning to afford him big-shot status, just as the casinos had. And for good reason. During a single weekend that fall, Robert bet $250,000 on a six-pack of college games. He and Fingers parked themselves in front of a satellite TV, then were horrified as game after game went against them. It happened rarely, but happy-go-lucky Buddha actually became anxious, saying he wasn't sure he could cover the loss entirely the next day. He looked like he might cry.

"All of a sudden, late Sunday night," Fingers recalled, "Robert stands up and says, 'I'm going to go make up the money.' And he goes over to the [Crystal Park] casino and wins a little over $200,000 in three hours playing pai gow. I was so relieved." And for good reason. When Robert paid up, Fingers lifted $37,500 from the pot.

After that harrowing weekend, Robert was the shark, and Fingers was his loyal pilot fish.

For a change of scenery, the dynamic duo zipped off to Las Vegas, where Gomez had in mind buying a new Jaguar, using $125,000 in chips he'd stored previously at the Aladdin. He claimed to have won the loot from Larry Flynt during a porn convention. Upon arriving, they cashed in the chips and headed to the Jag dealership. But on the way, they passed a Ford dealer, where Gomez spotted a fire-engine-red F-150 Lightning. "He said, 'Whoa, let's *look* at this baby,'" Fingers recalled. "While he was examining the truck, I went inside to speak to the salesman. I told the guy, 'Look, I'll push Robert into buying this thing, but in return you gotta pay me a $1,000 finder's fee.'" Sure enough, Robert plopped down $36,500 for the truck—which he sold four months later—and Fingers took his cut. Without knowing the first thing about National Finders or Miracle Cars sales techniques, Richie "Fingers" Sklar was ironically mimicking their business practices exactly.

In the California casinos, Fingers sometimes witnessed furtive meetings between Robert and James Nichols. "I was always impressed by James," he said. "He'd shake my hand, very quiet, very polite. But he would only really talk to Robert, and it was always out of earshot. James wouldn't gamble, and he wouldn't stay long. Just long enough to say a few words in private. I could tell Nichols was important by the way he carried himself. I figured the two were doing something illegal. I've been around huge players, cheaters, thieves, money launderers, scam artists, mob figures, and other crooks, but I must say I couldn't put my finger on where the money was coming from. No matter how much Robert lost, the money kept rolling in."

At the end of 2000, Gomez and his "Kato" permanently checked out of the Crystal Park Hotel and moved into a handsome rental property on an eight-home cul-de-sac in Downey. It wasn't a romantic union, although Fingers would later say, "I noticed that all of Robert's friends were small, thin Asian boys who were feminine." In the upcoming months, Gomez would bet approximately $2 million on professional and college sports. Fingers would skim roughly $80,000 from the losses.

"Nobody saw them much," said a neighbor. "Very quiet guys. A real odd couple. Definitely not Ozzie and Harriet."

Miracle Cars buyers now numbered in the thousands. Many of them had been promised midyear delivery of their cars. By the end of 2000, more than a few were hopping mad and wanted refunds. Both Baker and Conway were quick to comply, processing refunds in as little as ten business days.

To an outsider, it might have appeared that this car-selling business wasn't all that lucrative. There seemed to be as many refunds going out as fresh buyers coming in. But looks were deceiving. For one thing, Conway was tapping every buyer for a finder's fee—no longer a mere $50 but now $1,000—which she pocketed no matter what happened. For another, she was *reselling* the cars of those who bailed, often doing so at increased prices, and was collecting a *second* nonrefundable finder's fee on each.

It was, in fact, working out just swell. The year prior, Conway had cleared close to $100,000 in finder's fees. In 2000, she cleared *$991,810,* likely four times what the richest man in little Higginsville, Missouri, had earned in the same spell.

It was a mountain of loot, on which she unknowingly owed $320,379 in taxes. It was the sort of heaven-sent windfall that would send the average citizen running to an accountant. Conway did not do that. Her solution for handling her whopping income in 2000 was to file no tax return at all. That was a colossal blunder, but she wasn't alone. James Nichols, Gwen Baker, and Robert Gomez followed suit.

PART II

It was beautiful and simple, as all truly great swindles are.

—O. Henry, *The Octopus
Marooned*

14

A DARK CLOUD ON THE PLAINS

Situated on gently rolling plains fifty miles northeast of Kansas City, Higginsville, Missouri, calls itself the "Home of the Huskies." In December, the Higginsville town council broadcasts Bing Crosby tunes through speakers rigged along Main Street, and the electric company forgives everyone's power bill. There's still a popular roller rink in Higginsville, plus $2 movies at the Art Deco Davis Theatre. There's even a fully restored green and white Victorian train station, past which corn-fed farm boys drive their jacked-up pickup trucks en route to the King Pin bar and grill. And everyone waves to the mailman. The place could easily have been a backdrop for a Norman Rockwell painting.

Most of Higginsville's residents are of German ancestry. That includes the stocky five-foot-tall chief of police, Cindy Schroer (pronounced *Shray*-er), who eschews a uniform in favor of modest business skirts and starched shirts. Locals call her "Cindy," not "Chief," and you wouldn't know she was a cop except for a gold badge on a chain around her neck. To the townspeople, she's more a mother figure than a policeman. Apart from a few high-schoolers who've been busted for guzzling forty-ounce jugs of Coors, the citizens of Higginsville consider Cindy their pal.

From as early as summer 1999, Schroer had been receiving calls about Corinne Conway's Miracle Cars. "It was five or six a month," she remembered. "Always the same: 'Do you know anything about cars for $1,000, is it a good idea, is any law being broken?' I always answered, 'If cars are being sold at that price, somebody would already have snapped them all up—a dealer or someone. Too good to be true, is what I'm telling you.'"

Schroer poked around to learn what it was that Conway's Virtuous Women's International Ministries actually did. All she discovered was that there was no formal congregation, no sermon on Sundays, and that its headquarters right then was "in an alley in a trashy little trailer that had a telephone and an answering machine." In fact, she remembered, "It was a bit of a joke, because everyone asked, 'How virtuous do you have to *be* to get inside a trailer?' But the members *did* turn out to be deeply religious and conservative—I remember that the city administrator's secretary joined. Then they moved out of the trailer to the big building on West Nineteenth Street, with a day-care center in the basement. Paid cash for it. I began wondering what their source of income was. From the day-care center?"

A while later, standing in front of the post office, Chief Schroer ran into Fran Schwarzer, the owner of the Davis Theatre. "I said, 'Frannie, did you get your cars yet?' She hadn't, so I asked, 'Do you ever think it's a scam?' She said, 'Well, I have questions about this, such as how Corinne got the money for her new church. But this is a matter of faith, and if one person doesn't believe, it will cause the whole house of cards to fall. And I don't want to be that person.' She felt guilty even saying it. She's such a nice lady, bighearted, do anything for anybody."

Schroer nosed around some more. "The owner of the Super 8 told me that Corinne was putting up all sorts of people out there, and when she came to greet them, she'd be all dressed to the hilt, acting the role of the power player, all the attention focused on her. Then someone saw her driving a Ford Excursion with a Kansas plate, a high-dollar vehicle, and the joke was, 'Hey, is that the first Miracle Car to be delivered?' "

Schroer talked to Higginsville's economic adviser, who had toured the Virtuous Women's new digs. "She told me that when Corinne swung open a door in the basement, she announced to everyone, 'Now here's where the *real* action takes place!' and it was just this gorgeous office, really nice. Meanwhile, she's flying all over the world. I mean, has anybody else in Higginsville ever been to Africa? I don't think so."

Eventually, the owner of the local barbecue shack called Chief Schroer to inquire about Miracle Cars. "We talked for a bit," she remembered, "then he says, 'Oh, well. It's like gambling on the riverboat, sort of exciting to put up $1,000 for a chance on a $30,000 vehicle. So maybe it's worth it.' That's when I said to myself, 'Enough is enough.' "

Chief Schroer phoned Conway. " 'You know, Corinne,' I said to her, 'I just have a real bad feeling about this. What can you tell me that'll put my mind at rest?' She told me she was selling cars but wasn't *pushing* them, that she'd just mentioned it to a few friends and sales had skyrocketed. I said, 'Come on, that's a little self-serving. You mean all these cars just got sold by accident?' She said, 'No, it was word of mouth. You get rewarded for having faith. These blessings are part of a probate proceeding, and if you have questions, call Dr. Gwen Baker in Memphis.' Corinne thought some of the cars were stored there in Tennessee, with Baker, and said they were going to be delivered late in 2000. Then she got a little abrupt, told me, 'Listen, I'm a doctor, I'm *Dr.* Conway, and I'm smarter than that—you know, to be part of a con. Thanks for your concern, but I don't *need* your concern. I *know* these people, so leave me alone.' She was dismissive. She never said to me, 'Okay, Cindy, I'll check this out,' or, 'Oh, my God, you think it could be a swindle?' Which is what I was hoping she'd say. She had a kind of arrogance, like, 'I'm untouchable.' "

Now even more unsettled, Chief Schroer called Gwen Baker in Memphis, who wasn't so much worried that a cop was calling as annoyed that Conway had divulged a delivery date. "Corinne should *never* have told you that," Baker huffed. "This whole thing's in probate. We can't promise a date. It could be fourteen years! But if buyers want out, they can get their refunds any time, day or night."

Chief Schroer had never heard of a con in which you could make one phone call and get your money back, no questions asked. "And right then, wouldn't you know," she recalled, "Ray Sutherland, our middle-school principal, and his wife ask for their money back and get it instantly, with a 'Sorry we can't do business' and a friendly handshake. And, boy, that stopped me in my tracks. In a classic con, the actor collects as much money as he can, then—*bam!*—he skips out one night with the works, every cent. And in a normal con, the bad guy only goes after easy marks—the uneducated, the minorities, the poor. So if this thing was a con, it was totally backward. I mean, here the *ringleader* is the one who's the minority, and the victims are white college grads with common sense who're already driving new cars. So I was of two minds. I'd go back and forth thinking, It *must* be for real, then, the next day, It *must* be a con. I'll tell you, I began to lose sleep."

More citizens walked into the cinder-block headquarters of the Higginsville police department. "They always talked about being blessed, about the blessings," Schroer recalled. "The buyers were just doubting themselves, and no one was willing to sign a complaint. They just wanted me to reassure them. So I didn't have a victim. Yet it seemed as though one in three people in town was involved. I mean, our most prominent lawyer had bought cars. I said to him, 'Tom, what were you *thinking?*' And he's like, 'It's okay—if I don't get my cars, I can sue her!' "

Chief Schroer got the feeling that the tentacles of this thing were beginning to squeeze the life out of her idyllic little town on the lonely plains. She began to dread yet another passerby asking, "Cindy, have you heard anything about the cars?" It was like a *Twilight Zone* episode in which aliens had taken over all 4,600 citizens' brains, and now they couldn't eat, sleep, or enjoy high-school football. They'd become obsessed with invisible cars from an invisible source conferred on them by an invisible deity. Schroer had a nagging suspicion that the source of the evil was some place far away and that the little Higginsville PD had about a one-in-a-million chance of eradicating it.

That's when she parked herself in her tiny office and began filling out an incident report. "Which was weird," she remembered, "because there still wasn't a victim. People wanted their cars, not retribution. So it's just me. I didn't know what else to do. Basically, I wrote, 'Since July 1999, I've been hearing about these cars, that numerous persons in Higginsville have made an investment of $1,000 to $4,000.' I wrote, 'I *know* we are going to have numerous victims,' even though I didn't know it for sure. I didn't tell Corinne that I'd filled out a complaint. I still didn't want there to be a confrontation."

On the cover of the incident report, Schroer wrote "Fraud," then, in the waning days of 2000, sent it to the office of the attorney general of the state of Missouri.

In three years and four months of uninterrupted Miracle Cars sales—beginning with Rose Nichols in California, continuing to Gwen Baker in Tennessee, to Corinne Conway in Missouri, to Kim Krawizcki in Pennsylvania—not one member of America's 428,000-strong police force had spent more than five minutes investigating whether a single Miracle Car ever existed. Chief Cindy Schroer was the first. What's more, she had filled out precisely the right complaint in precisely the right state and had handed it to precisely the right man.

Which is how a five-foot-tall blond lady cop in a homey little town on the windswept plains—where the most serious crime was mailbox bashing following the Huskies' homecoming game—came to represent the beginning of the end of the most notorious retail automotive fraud in U.S. history.

Chief Cindy Schroer's complaint found its way to Kansas City, where it kicked around for a spell in the office of U.S. Attorney Todd Graves. Initially, nobody was wildly enthusiastic about pursuing the thing, even though the alleged fraud met the unofficial guideline of exceeding $25,000—the minimum required to trigger an investigation by the feds. If this was a fraud, it appeared to be a local endeavor perpetrated by a devout Christian woman with an overstimulated imagination but no criminal history. Who wanted to indict a sixty-year-old doctor of divinity who was viewed in her little town as the female equivalent of Billy Graham? What sort of predatory prosecutor would want to trot such a figure before a jury? Maybe this Conway woman would refund every buyer in Higginsville and the problem would just go away.

Then an assistant noticed that Conway was funneling car-sales proceeds to Memphis. *Bingo!* That meant this whole mess crossed a state line, and "interstate fraud" allowed you to foist it off on out-of-state investigators, at least temporarily. All the U.S. attorney had to do was tell the Tennessee FBI, "Hey, guys, look into this," and they'd take the case away for a few months. And when they came back, they'd likely give the U.S. attorney a thumbs-down—suggesting that Chief Schroer and her local PD should handle it. And if they gave him a thumbs-up, well, the agents by then would already be lugging around their own boxes of evidence, and maybe the U.S. attorney in Tennessee would want to pursue it, leaving Missouri to move on to bigger things.

But it didn't happen that way. The FBI in Memphis had recently been swamped by a spate of bank robberies, and they were simply overwhelmed. It wasn't long before the case bounced back to Kansas City.

In matters of fraud, U.S. Attorney Graves knew that the last thing you wanted was a big strapping Clint Eastwood kind of guy pounding on doors and pointing guns at people. It *never* worked that way. What you wanted was one guy who could intercept and interpret documents and another who could walk into any bank in America and demand to see financial records. By happy coincidence, Kansas City was home to a crackerjack U.S. postal inspector and a wily special agent in the U.S. Department of the Treasury's Criminal Investigation Division. Both were free at the time, and both were regarded nationally as all-stars in their fields. In gumshoe parlance, they were "slow-motion stranglers"—a pair of follow-the-money feds who assiduously collected tiny detail after tiny detail until they'd built a case the size of a congressman's house and the perp was smothered. *Slowly.* Sad stories didn't sway these guys. Cleverly concealed funds didn't dissuade them. Criminals who hid behind religion enraged them. In their careers, both had busted not only gray-haired grandmas and grandpas but also white-collared pastors and priests.

Special Agent Gary Marshall was one-half of Kansas City's "daunting duo." Thin and wiry, with a sharply pointed nose and wire-rimmed spectacles, he combed his black hair straight back—keeping it in place with old-fashioned Brylcreem—and was fond of narrow black ties and *Men in Black* suits that hung loosely from his bony frame. He looked like a 1950s version of Bartleby the Scrivener, except his eyes could go black and cold, like an eel's, and there was a flinty edge to his demeanor. Marshall had commanded an M48A3 tank with the U.S. Cavalry in Vietnam. He ran search-and-destroy missions around Saigon and the DMZ, where he saw some awful things. After the war, he earned an accounting degree, then joined the IRS in 1973 as a criminal investigator. With twenty-seven years of experience, he was now at the top of his game and had seen it all—everything from ignorant flimflammers who were running laughably obvious numbers rackets to an ethanol plant claiming fraudulent energy kickbacks to an insurance company trying to bribe state commissioners. Only months earlier, Marshall, then fifty-three, had said to an assistant U.S. attorney, "If you get a really good case over there, let me know."

The second half of the duo was Steve Hamilton, fifty-one, who looked a whole lot like Robert Duvall—bald on top, with a fringe of reddish-blond hair. Raised in Pleasant Hill, Missouri, he had the down-home good looks of a Midwestern farm boy with the strangely unsettling voice of John Malkovich. Like Marshall, Hamilton had served during Vietnam—did four years with the U.S. Air Force and was stationed for eighteen months in Thailand. When he returned, he earned a degree in criminal justice, then put in twenty years with the post office's Inspection Service. Hamilton possessed a perfectly disarming smile and a telltale set of laugh wrinkles, but he also possessed a set of stainless-steel handcuffs that he hid in the small of his back.

If you opened your door one day to find Marshall and Hamilton standing on your stoop, you'd instantly confess to cheating on your taxes and once on your wife. They were special agents right out of central casting—tight-lipped just-the-facts kind of guys, with no sense of humor, guys just *waiting* for you to utter a lie. Joe Friday and Popeye Doyle had nothing on Marshall and Hamilton.

The U.S. attorney's office assigned the so-called Miracle Cars case to these two men, who immediately split up their assignments. Hamilton began trying to decode the whole John Bowers can of worms. Where was the estate held in probate? Who was the executor? Who were the lawyers? And Marshall began quietly subpoenaing bank records. For the first few months of 2000, both men assumed Corinne Conway in Higginsville was the ringleader. It sure looked that way.

"It was initially puzzling," Marshall recalled. "In a case involving massive fraud, you can't see the whole picture right away. Rarely. So you look at one document at a time, follow where it goes, try to understand just what that single piece of paper means. You don't jump to conclusions. So I looked at this one check from the football player Neil Smith. It was for $42,500, apparently to buy twelve cars. And it went to Corinne Conway in Higginsville, who forwarded it to Gwen Baker in Tennessee. Then she forwards it for deposit in an account she holds jointly with a guy named James R. Nichols, but that bank is way the heck out in Lakewood, California. And then Nichols takes out $1,000 for himself, then writes a personal check for $30,000 to purchase a $30,000 cashier's check—which means his name appears nowhere on it—and that's made out to the Hollywood Park Casino. And then on *that* check, somebody writes 'Hold for Buddha,' and this Buddha person, if it even *is* a person, cashes it for $30,000 worth of poker chips. A trail leading into a very dark forest, right? Same with dozens of other checks following a similar path, except they'd wind up in different California card parlors at the very end. And even then it was IC Enterprises or El Dorado Enterprises or HPC Services. At first, we didn't realize that those were casinos, too."

"While Gary was doing that," said Hamilton, "I was trying to assume all of this was legit. You know, don't start out with a big attitude. If I could just get a court-case number and talk to Judge Jack Lomeli, maybe I could clear it up in a few days, right? The people I talked to said that Bowers died in New York and his estate was being disposed of there. So I started calling the New York counties that might be handling it. You know what? There are *sixty-two of them*. I called each county and explained a little about the case, how colorful it was, and that would get the clerk interested, and they'd go search for John Bowers for me. I went hoarse during all those phone calls—the romantic life of a federal agent, huh? But, eventually, I *did* manage to track down two estates belonging to men named John Bowers. One was for $15,000. The other was for $140,000. Nothing close to $411 million. So then I started looking for a New York attorney named Shawn Houston. The closest I came was Samuel Houston. Then I looked for Judge Jack Lomeli. Found a *Gloria* Lomeli, and then, after a while, there it was, a *Jack* Lomeli in California. Yippee, here's our man, right? Unfortunately, he didn't handle probate at all, hadn't ever heard of John Bowers, didn't have a clue about any estate cars."

Marshall and Hamilton scratched their heads. On paper, the whole story emitted the fetid odor of fraud, yet they still didn't have a scrap of evidence to prove it. "So then I said, 'We just gotta go interview the casinos,'" Hamilton recalled. "Well, talk about uncooperative. Casinos are not big on federal agents. *Until* you show up with a subpoena. Then they're sweet as little puppies. The casinos were negotiating these third-party checks in huge denominations. They must have suspected something, right? But they weren't going to delve too deeply. As long as the checks were good, turn a blind eye, you know? Let it go. But guess what? They all knew Buddha. Boy, did they know Buddha."

"We still didn't have much," remembered Marshall. "Are there cars out there? Is there a will, an estate we just haven't located yet? Could be. But I remember saying out loud, 'I have a sneaking suspicion that Corinne Conway isn't at the top of the food chain, here,' and Steve said, 'Me, neither.' Then I asked him, 'Why would these people go to so much trouble to earn all this cash only to pump most all of it into the riskiest place under the sun?' There was about a five-second pause, and we both said at the same time: *'Laundering. They're hiding it.'* "

The two agents drove over to the Charles Evans Whittaker Courthouse in Kansas City. They took the elevator up to the fifth floor and walked into the U.S. Department of Justice, Western District, Missouri. They sat down with an easygoing assistant U.S. attorney named J. Daniel Stewart and said, "We're not sure what we have, but this thing seems to lead everywhere. It looks like a monster."

Except for Robert Gomez occasionally pretending he was with the FBI, James Nichols didn't know the first thing about federal agents. But he knew he had walked away from a California court-room filled with lawyers and a detective and a judge who never questioned the existence of the Miracle Cars. And now he was using that experience as an object lesson for skeptical investors: *You want out? Of course you can get out, and all your money will be returned, too. Don't believe me? Go talk to the judge if it makes you feel any better. On the other hand, if you just wait a little longer, your reward will come—horsepower from heaven!*

It was a powerful argument.

Although James right then controlled a ton of money, his own car situation wasn't so great. At the start of 2001, he wrecked his second BMW M3. But the solution wasn't difficult. "I got per-mission from Robert to get another car," he told his mother. "Robert said I was entitled to a wire transfer of $50,000 that had just come in the week prior." He purchased a replacement M3 in

February. Four months later, he bought another. One month after that, he bought another—this time it was a convertible, the finest of his five, a real stunner that had cost $63,500. It was the most sought-after M3 on the market, a genuine rarity.

Still his enthusiasm for fast machines waxed. "The whole estate-cars thing was very tiring," he said, "and I was quarreling with my spouse, and everyone seemed to feel like what I needed was a hobby to help me relax and get in touch with all my old buddies, who I hadn't seen in ages. So we all went out to look at motorcycles. Robert and my friend Steve Finnie drove down to European Cycle Specialties. And I saw a new Ducati M748 there." Robert could see that James wanted the bike. He handed his pal what was stuffed in his pockets at the time—a measly $4,260— and told James to withdraw the ten-grand balance from the Lakewood account.

Sixty days passed before James changed his mind. "I realized it wasn't enough power for me," he said. "I hadn't been on a motorcycle in a while, and I knew I needed to upgrade." So back he went. This time he bought a Ducati M996 for $17,608.

But he still wasn't through. As part of his new-hobby regimen, James decided he wanted to build a dedicated autocross racing car—another M3, naturally—that he could enter in events staged by the BMW Car Club of America. That's when Kimberly Hall put her foot down, suggesting that their driveway now resembled an imported-car dealership. Moreover, the neighbors were talking. James "defused" the situation by purchasing a $29,216 BMW 323i—not for himself but for Kim. "I felt a better car for her was proof that I meant what I was telling her about us reconciling," he explained.

By the summer of 2001, James's car purchases had amounted to $343,023.

But it didn't make much of a dent in the business. After all,

Dr. Baker in Memphis was still on a roll. She'd just hired Janice Siglar—wife of NFL celeb Ricky—to act as a regional finder, awarding her a $10,000 advance commission. Better yet, Baker had just received a letter from a man named Ryan Landie, a car dealer in Kansas City, asking if he could purchase 126 cars, among them eleven 1998 Range Rovers at $5,000 per. The total that Landie proposed to invest—he hadn't actually sent the check yet—amounted to $441,900. Another whale.

In response, the boys in California informed Baker she'd soon realize a salary increase and that she should see about installing more phones and more employees to answer them. Robert asked for one favor in return. He told Baker: "I'm very upset. I'm not supposed to be involved in the selling of the vehicles. If the attorneys and Judge Lomeli find out that I am, I could lose my whole estate." He then asked Baker to type up a letter in which she clearly stated that the heir had *never* sold any cars himself and hadn't accepted any car-sales proceeds.

"But I would be lying," Baker replied.

"You wouldn't really be lying," he countered, "because you haven't actually given me any money *directly* from cars."

"Well, I guess I could look at it that way," Baker said.

"Because, Gwen, I just don't want to lose my estate," Robert replied in a pained, adolescent voice. "When I think of losing $400 million, I could just kill myself."

It wasn't the first time that Robert had mentioned suicide. Baker suspected he was just being dramatic, but Robert was such an odd person that she couldn't be certain.

She wrote the letter and mailed it immediately. Robert was, after all, the heir—this was his show. While she was at it, Baker appended a copy of a letter she'd received from the lovable Pastor Holt. Holt was sniffing around for the $75,000 balance of the "pledge" that James had made to his congregation. "As you continue to give," Holt gently reminded, "God will continue to give back."

Right then, Robert was certainly capable of giving back but didn't. A third-party banker named Raymond Garcia, a former cop, had just witnessed him win $850,000 in a single day. Garcia, however, felt that there may have been some "cheating through intimidation." Robert was regularly playing six pai gow hands simultaneously. After all the hands were dealt, the dealer would turn the third-party banker's hand and set the cards. Then Gomez would open each of his hands, glance at the cards, and turn them facedown, declaring each a winner or a loser. He did this with such Gatling-gun rapidity and with such exaggerated gestures that dealers couldn't always verify whether he was telling the truth. But if they asked to look at his cards again, Buddha would fly into the sort of tantrum you had no trouble remembering for a lifetime. "He once hurled a chip rack at a guy," remembered Garcia, "and the man had to go to the emergency room for stitches. But the casino took care of the whole thing. Why? Because in one session they made $60,000 in collections."

Robert forgot about Pastor Holt and celebrated his victorious day by buying more Buddha statues. He already had more than a hundred in his house. He preferred those that were solid jade or gold-plated. And he began telling people that, with all his winnings, he'd recently purchased a new home in Bel Air for his beloved mother, and that she now had servants who ironed her sheets each night before she went to bed.

Given his background in law enforcement, Garcia knew bullshit when he smelled it. There was almost certainly no home in Bel Air. But Garcia *did* find himself wondering where on earth Robert really *was* stashing his winnings. Sure, the boy was regularly seen driving flashy wheels—a couple of Lincoln Town Cars, a Lexus GS400, a Ford Lightning truck, and a Cadillac DeVille.

But that wasn't enough to soak up the millions that Gomez was both bringing in and hauling out. If he was stashing everything in safe-deposit boxes, well, those had to be mighty big boxes.

Ironically, Robert didn't shy from the subject. When asked what he planned to do with all his loot, he replied, "You never heard of a guy who buries everything in his back yard?" Then he laughed like a hyena, but Garcia wasn't so sure it was a joke.

Robert took Garcia to Arnie Morton's steakhouse. He took freelance writer Max Shapiro, too. "Robert asked me to write a story about him," remembered Shapiro. "He told me, 'I've got plenty of stories. Your readers will *love* me.' He added, 'Tell your readers I just beat up Frenchie,' who was an obnoxious player at the Bike. I remember thinking, Robert has soft, delicate hands like a girl, and he needs those hands for what he does for a living. I had a hard time imagining him in a fistfight."

It took a while, but James and Robert eventually found out that Philadelphia finder Kim Krawizcki was charging $5,000, $6,000, even $7,000 finder's fees. Right away, both Gwen Baker and Corinne Conway became jealous. What's more, it was enraging buyers who later learned that the Midwest finders charged a whole lot less than Kim. Why would the estate sell a Mustang convertible for $2,200 in Tennessee and $7,200 in Pennsylvania? Some of those buyers phoned James at the Kemp Avenue office and raised holy hell.

Baker and Gomez got on the phone with Krawizcki. "You gotta stop, or we're going to throw the book at you," Robert warned, not explaining what the "book" might be. He told her that, to put things right, he was going to have to consult with an attorney in New York and that he might also "have to calm down the FBI in Philadelphia." Baker chimed in, "Please, Kim, just do as my godsons say, and they'll do their best to keep you out of jail."

Then they made some subtle threats, intimating that they could fire Krawizcki and replace her with Pastor John Alexander in Atlanta. After all, Alexander seemed very promising, very aggressive. Plus, unlike Krawizcki, the man had his own church. It was in a strip mall, sure, but it would nevertheless be Bonus City as far as car sales were concerned.

The FBI? *Jail?* Krawizcki didn't know what they were talking about. "And I got even more furious," she recalled, "when I heard that Dr. Conway said she didn't even know I was charging the [larger] fees, that she hadn't given me permission. And I'm like, '*Hello,* you're cashing the thousand-dollar checks every single day.'"

In a huff, Krawizcki called the executor himself. "I'm on the next plane to California," she warned, "and I'm not leaving until we have a face-to-face."

James sighed. Why was everyone so angry? Why couldn't everyone do as he did and maintain a low profile?

Krawizcki arrived in L.A. in March 2001. "They picked me up in a limo," she remembered, "and I met James at a restaurant near Disneyland. He arrived in some sort of sports car. He was wearing this beautiful suit and tie. Polite, soft-spoken, very handsome. An extreme gentleman. So I showed him all my documents, receipts, the works, so he could see no one was getting cheated. And he goes, 'Well, you misrepresented the estate, Kim, but I believe you're innocent. And what we're going to have to do, now, is give free cars to the buyers who paid these excessive fees.' So it was cars in lieu of cash, and I was told to help facilitate that. I reminded him that I liked Pastor Alexander and had done considerable business with him, but I didn't want to be replaced by him. And all James said to me was, 'Yeah, well, we just hooked him.'"

Krawizcki flew home to Philadelphia and called every single client she had, informing all that they'd be receiving one or more free cars. "Some were thrilled, some didn't care, some were mad," she said. "But after that, I felt like the rest of the Miracle Cars team gave me the cold shoulder. They were getting ready to banish me. I was out of the loop." There was dissension in the ranks.

15

MEN IN BLACK

When fifty-six-year-old Dan Stewart first heard the term "Miracle Cars," he had already been an assistant U.S. attorney for twenty-three years, six of them in Chicago following his graduation from Northwestern. In 1974, he had married Linda Arnce, who was one of the FBI's first female agents. "Our kids [Andy and Lauren] thought it was unfair that their father was an assistant U.S. attorney and their mother was an FBI agent," Stewart said. "They had feds crawling all over 'em. But they got over it."

In or out of his Kansas City courthouse office, Stewart was the antithesis of the hard-bitten government prosecutor. He was modest, shy, soft-spoken, and eager to please. Even when he wasn't wearing a cardigan, he bore a striking resemblance to Fred Rogers and possessed the TV host's gentle, easygoing nature. He was not afraid of confrontations but went some distance to avoid them.

Stewart had been assigned to the Miracle Cars case. As the point man, it was his job to deploy the "slow-motion stranglers"—Special Agent Gary Marshall and Inspector Steve Hamilton—in a coordinated low-profile investigation that wouldn't panic the victims or tip off the perps. At least for the time being.

What Stewart, Marshall, and Hamilton did first was simply chat with a few local investors. "I was shocked by what they said," Stewart recalled. "Almost to a man, they'd tell us, 'This *can't* be a hoax, because I've gone to meetings with my minister.' Or they'd say, 'These people involved with the estate, they're people of faith, so it *can't* be untrue, because religious people wouldn't lie.' "

"It floored me," remembered Marshall, "because even when I'd tell victims, 'Listen, I have serious doubts that these cars exist,' they'd come back with, 'Well, that's *today* you don't know whether they exist, but that doesn't mean they don't—I have faith that this blessing will occur.' I'd walk away shaking my head."

Stewart had assumed that most of the buyers were motivated by greed. But around Kansas City, it didn't seem that way. "These were decent people, a lot of them poor," he noticed. "They'd taken out loans for a thousand, two thousand. And others had used credit-card cash advances and now were paying twenty percent or whatever, and what had started as a small inconvenience was now a financial disaster."

Stewart interviewed Thelma Carnes, the seamstress who created the red Miracle Cars blazers for the football stars. And he interviewed an elderly black woman named Rosie Ingram, a cosmetology instructor. Her husband, Otis, had been in an accident and was desperate for a reliable automobile. Rosie and Otis prayed for help. "And when Corinne Conway came along," she told Stewart, "I thought God Himself had selected us for His blessing."

"You'd finish an interview like that," Hamilton recalled, "and you'd get in your car and think you were gonna cry, it was so pitiful. I'm accustomed to people lying to me, giving me alibis and excuses. This was different. These people believed the estate was real, and a lot of them would hardly talk to us. They'd say, 'You guys do *not* know what you're talking about.' Some of them laughed at us."

When the small investors wouldn't talk, Stewart moved to Plan B. Examining the documents that Agent Marshall had already uncovered, he noticed that football player Neil Smith was a monumental investor. "I happened to know his attorney," recalled Stewart. "So the attorney tells me, 'Well, sure, go ahead and talk to Neil, but just reveal the broad elements of the scheme.' So one day—it's pouring rain—we all drive out to Blue Springs [a Kansas City suburb on the Missouri side]. We ring the doorbell, and here's Neil in his bare feet, and he's about seven feet tall and in great shape, just huge. I'm looking straight up so I'm not talking to his stomach, you know? Neil and his wife, Shari, have this pure white carpet, like lamb's wool. Neil says to us, in this rumbling voice, *'Take off your shoes.'* He sounded like the Jolly Green Giant. And we later joked, 'If he'd asked, we'd have taken off our *clothes.*' So Gary shows him a summary of where the money went. He looks at it, studies it, and when he gets to the end of the flow chart, he sees the word 'casino.' Well, I thought the guy's head was going to explode. Really, I'm sort of eyeing the door in case he goes nuts. He told us he thought his money had been sent into a trust account. Then he goes, 'But the cars, *those* are still real, right?' I was amazed, just amazed."

"He didn't know how much he'd actually invested," recalled Hamilton. "He was mad at two things: where the money went and how *much* of it went. He thought he'd invested only half of what he had [$522,900]. He asked me, 'Are you sure this is all mine?' I think his wife had been investing more than he knew. And Gary says to him, 'It's *alllllll* yours.' And he looked at his wife like, 'We'll discuss this later.' "

Stewart, Marshall, and Hamilton then drove over to Ricky Siglar's house in Overland Park, Kansas, and the scene repeated itself. Siglar had a whole network of investors, including other pro athletes with similarly wondrous savings accounts.

"Ricky asked us, almost begged us, to be allowed to go into a room alone with Robert Gomez for fifteen minutes, said he'd solve the problem," remembered Stewart. "But both the Smiths and the Siglars are very religious, very sincere, and they had trouble believing that people of their own kind would do them dirty. When we left, I could see they were wrestling with that. I mean, emptying a guy's wallet is one thing. But to shake his faith while you're at it? That's a double whammy."

As fraud investigations went, this one was a freak. People had been ripped off coast to coast. Yet the victims hadn't much wanted Chief Cindy Schroer's help, and now they didn't much want the feds' help, either.

In Seattle, investor Matt Jones demanded to know why he'd been tricked into paying more than $100,000 in finder's fees. In San Juan Capistrano, car dealer Greg Ross was agitating to see some VINs. In Grove City, Ohio, Robert Fluellen insisted that cars better begin arriving on tractor-trailers, or someone would hear about it. And in Tucson, Richard Gil, the president of a biotech company, wanted proof that James R. Nichols even existed.

Many investors had been waiting for cars for more than two years. If they didn't get some answers, they wanted their money back, and fast. Matt Jones, in fact, had already threatened to call the cops and had begun tape-recording his conversations with Corinne Conway.

James was feeling the heat, and he didn't like it. Robert was of little help. He was busy playing big shot in the casinos, taking aim at the "stationary targets," the amateurs. There *had* to be a way to calm these people. James phoned Gwen Baker and instructed her to invite the "problem investors" to a formal business-powwow brunch on March 19, 2001, in California. He rented a room in the Smoke House restaurant in Burbank, the home of American mainstream TV, which would impress the sodbuster Midwesterners. There was a long table in the room, with a starched linen tablecloth, and a dozen Impressionist watercolors hung from the walls. Sixteen investors flew in from all over the country, eager to learn when their cars would be delivered, eager to give James an earful.

James sat at the head of the table, with Gwen Baker to his immediate left. He was wearing a stunning black Hugo Boss suit with a white handkerchief jutting from his breast pocket, and Baker was in a formal gray suit with tall collar. As the meeting began, ice-cold mimosas were served. They had a calming effect.

Attendees included not only the problem investors but also the recently recruited Atlanta finder, Pastor John Alexander, who, along with his wife, Jane, was attending in the capacity of all-around cheerleader. The heir to the estate was nowhere to be seen. When James was asked why, he responded, "Because Mr. Gomez is a hazard to himself."

As attendees sipped their drinks, James stood to address the flock, his arms outstretched like a preacher's. He introduced himself as the executor of the estate, and explained how he'd once worked for the late, great John Bowers, Robert's adoptive father. "Mr. Bowers trusted me before his death," he declared. He explained that his job was to minimize Robert's various delinquent tendencies—alcohol, drugs, and, most recently, gambling —and that he expected to be rewarded for this service with a modest engineering job at Mission Foods in Texas, where Bowers had formerly worked. James related that Robert's self-destructiveness may already have induced liver cancer. The group sighed and clucked, and Baker offered a quick prayer.

James stated that his own health was shaky, given all the hours he'd spent at computer terminals, just about burning out his retinas. At least he didn't have to maintain the cars, he said, smiling. The estate had hired "thirty-some mechanics" to do that. He assured the group that their funds were safe in a noninterest-bearing escrow account in Chase Manhattan Bank. One investor asked, "All that money, wouldn't it be better if it was earning a little interest over the past two years?"

"Absolutely not," James snapped. "It would be inappropriate. An estate is not a moneymaking vehicle"—a brief moment of personal irony, perhaps. Then he raised the subject of excessive finder's fees, and stated that no such fees had been approved by the estate's board of directors, that he and Robert were just sick about it, and that "a class-action suit was being contemplated against Doctors Conway and Krawizcki." The solution, he said, was that investors who had been overcharged would be compensated with additional cars—anywhere from ten to fifteen of them—delivered free of charge.

Gwen Baker seemed pleased to hear her fellow National Finders were in hot water, and Matt Jones seemed satisfied, too, especially when James whipped out a legal-looking contract in which the bonus cars were guaranteed in writing. Jones, Nichols, and Baker all signed the contract. Other investors followed suit. Some of the group's anger had been dissipated.

Then Baker stood and handed out copies of a document printed on the James R. Nichols Private Investing letterhead. Among the Miracle Cars participants, it would ever after be known as the "Smoke House letter." In part it read:

> It has been brought to my attention by the master attorney Shawn Houston, who is closing the probate of the estate, that we have confirmed a closing date of March 25, 2002. Such date has been set forth by the Arbitration Judge Jack Lomeli and has been accepted by the board of directors of the estate. I have confirmed such dates with all investment

groups involved and would ask of you to close all open accounts with myself.

On behalf of the heir to the estate, I would like to extend my gratitude and appreciation. Due to the security and safety of the heir, installed "gag" order remains in effect. Attorneys involved wish to keep this correspondence and date extremely confidential.

Sincerely,

James R. Nichols

Assigned Executor

Several invitees read only as far as the "2002" date before their blood began to boil. An airline pilot shouted, "I cannot wait another whole year." Two other investors demanded, "No more delays, unless we see the cars *right now.*"

A mutiny was brewing. James hadn't expected this reaction. He thought the investors would be thrilled with a document that absolutely, positively specified a date beyond which probate proceedings would not venture. "Hold on, please, *hold on,*" he pleaded, trying to regain control. "Let me see if I can get Shawn Houston on the phone, and maybe he'll allow you to see the cars." He withdrew his cell phone, then walked out of the banquet room and out of the restaurant itself. But he didn't call Shawn Houston. Instead, he called Robert Gomez.

While James was on the phone, Gwen Baker took her own shot at calming the troops. "I've *seen* the cars," she declared. "In Long Beach. And, oh, what a pretty sight it was!"

"Gwen," Matt Jones countered, "we want the phone numbers of the estate's attorneys."

"Come *on,* are you losing faith?" she replied, her standard comeback. "We must pray for patience."

When James returned, he was trailed by Pastor Alexander,

who followed him to the head of the table. There, Nichols, Baker, and Alexander briefly huddled in three-way prayer.

"Alexander had totally kissed James's ass throughout the whole proceeding," Greg Ross later grumbled. "It was like he'd been paid to be pious, and it was corny to see them bow their heads in what was intended to be a business affair." When Alexander solemnly uttered, "Amen," Ross asked, "Who, exactly, is on the estate's board?"

"Eleven directors, thirteen attorneys," James replied, volunteering no names.

Ross felt certain his fellow investors would again acquiesce to James's entreaties. "He was a commanding presence, just this supersharp kid who absorbed every statement, every detail," Ross recalled. "He'd think, pause, speak slowly and carefully, never jumping back with a quick comment or off-the-cuff statement. You felt like you were listening to someone with real weight."

The Smoke House meeting lasted ninety minutes. No legal documents from the estate were produced—no will, no gag order, no monthly statements from Chase Manhattan Bank, no letters from any judge. Also, no Robert and no cars. But there had been some champagne, a tasty brunch, and James had conducted himself like the chief financial officer of a Fortune 500 company. "He was just totally professional," recalled investor Richard Gil. "Charismatic, a powerful speaker, a strong voice, intelligent." In fact, Gil asked to have his picture taken with James, although what he really needed was proof that Nichols the executor existed. It was what the research doctors at his biotech company back home in Tucson were demanding.

After the meeting concluded, Matt Jones sauntered casually to the parking lot to photograph the license on James Nichols's latest BMW M3. He meant to do it surreptitiously, but James noticed.

"He thought my car was an M5," Nichols later related. "He was obviously delirious. An M5 has four doors. An M3 has two."

When Richard Gil arrived home in Tucson, he showed the research doctors his photo of Nichols. Then he studied a piece of paper he'd been given during the meeting, on which the name of the estate's official financial adviser had been recorded. The adviser's name was Girard. But when Gil went to dial the number, he noticed a funny thing. Girard's number was identical to James's.

In theory, the Smoke House meeting had been a good idea. The Smoke House *letter*, on the other hand—delaying delivery for another year—had left investors smoking mad.

Car dealer Greg Ross had developed quite a reputation in Southern California as a man who could acquire any car that any buyer desired. He could glance at an auto from fifty feet and recite many of the digits that would necessarily appear on its VIN. James Nichols and Robert Gomez held $120,000 of Ross's money, and they were beginning to give him the heebie-jeebies. Ross decided to take one more shot at researching the estate of John Bowers, and if it didn't come up smelling like roses, he was going to bail faster than a tipsy paratrooper.

On March 30, eleven days after the Smoke House meeting, Ross phoned Gwen Baker in Memphis and told her he *had* to speak to the manager of the bank servicing the estate. He made it clear he would not be put off. Baker called Robert Gomez. Gomez told her, "It's gonna be a big hassle, and the attorneys will pitch a fit, but I can put it together." A day or two passed, then, sure enough, a man named Bob Burrows phoned Ross at his office.

"He had a strong, deep voice, with an unmistakable African American accent," Ross recalled. "He said he was the mortgage and escrow officer, that First Bank & Trust just had a holding account, that no money stayed in it long. He said it was because they were trying to avoid threats on Robert's life, because of his street background and having all this money and all. He said the money came in and then quickly moved to an escrow account elsewhere. He told me, 'I've known Robert and James for twenty years, and there's $20 million in their main account.' I was careful to get his phone number so I could call back if I had other questions later. But he told me, 'Well, don't call back for a week, because my wife just had a baby.' "

Ross hung up feeling a little better. But it didn't last, not even for two hours. He had other questions, wanted to probe more deeply, and now he didn't care if Burrows himself were breast-feeding. "Late Friday I called back, and they said Burrows was out, but they said they'd have him paged at a branch of the bank in Newport Beach. When nobody called back, I became totally paranoid. So I drove over there and looked inside, hoping to see a black manager. Nothing. Then on Saturday morning, my phone rings, and it's Gwen Baker. She says: 'Greg, are you checking up on us? Nobody has faith anymore. It breaks my heart.' And now I'm thinking, How the hell did Baker in Memphis know I was trying to check up on Burrows in Newport Beach? How could that be? Who would call her to tell her that?"

Ross spent an additional three and a half days sweating bullets, waiting for Burrows to call. Finally, on Wednesday, the phone rang.

"The guy says, 'Hello, this is Bob Burrows,' " Ross remembered. "But now he's got this strong New England accent, maybe even British, you know? So I said, 'Mr. Burrows, what do you do for a living?' He says, 'I'm a loan officer with First Bank & Trust.' I said, 'Okay, do you know James Nichols?' He says, 'No, I don't.' So I sort of clenched up. Then I asked, 'Are you maintaining an account for the estate of John Bowers?' He says, 'I don't handle estate accounts.' And then I popped the big one, and now I'm completely holding my breath and my heart is pounding. I said, 'Uh, Mr. Burrows, did you and I talk last Friday?' "

He replied, "Mr. Ross, I don't think we've *ever* talked."

"The bottom fell out of my stomach," recalled Ross. "I was dizzy for a second. You know those movie scenes where a guy gets some news so bad that he just drops the phone? That's how I felt. It's like going into a room and turning on a light, and suddenly you see all the rats scurrying away. I thought, My god, not only is it a con, but they've got a troupe of actors and operatives all over the country."

Ross hung up but remained right where he'd been sitting. He held his head in his hands and tried to think what to do next. At first he was terrified. He felt that his office might be bugged or that someone had tapped the phones. How else could Baker have known he'd been talking to Burrows? And if she knew he'd talked to the fake Burrows, she might also know he'd talked to the *real* Burrows. And if so, would someone be on his way over right this instant to put a bullet in his brain? People got killed over as little as $100, never mind $120,000.

It took a while, but when the fear passed, it was replaced by fury. Ross wanted to call every Smoke House attendee and form a posse that would ride to Kemp Avenue and string up James Nichols and tar and feather Robert Gomez.

"Finally, I calmed down," he recalled. "It occurred to me that goal number one was getting my money back. If I started telling these people, 'You dirty thieving bastards, I *knew* it was a lie!' it was gonna work in their favor, not mine. My plan became, Don't let 'em know. Not yet. So I drafted a very calm, matter-of-fact letter to Gwen Baker. It said, 'Thanks for the chance to buy these cars, and I'm definitely coming back later with an even larger investment, but right now I need my original $120,000 back, just for the time being, no harm, no foul, it was great doing business with you.' Real relaxed, real friendly, you know? Then I sat down and waited ten days. The longest ten days of my life. But you know what? It worked. My money came back. I felt like a fish who gets reeled all the way back to the boat, then the hook slips out at the last possible second. It was like, *Thank you, God, I got away.*"

Ross filed a complaint with the local sheriff. But when the sheriff learned that Ross had been refunded his money, he said, "Well, now you haven't lost anything. You were just inconvenienced. Now there's no crime. There's no one to bust."

Ross was annoyed but remained giddy about getting his money back. He phoned superinvestor Matt Jones up in Seattle. "I said, 'Matt, come *on,* don't you think this is screwy? The deal's no good, man, you gotta get out.' Matt said to me, 'Well, I'm in real deep. My lawyers are on it. But it still looks okay. I'll wait a little longer.' I said to myself, It looks *okay?* Wait for *what?* Wait for them to run? How do you get your money back then?"

In the spring of 2001, James Nichols told his mother, "My stress level is just going up and up." He mentioned to Robert Gomez that he was thinking about resigning as executor of the estate. Robert replied, "Are you nuts? If a few investors back out, who cares? We'll get more. We always have before."

Which was absolutely true. But it wasn't Robert who had to keep the peace. The three women—Baker, Conway, and Krawizcki—were again acting as if they wanted to gouge out one another's eyes, and James wasn't sure how much longer he could play the role of mediator, calming antsy investors.

During the month of April, a scant $35,000 in car-sales proceeds dribbled into the First Bank & Trust account in Lakewood. James had written a lot of big checks that month and had unwittingly emptied the account. He now owed $60 in insufficient-funds charges. It was embarrassing. The Lakewood clerks, who had previously doted on the handsome young man in the beautiful black sport coats, were now giving him the stink eye. What was going on?

In truth, it wasn't as bad as it looked. He hated to do it, but James got on the phone and called a few folks who hadn't yet invested but had written letters of inquiry—the people who annoyingly wanted VINs and photos of the cars. He told them that Nichols Private Investing (his company) had been in touch with Global Financial (Krawizcki's company), who'd been assured that Auto Emporium (Baker's company) was within weeks of shipping cars to the Faith Car Club (Conway's company). Then he called the National Finders and encouraged them to step up their efforts. It worked like a charm. Within thirty days, Gwen Baker watched as $656,497 flowed into her Auto Emporium account in Memphis.

But everyone *did* seem to be coming up with whopping expenses. For starters, there was Baker's $30,000-per-month salary, for which she filed receipts saying, "Business Expenses, per Shawn Houston." And then, using Miracle Cars proceeds, she had to buy a new $29,532 silver Chevrolet Camaro for her daughter Kimberly Baker. And Robert was still bitching about the $12,500 he'd spent entertaining investors in Las Vegas. And that was followed by yet another miserable Vegas trip, during which he'd immediately lost $34,100 at the Luxor and $20,000 at the Aladdin, which wasn't really a problem until he had words with the cage manager, who filed a CTR. And when the cage manager had the temerity to ask for a Social Security number, Robert had started cursing, causing the man to write in huge letters, "SSN REFUSED!" which wasn't the sort of message anyone wanted to be sending to the IRS.

Robert soothed his bruised psyche by locating a Vegas jeweler to appraise an eighteen-karat gold-and-steel Rolex Oyster Perpetual he'd just been given by one of the California casinos. The jeweler assured him it was genuine, valuing it at $4,995. Big deal. He had $50,000 worth of free jewelry back home, including a $10,000 ruby-encrusted Movado that made the Rolex look like a county-fair trinket.

But James remained nervous. The cash flow was jerky, not consistent. He temporarily slashed Robert's allowance from five figures a week to four. Robert didn't care. He just went back to writing $25,000 checks on which he was forging Nichols's signature, buying them back at the end of the night. In this enterprise he remained careless. Twice he forgot to make out the checks to anyone at all. Once he signed Nichols's name as "Nichol," then returned later to add an upper-case *S*. And on a $50,000 check written to the Club Caribe Casino, he'd added in the lower-left corner, "O.K. per Robert Gomez." He was preapproving his own forged checks—quite a trick.

Then, more bad news. One of Baker's regional finders—the bishop who'd attended the Vegas junket, in fact—had been circulating promotional brochures claiming that the great John Bowers had worked for Mission Foods, the company that daily produced 14.5 million corn tortillas. One of the brochures landed in the wrong hands.

A man named Salvador Elias called. He was a legal officer for Gruma Corporation, which owned Mission Foods, and he wasn't happy. Elias informed Baker that as many as ten persons had called, all inquiring about John Bowers. He said to her, in no uncertain terms: "Ma'am, there is no John Bowers who ever worked here, you understand? *No John Bowers.*"

Baker immediately called the heir. "Robert told me that his father was associated with a *different* Mission Foods," she recalled.

"Mission Foods in *Mexico,* not America. And then he changed the subject."

Baker was troubled. Robert's explanations were sometimes a little too facile. She resolved thereafter to record in her Day-Timer whatever he said on the phone, including time and date. And then she told James about her conversations with Elias and Robert.

James rubbed his eyes and groaned. All these tedious setbacks were working on his nerves. He'd become jumpy and irritable and was again arguing with Kimberly Hall, who described their relationship as "a work in progress." And then came the capper—the news that Greg Ross had demanded a full refund, the whole $120,000. James walked into his mother's bedroom, closed the door, sat on her bed, and told her he was again thinking about resigning. Rose replied, "It's better that you do. The money isn't worth your health." She had felt the same way forty-four months prior, when she'd been selling cars herself.

James sat for a moment, thinking. Then he said, "But if I resign, you and Gwen and Aunt Gladys won't get what you're due. I *have* to stay in to protect your interests."

Gwen Baker thought that was quite gallant of him.

16

INNOCENT BYSTANDERS

I n the spring of 2001, Linda Janowski discovered the joys of the California card parlors through a coworker named Val Morella. After a hard day's work, Linda found it relaxing to eat dinner at a casino, then watch the boys fling wads of cash at one another. She wasn't a skillful gambler herself but was learning. And everyone was kind to her. Linda was no spring chicken, but she wore expensive pantsuits and possessed a figure that caused men to gawk. The boys in the casinos liked showing off for her. Plus, she was funny and smart.

Janowski, then forty-three, was the finance director at South Bay Toyota in Gardena. It was her dream job—she was the third most powerful person in the dealership—but it had taken her twenty years in the car business to achieve that status. Now she was earning big bucks, $18,000 per month, more than 200K per year. "Not bad for a little Jewish girl from New Jersey," she liked to say.

One night, her friend Morella said, "Have you met Buddha? He bets as much as $30,000 a hand. You won't believe it."

"When I saw him, I said, 'Really? *That* young kid?'" she remembered. "He appeared to be about fifteen years old, you know? But he was as sweet as could be, cute. Even though he was a professional player and everybody knew him, he'd take time to play heads-up poker with me, just to be nice. One time we were playing, and suddenly he stands up and shouts, 'Hey, Larry!' And it's Larry Flynt, for real. My God, you know, it's so cool, he's friends with Larry. I'm in awe, because back then I was still into the whole Hollywood celebrity thing—you know, Vanna White is buying a house down the street, Dennis Rodman is driving past in a Ferrari, and now I'm playing cards with a kid who's friends with Larry Flynt. And Robert was good, too. I once saw him start with $100,000 and make half a million at pai gow. *Half a million.* He had balls, that boy, I'll tell you. But he was rude to the dealers, and sometimes it was embarrassing. He hated them to make eye contact. He'd scream, 'Don't look at me, look at the goddamn *cards,* you whore!' And 'whore' was about the nicest word he used. It was usually the c-word. And if he was losing, he'd say, 'Get a new dealer, get her out, *now!*' and they'd do it. The casinos really worshipped him—took him on a cruise to Mexico, Lakers tickets, jewelry, whatever he wanted."

Gomez and Janowski became friends. "With no warning, Robert would call me at the dealership late on Friday afternoons," she remembered, "and he'd say, 'Linda, we're flyin' to Vegas, no need to pack, I'll buy everything you need when we get there.' And off we'd go. Robert would have this giant two-bedroom suite in the Bellagio, all comped, and I'd stay in one room, and he'd stay in the other with this little Filipino friend who was always by his side—Tony, little Tony Zaldua. Everybody called him 'Robert's geisha girl.' I'd usually gamble alone, because I wasn't into the huge-money stuff. Then later I'd just watch. And then Robert bought me a beautiful necklace. One time my sister tagged along, and it was the same for her, everything free. We had a ball."

Gomez told Janowski that he'd inherited his wealth from his

grandfather. He told her that his biological father—now living in Beverly Hills—was a terrible womanizer and had become resentful when Robert was put in charge of his grandpa's estate, "zeroing out his dad." He told her that his mother lived in a West Covina mansion, that she drove a Lexus and pretty much lived in the lap of luxury.

Janowski was mesmerized by a lifestyle so reckless and carefree. She'd never met anybody like Robert Gomez.

One afternoon, Robert walked into South Bay Toyota and told Linda he wanted to buy a car. "It was a huge black Sequoia sport-ute," she recalled. "It cost $45,000. As a trade-in he had this Ford Lightning truck he'd bought in Vegas. But then he tells me, 'Listen, Linda, the problem is that I don't have any credit because I'm a professional gambler. Banks don't give gamblers loans, you know? What's more, I don't put *any* vehicles in my name, *ever,* because I don't want tax problems.' So his solution was to put the Sequoia in the name of my friend Val Morella. It's what's known as a straw purchase. I don't know how ethical it is, but it's done all the time."

Gomez drove away in the luxurious Sequoia but returned to South Bay only a month later. He told Janowski that he'd heard the truck had "rollover problems" and that, in any event, he'd fallen in love with a Ford Expedition. "So we gave him $38,000 for the thing," she recalled, "making $7,000 or so on the deal, and Robert walked away happy, and the dealership was pretty happy, too."

The deals between Janowski and Gomez had just begun.

Not long after, Janowski wanted to buy a new house but came up $60,000 short, because most of her money was tied up in a separate piece of real estate. It occurred to her, however, that a man who could make $500,000 in one night of gambling might be in a position to lend her a piddling sixty grand.

"Robert immediately said he'd do it," Janowski recalled, "and he was as kind as could be. But he said, 'Linda, in return, there are two things you can do for me.' First, he was sick of living with Richie Sklar in Downey and wanted to move into his own condo on Country Club Lane in Long Beach. It was right on a golf course, really beautiful, and it even had a floor safe in the master bedroom. He said to me, '*You* sign the rental agreement, then *you* pay the rent, which is $2,500 per month. In one year, that comes to $30,000.' "

Janowski wasn't thrilled with the idea—why should her name be on the lease? On the other hand, why would a kid who was quite obviously a millionaire burn her?

"Then he tells me part two of the deal," Janowski remembered. "He said, 'Next, I want you to open a player's account at the Bike and apply for $30,000 of credit, which they'll give you in an instant because of your great job and all.' " This, too, seemed harmless. After all, this was her best pal, Buddha, whom the casinos adored.

Robert ponied up the $60,000 loan in dribs and drabs. He'd hand Janowski whatever bills happened to be in his pockets at the time—"six thousand dollars here, seven thousand there," she recalled. What she didn't know was that Robert had already talked to his employee friends at the Bike, who secretly added Gomez's name to Janowski's new player's account, as if he were her husband. Now it was a joint account. It hadn't been difficult, either. On the application form, Bicycle Casino employees had written of Janowski, "Owns five properties, excellent credit." On an adjoining page, they wrote of Gomez, "BIG PLAYER, once to four times per week, pai gow poker, private games." With so glowing an endorsement, Robert had the Bike raise Janowski's credit limit to $50,000. It meant he had access to that sum any time of the day or night, and if he didn't feel like paying it back, well, Linda Janowski would be responsible. But he didn't tell her any of this.

It was not the sort of thing that one friend would do to another. But it was small potatoes compared with what came next.

Robert Gomez moved into his elegant new condo on Country Club Lane. A scene from the movie *Ferris Bueller's Day Off* had been filmed in his back yard. Robert's new friend, Tony Zaldua, moved in, too. Linda Janowski was paying their rent.

"I would prefer not to have my name advertised at the front security gate," Robert instructed the owners' association. "Only my immediate family visits me here."

Which wasn't exactly true, because on weekends he hosted low-stakes poker parties for his pals—bookies, shoeshiners, groupies, and random pilot fish like "Fingers" Sklar. As his friends gambled, Robert would stroll from player to player, evaluating each man's cards, munching Doritos, and whispering words of advice. His friends usually listened. When they'd bust out, Robert would laugh until his breasts bounced, then he'd reach inside the Buddha statue on the hearth. "Here, this'll make you feel a little better," he'd say, dropping a handful of twenties or fifties in front of whichever player had lost the most. Then the action would resume. "At my house," he told friends, "no one's a loser. Come on and play like big daddy!"

For the most part, his house was clean and tastefully decorated. "Leather furniture, the most expensive flat-screen TVs in every room, but it never looked like a fraternity house," recalled Linda Janowski. And Robert was developing a massive collection of sports paraphernalia. On display were World Series baseballs under glass, plus jerseys that had been worn by Michael Jordan, Shaquille O'Neal, and Kobe Bryant. "Then amidst all that, he'd display something totally out of place, like really ugly crystal figurines that cost a thousand dollars apiece. He did it because he thought it was funny."

Robert was sometimes as lazy as a basset hound. But when the funds for his beloved gambling were threatened, he reliably leapt into action. When he heard that car dealer Greg Ross had bailed out of the Miracle Cars operation, Robert began wondering whether the investors needed the sort of reassurance that James had intended to supply during the hapless Smoke House meeting.

At eleven-thirty in the morning on July 17, 2001, Robert unexpectedly showed up at South Bay Toyota. He practically begged Linda Janowski and her coworker, Val Morella, to accompany him to lunch. Linda agreed but warned that they'd have to be back by one P.M. She had a managers' meeting to attend. The trio ate at a Mexican restaurant, and when they returned, Robert inexplicably hung around Linda's office, apparently bored and making a general nuisance of himself. At one point, he began fingering a stack of South Bay Toyota letterhead.

"This is nice," he said. "Do you mind if I look at this? I'm thinking about starting a company that transports cars, and I'm curious about company logos."

Janowski was on the phone, preparing for her meeting, and she didn't appreciate this distraction. But she took time to tell him, "Robert, that's the old letterhead. We use it for scrap." Then she pointed to a pile of new letterhead.

"Well, these are cool, too," he said. "Do you mind if I take a sample of each?"

"I don't care what you do," she snapped, "because I have to go to my meeting now." Then she walked out of her office, leaving Buddha, the king of pai gow poker, standing by himself with a piece of stationery in each hand.

And that was the very day, by coincidence, that a curious document emanated from a fax machine at South Bay Toyota, 18416 South Western Avenue, Gardena, California. The one-page fax was addressed to James R. Nichols, in Carson. In part, it read:

This letter is to confirm we are in receipt of 322 vehicles that were previously contracted to South Bay Toyota for the agreed upon maintenance and servicing. This maintenance should take approximately six to eight weeks. In accordance with Toyota's 220-point inspection, each vehicle will be thoroughly inspected, road-tested, and will meet the requirements of a genuine Toyota certified vehicle. Should you require any additional information, please do not hesitate to call.

The fax appeared to be signed by Thomas Burchett, general manager of South Bay Toyota, and it immediately wound up on Gwen Baker's desk in Memphis. Lo and behold, it was exactly what she needed to allay investors' fears. Here was proof positive, from the manager of a huge car dealership, that at least 322 of the Miracle Cars were being conscientiously maintained, just as James had claimed. All she needed now was a similarly persuasive document showing that some of the cars had already been shipped.

As if sent from heaven above, another fax arrived. This one was on the letterhead of Payless Towing & Storage, 1300 North Lakeview Avenue, Anaheim, California. It was a copy of an invoice for $28,620, made out to the attention of "James Nichols Private Investing." The invoice showed that 11 models of luxury automobiles—among them 113 Mercedes-Benz S500s, 24 Cadillac Sevilles, 4 Porsche 911 Carreras, and 92 Toyota 4Runners—had been shipped from Payless's lot in Anaheim to Fontana. Why late-model cars would need to be trucked from Anaheim to Fontana, only twenty-five miles distant, went unexplained. Wouldn't it have been the briefest of trips for superanxious buyers, and wouldn't the estate have saved $28,620 in shipping fees? As usual, not one person ever asked such questions, at least out loud.

And then a third fax arrived. It was on the letterhead of the

Union Pacific Railroad and was a quote for shipping cars from Los Angeles to Memphis. Gwen Baker was delighted—more proof that cars were about to be delivered nationwide! But when she telephoned Lori Bloom, the railroad employee who had signed the document, Baker was informed that Bloom hadn't worked in that department for more than a year.

She called the Kemp Avenue office to clear things up. Instead of reaching James, she connected with Rose, who seemed strangely uncommunicative. When Baker mentioned the Union Pacific document, Rose responded with a biblical parable about a lemon tree. "I thought Rose wasn't telling me everything," Baker later said. "She wasn't being honest with me about everything she knew." Baker felt the same about James. And she was still taking notes whenever Robert called.

For the time being, however, it didn't matter what Gwen Baker thought. Within hours, investors in Ohio, Pennsylvania, Georgia, Illinois, and Washington had all three documents shooting out of their fax machines. It wasn't as comforting as seeing the Miracle Cars themselves, but it was the next best thing. Here were the cars on paper, described by disinterested third-party contractors.

Seattle investor Matt Jones, perhaps the twitchiest of the investors—especially after his conversation with Greg Ross—called South Bay himself, just to double-check. He got transferred from employee to employee but eventually reached a man who seemed vaguely to know what was going on. Some three hundred Toyotas being serviced in six to eight weeks? That sounded about right, the man estimated—the dealership could handle that. Jones forgot to record his name. But he was hugely relieved. He thought to himself: See, I was right. Greg Ross bailed too soon.

Miracle Cars sales again picked up. From May 14 to June 14, 2001, $360,100 rolled into the First Bank & Trust account in

Lakewood. Included was an $8,000 wire transfer from Pastor Alexander's wife, Jane. It looked like the Atlanta couple was reaping God's blessings in the Confederate States. That was good news. James bumped Robert's allowance back up, handing him a couple of celebratory cashier's checks made out to Hollywood Park Casino—one for $104,500, the other for $145,000. There'd been a few shaky months, but the Miracle Cars operation was back on track. No one was happier than Robert Gomez.

In August 2001, Gwen Baker flew to Los Angeles and stayed with her daughter Kimberly Baker, in Agoura Hills. While in southern California, she didn't learn anything new from Rose Nichols, who was still reciting inscrutable lemon-tree parables, and she didn't learn anything new from James Nichols, either. He'd become oddly reclusive.

But Robert Gomez was still his fat and jolly self—cheerful, chipper, funny, enjoying life to the max. In fact, Robert phoned one morning just before Baker was to fly home to Memphis.

"He asked if I could drop by First Bank & Trust [where she was a cosignatory] to get a cashier's check," Baker recalled. Robert told her that James had rushed off to San Diego to work on someone else's estate. "I told him I was busy, on my way to the airport. He said, 'No problem, I'll meet you at the airport and pick it up there.'" Robert instructed Baker that the check's remitter should be James Nichols, and that it should be made payable to IC Enterprises in the amount of $200,000.

When she heard the amount, Baker began dragging her feet. She resisted further when he added, "This is just between the two of us. No need to tell James. He's all stressed out about the estate right now, and I've become half afraid to talk to him about anything, in case he has a mental breakdown or something."

Baker wasn't crazy about this plan. Conscientious business

execs didn't hide six-figure monetary transactions. But she changed her mind when Robert said: "Then, after you get the check for me, take a little something for yourself—I mean, for office expenses back in Memphis." When she asked how much, he said, "Oh, about $8,000, I'd say."

Baker obtained the $200,000 cashier's check, plus eight grand for herself, and met Robert at the airport. He seemed quite happy. Later that night, so was Ivy Chu, the "IC" half of "IC Enterprises," who owned Crystal Park Casino. When Ivy saw the $200,000 check, she instructed her casino manager, "Hand-carry this to the bank, *first* thing in the morning." But the check really didn't make a monstrous dent in the Lakewood account. In August, $750,900 worth of car-sales proceeds rolled in. In fact, James never even noticed that $208,000 was missing.

Buddha carried on with his gambling, laying what he called "bad beats on the bumpkins." Few gamblers win in the long run, but Robert seemed regularly to overcome the odds. Linda Janowski could tell when he was winning, because that's when she'd receive gifts. "When I moved into my new place," she remembered, "here he comes with a five-thousand-dollar Sony flat-screen TV as a housewarming gift. Then one night I was going to a party and didn't have anyone to take with me. I was feeling sad, and then I saw Robert, who was wearing a gold-and-diamond bracelet. He said to me, 'I can tell you love this, so I want you to have it.' And he gave it to me—twenty carats' worth of diamonds, I'll bet. I got the size reduced so it would fit my wrist. It was the most beautiful thing anybody ever gave me. I wore it into South Bay to show everybody I worked with. My boss said, 'Linda, you're so gullible—something's going *on* with that kid.' "

Janowski flew with Robert to San Francisco—where he gave her a selection of Montblanc pens—then on to Vegas. "We were in the high-roller pit in the Aladdin," she recalled, "and he went through half a million dollars in ten minutes. *Phew!* Blew it. All gone. He left mad, *furious*. But then he lightened up and said, 'Linda, let's get a picture of the two of us together.' He did that all the time, with his arm draped around me or around girls in the casinos, mugging, making faces for the camera. His house was full of those pictures. I think he wanted his friends to see him with the ladies. You know, in the casinos, all the big gamblers are John Wayne types, very macho. If you're gay, it's bad for business."

After Robert showered gifts on Linda, however, it was never long before he'd require a favor in return. Holding a satchel, he showed up one night at Janowski's front door. "He said his house had just been burglarized," she recalled, "and he wanted me to put his jewelry in a safe-deposit box, in case it happened again. He gave me seven or eight Rolexes, rings, gold, more men's bracelets. I'd once questioned why he had guns in his house, and now he says, 'See, *this* is why—I get robbed all the time.' After that, he put in an expensive burglar alarm."

A few weeks passed, then he showed up with another bag. "This time it was a bunch of videotapes he wanted to drop off for safekeeping," Janowski said. "He didn't tell me, but I found out they were porno tapes—young black men, boys really, who were masturbating in Best Western motels, with people yelling in the background, and maybe one of them was Robert. It was very strange material." Linda Janowski couldn't say for certain, but she got the feeling that Robert was "cleaning" his house in preparation for uninvited visitors.

Gomez's summer-of-2001 antics weren't concluded. Next, he phoned Gwen Baker in Memphis. He instructed her to begin *wiring* car-sales proceeds instead of sending checks by FedEx all the way from Tennessee. "No need to tell James," he said again. "James is just overwhelmed with a separate estate he's handling, and he's not putting enough attention on my father's estate, and I want things to hurry up and end."

Again, Baker was hesitant. If the boys wanted wire transfers, it meant they weren't interested in seeing the buyers' checks, and they'd thus have no way of knowing how many cars had been sold or to whom. They'd have to rely entirely on the National Finders' records. It actually leveraged Baker's position—now it would be easier to skim money in Memphis, if she were so inclined. But she wasn't thinking about that.

"Robert, I'm not sure I'm comfortable with this," Baker said. "For one thing, your books will be off, so I think we should first talk to—"

"If you help speed things up," Gomez interrupted, "I'll see to it you receive a handsome bonus." This time the bonus wasn't a mere $8,000. This time it was $50,000.

Baker liked the sound of that. After all, she still owed a bit on the various properties she'd purchased in Cole Farms subdivision. So she began wiring the money, exactly as Robert had instructed. The first batch of wires totaled right around $100,000.

17

UNDERCOVER RESEARCH

Back in Kansas City, Assistant U.S. Attorney Dan Stewart watched in awe as Special Agent Gary Marshall strutted his stuff. Marshall was patiently and painstakingly following the money, one check at a time. During June and July of 2001, he had been examining dozens of such checks, including one that cosmetology instructor Rosie Ingram had written to Gwen Baker. He noticed that, like the others, it wound up in the Lakewood, California, account. It had been one of several checks that James Nichols then used to obtain a cashier's check in the amount of $55,000 from First Bank & Trust, made payable to IC Enterprises—the Crystal Park Casino. Nichols then took out $1,650 in cash for himself. On the same day, that check was presented to Crystal Park Casino by Robert "Buddha" Gomez, who traded it for $53,350 in chips.

"Investors kept telling me their money was going into an escrow account at Chase Manhattan Bank," remembered Marshall. He and Inspector Steve Hamilton developed a running joke, asking each other, "Is it just me, or does the Crystal Park Casino look like a bank?"

Dan Stewart continued to interview victims. "I was amazed

at their divergent backgrounds," he said. "There was a retired Marine Corps major who said he'd taken $60,000 out of his retirement savings to invest in the cars. There was a young African American man from New York who obtained cash advances on his credit cards. He was planning to go to college on the money he'd make from selling his cars. And there was even an attorney with strong religious beliefs who told me he'd borrowed money to invest in the cars. He asked, 'How am I going to pay it back?' as if I'd know the answer. There were periods when I'd talk to one person after another like that. I'll tell you, it was depressing."

In the last few days of July 2001, Marshall, Hamilton, and Stewart sat down to talk in a little-used storage area on the fifth floor of the courthouse in Kansas City. They'd already nicknamed it the "war room," and they'd reserved eight filing cabinets to hold all the incoming documents and canceled checks. The three men quickly reached a consensus that the Miracle Cars scheme was likely a far-reaching fraud enacted by multiple conspirators who had duped thousands of buyers out of millions of dollars. So far, the agents had failed to find any probate proceeding for the decedent, John Bowers. They'd failed to find a Judge Jack Lomeli. They'd failed to find attorneys Houston, Gaines, and McNeil. And they'd failed to find any cars. They weren't even certain they knew all the actors. Sure, the money flowed mostly to the two boys in Los Angeles, but that didn't necessarily mean James and Robert were the kingpins. Where did the money go after Robert Gomez won in the casinos? Were the casinos part of the scam? Was all of this a new arm of organized crime whose purpose was to empty the collection plates in America's grassroots churches? The feds didn't know, but it almost looked that way.

It still appeared that the main characters, the in-the-trenches money earners who were daily fleecing congregations coast to coast, were the National Finders—Baker, Conway, and Krawizcki. If the three women were selling cars that did not exist, then they were committing crimes under the noses of federal agents watching silently from the shadows.

"I didn't want to blow our cover," said Stewart, "but I also had a moral obligation to do something if I thought a crime was ongoing. I'm not allowed to just watch from the sidelines, saying, 'Wow, will you look at that, these folks are really clever.' It seemed like a good time to go out and meet a few of the principals, one by one. My plan wasn't to accuse them of anything or say, '*Aha!* Now we've caught you,' or 'Hey, there *aren't any cars!*' because we still weren't positive of that. But what I *did* want to see, after we sat down and said, 'We're real uncomfortable with this, it really smells fishy,' was whether they'd continue to sell. That would tell us a lot."

What the Kansas City feds did first was talk to Kim Krawizcki in Philadelphia. It was the perfect place to start. Krawizcki, by then, had sold nearly four hundred Miracle Cars. Perhaps her most stunning sale had been to national TV evangelist Kenneth Copeland, who had purchased cars totaling $116,450. Various Copeland relatives signed on for an additional $102,500. And the official Kenneth Copeland Ministries was in for an extra $46,000. In their own way, the sales to Copeland were more impressive than the sales to the pro athletes. Under the cloak of religion, Krawizcki had tapped the coffers of a nationally known religious organization filled with pros as adept at collecting money as presidential campaign managers. They were men who had seen it all. *Until* they met pretty little Kim Krawizcki, with her slim figure and charming overbite.

Including the Copelands, Krawizcki had grossed $3,564,528. From that sum, she had given Conway $406,000 in secondary finder's fees. And then she'd taken $1,824,848 for herself. The remainder went to the boys.

But now the good times were over. Krawizcki was getting the cold shoulder from Baker and Conway. She was out of the loop and her sales had stalled. In fact, James Nichols had effectively replaced her with Pastor John Alexander, and Kim knew it. She'd been benched.

When the agents told Krawizcki they had doubts about the estate, her reaction was everything they'd hoped for. "She was totally mortified," recalled Dan Stewart.

"It was like having *Law and Order* show up at your house," Krawizcki said. "I sat down at noon, and when I looked up, it was dark. I hadn't moved. I stopped washing my hair, brushing my teeth, changing my clothes. I'd sit and watch TV and not know what was going on. I was scared to death I was going to jail. Then, finally, I said out loud, 'How *dare* you do this to me,' " referring to Baker and Conway. "They'd pretended to be so motherly. Then they betrayed me."

Within a week of the agents' appearance on her doorstep, Krawizcki began liquidating everything she had in order to pay back investors. Ironically, it was lucky she'd initially been so greedy about finder's fees. She had spent relatively little of her $1.8 million income—on which she'd dutifully filed tax returns—and now she was in a position to write scores of refunds. She couldn't cover the finder's fees that investors had ponied up, but she *could* refund the cost of the cars themselves. A surprising number of investors were satisfied with that. They simply walked away, not willing to forgive, exactly, but more than willing to forget.

Krawizcki asked Dan Stewart, "Is there anything else I can do?"

"It dawned on me then," Stewart recalled, "that she absolutely *did* believe the estate had existed, had really bought into it with all her heart. She sold cars to her dad and to her brother. As far as finding a ringleader went, right away we knew it wasn't

Kim. I felt she was trying to be an honest person. So I said, 'Would you let us tap your phones? We'd like to know what the other participants have to say.' "

Krawizcki readily agreed. It didn't take long before the feds hit pay dirt.

During the first week of August 2001, at the request of the Kansas City feds, the FBI tapped Kim Krawizcki's phones. What they heard was classic:

AUGUST 2, 2001, 4:10 P.M.
KIM KRAWIZCKI: Hi, Dr. Baker, it's Kim.

GWEN BAKER: Hi, how are you?

KK: I just got contacted by the FBI, and they want to meet with me and ask me all these questions, and they want me to give them paperwork, and, you know, I didn't know if I meet with them, do I violate the gag order? I just don't know what to say to them.

GB: Oh, my goodness! Well, let me call my godson [Robert Gomez]. I just got off the phone with him. When do they want to meet with you?

KK: They didn't say. They said the FBI had already contacted you, and the heir, and people in Philly.

GB: No, I didn't meet with them.

KK: Well, I said, "Look, I don't have any information for you, and I'm not going to talk to you over the phone. I don't have what you want." Then they called today and said, "We need to meet with you, we need to sit down, see all your paperwork," and, um, the whole nine yards.

GB: Okay. Okay. I'll call the estate right now and let them know, and they'll take care of it. Then I'll call you back to let you know what they say we should do.

KK: Okay, great.

In only fifteen minutes, Gwen Baker called back.

GB: Hello, Kim, I called my godson. He said, "You don't have to respond." He said, "You didn't get a summons." He said the people you've dealt with, all that were overcharged, they've been taken care of, except for the ones that want to stay in. He said, "So you really have nothing else to do with it—you don't have to respond." The only way you respond is if they summons you.

KK: And they would do that by documentation, like a subpoena or something?

GB: Yes, absolutely. [Robert] said he'd take care of it.

KK: So if they contact me back, I just say, "I don't need to talk to you until you subpoena me"?

GB: No. Don't give them any suggestions. Just tell them that you don't have anything else to do with it, and that you have no documentation, and whatever documentation you have I suggest you destroy where they can't find it. Their people are known to break into homes when you're gone. You understand what I'm talking about, don't you?

KK: Right.

GB: So I suggest you get rid of it, one way or the other. Don't have it hanging around there, 'cause they can sure confiscate it.

KK: Can they really? Now, if they do subpoena me, at that point, what do I do?

GB: Number one, call us first, and we'll have an attorney jump on it immediately.

KK: Why are they doing this?

GB: People from all over are calling, acting crazy, bombarding the offices from California to New York, from Washington to Florida.

KK: Yes, they're like, "It's a scam, there are no cars, no one's seen cars."

GB: The burden of proof is on them.

KK: Yes, I mean, obviously, it's extremely upsetting to have the FBI knocking on your door.

GB: Now are you sure that's who it was?

KK: Well, when you call back that number, they answer, "FBI."

GB: Oh, okay. They can't investigate without it being formal, because if they investigate a person without their knowledge, that's illegal.

KK: If they knock on the door, do I ask for some kind of documentation?

GB: Yes, I would.

KK: And if not, just not let them in?

GB: I don't know about that part. But you don't have to answer any questions. Please don't. I think a lot of times what they do, they search and seize. We've had people from the police department do that before. I've had several do me like that.

KK: Well, the big thing they keep pushing is, "Nobody's seen the cars, nobody's seen the cars."

GB: They're trying to find out for themselves. That's not an official investigation. They're pulling at straws right now. Really, they can't investigate without acknowledging or informing that person. It's an invasion of privacy. They want to see if you're gonna run and hide, see what you do.

KK: If they come to the door, can I show them a copy of the gag order?

GB: You don't have to do anything. You don't have to answer any questions. Tell them you will not speak without an attorney present. That's how it has to be.

KK: If I destroy all of my documentation, and they subpoena me, *then* what do I do?

GB: Nothing. You don't have it. They can't make you keep it. That's not against the law.

KK: Okay. So I can just paper-shred everything.

GB: Uh-huh.

KK: Wow. Okeydokey.

GB: All of this is happening for a reason, Kim. God's going to give the glory in the end. We're not running and we're not hiding, because the estate is real, the cars are real, and it's going to be a lot of pie in their faces. Can you see the glory of God coming through in all of this?

KK: Yeah, I hope to, somehow.

GB: And, Kim, you know what? If people don't understand, they don't understand.

Then, four days later, in a conversation on August 6, 2001, at 1:10 P.M.:

KK: What do I do if the FBI calls back again?

GB: Maybe it's a good idea if you record a message that you're out of town for two weeks. Like, "Please leave a message, as soon as I get back, I will call you."

KK: I appreciate all your help.

GB: It will be all right. Only six months to go and it will be over with.

KK: So [car delivery] is still on for the end of March [2002]?

GB: Oh, yes, everything is still on schedule. They have promised us it'll be over with by that time.

And in a conversation four days after that, on August 10, 2001:

GB: Now I can tell you what Robert told me. I can't vouch and say it's the absolute truth, but he did tell me that [attorney] Shawn Houston checks periodically with his friends [in the FBI] to see if there is any kind of investigation going on, and so far the answer is no.

KK: Couldn't we just stop these stupid calls by just showing them the cars and be done with it?

GB: Well, you've got to realize there is a game going on. The Christians have to realize this is God's business. What actually is happening here, Kim, is there are true believers who are falling apart. I had a person in a couple of churches tell me they didn't want to hear that. About God, believing in God. So, when people talk like that, I just cry. No sense in trying to make them see. That's just a blind person in the church, and you cannot make a blind man see.

KK: Yeah.

GB: Because people don't realize you can't separate people from God. God is your wisdom. And if people want to say, "Well, this is a church here, and that is just business over there," they don't know any better. So I just keep quiet. And then when you tell them to take their money back, they don't want their money back.

KK [laughing]: And then you're like, okay, *now* what do I do?

GB: There hasn't been one person who had to call an attorney or the police or the attorney general to get their money back from us,

James Nichols ran his office out of the bedroom of his parents' home in Carson, California. (Photo by the author)

The Miracle Cars scheme first went public in Christ Christian Home Missionary Baptist Church in Compton, California. (Photo by the author)

Top: It was easy to see why Gomez was nicknamed "Buddha." Until the very end, he was as lucky as Buddha, too. (Photo courtesy of Robert Gomez) ***Bottom:*** Happy-go-lucky Robert Gomez later couldn't recall ever owning this Lexus. It certainly wouldn't have been in his name anyway. (Photo courtesy of US Attorney's Office, Western District of Missouri)

In his tailored suits, James Nichols looked like a Hollywood movie star. (Photo courtesy of US Attorney's Office, Western District of Missouri)

Above: Nichols became a knowledgeable car enthusiast, planning to open a custom parts business in Las Vegas. (Photo courtesy of James Nichols)

Gwen Baker once told buyers: "God wants you to prosper. God wants you to roll!" (Photo courtesy of US Attorney's Office, Western District of Missouri)

Corrine Conway was the founder and president of the Virtuous Women's International Ministries in little Higginsville, Missouri. (Photo by the author)

At first, Robert Gomez said he considerd the bicycle casino his "home," but later he preferred the Hustler. (Photo courtesy of *Car and Driver*)

Gomez squared off against Larry Flynt in the Hustler Casino and once cashed a check there for $518,731. (Photo courtesy of *Car and Driver*)

Former Kansas City Chiefs football player Neil Smith accepts his honorary Miracle Cars blazer. Fellow NFL star Ricky Siglar got one, too. (Photo courtesy of US Attorney's Office, Western District of Missouri)

Top: James Nichols went through five BMW M3s worth $192,560. (Photo courtesy of James Nichols) *Bottom:* Nichols didn't confine his love to BMWs. He got into expensive Ducati motorcycles, too. (Photo courtesy of US Attorney's Office, Western District of Missouri)

In March 2001 investors flew to Los Angeles to attend a swanky meeting at the Smoke House restaurant. (Photo courtesy of *Car and Driver*)

James Nichols presides over the investors' meeting in Burbank. Sitting beside him is Gwen Baker, who did her best to soothe angry investors. (Photo courtesy of US Attorney's Office, Western District of Missouri)

Above: By following car-sales proceeds, federal agents Steven Hamilton and Gary Marshall were the first to unravel the scam. Marshall would win a national award for his efforts. (Photo by the author) *Right:* Kansas City attorney Tom Bradshaw was relentless in his defense of James Nichols. (Photo by the author)

Agent Elijah Zuniga dogged Robert Gomez in the casinos, finally arresting him at dawn in the Hustler Casino. (Photo courtesy of Elijah Zuniga)

It took more than a year out of their lives, but Assistant U.S. Attorneys Curt Bohling and Dan Stewart brought an end to the $21 million Miracle Cars con. (Photo by the author) and I've been doing this for over three years now. All the ugly threats, that's not necessary, and it just hurts my heart to see people in the church acting like this. They have been my worst clients. It is so sad that the people you want to pledge [cars to] are the ones who want to cheat you. So I stopped [selling to church members]. I'm just gonna go to the people who already got money, the big buyers, because I have tried working with the churches and it's just not working.

KK: If the FBI calls, well, then I want a copy of the gag order.

GB: You just have to tell them someone from the estate will contact them, because, you know, you weren't really a representative of the estate. Tell them, "I'm really not working with the estate. Someone from the estate will be contacting you." Just like that. Put it on the estate.

KK: Great. Thank you.

When Inspector Steve Hamilton read the transcripts of the phone conversations, his jaw fell slack. Gwen Baker had put herself in the worst sort of jeopardy. She'd already inserted one leg and one arm into a furiously rotating threshing machine. "It's almost like a cliché," Hamilton said, laughing, "that if someone says to you, 'Shred the documents,' your response should be, 'So, I take it we're all going to jail?' " Hamilton wondered if this was going to be easier than he thought. It wasn't.

His first contact with Baker was on the telephone. Hamilton politely introduced himself, then asked, simply, "What can you tell me about these cars?"

Baker was blasé, a little impatient, as if she were sick of such inquiries. "She told me, 'The estate exists, the cars exist, and I'm acting on good faith,' " Hamilton remembered. "She was a little abrupt, a little arrogant about it. It sounded like a speech she'd given before, and she was annoyed she had to deliver it again. She said, 'Of *course* I'm not defrauding anyone—don't be ridiculous. These are blessings, and I'm trying to do God's work.' She told me she'd never met John Bowers, didn't know much about the man."

Special Agent Gary Marshall likewise considered Baker a tad belligerent and dismissive. "We interviewed her most of one day, into the evening, and some of the next day," he recalled. "But she was *never* going to believe those cars didn't exist. She said to me, 'No, no. You're talkin' crazy, now. Those two boys, my godsons, just wouldn't do me like that. It's a matter of faith.' " Baker went on to recite the broad elements of the operation, but it was nothing the agents hadn't already heard.

Hamilton and Marshall then contacted Corinne Conway in nearby Higginsville. The conversation was nearly identical. Unlike Baker, however, Conway had never met Robert Gomez face-to-face. Marshall asked, "When you saw the delivery dates being rolled back—1999, to 2000, to 2001, and now to 2002—wouldn't a reasonable person question the estate's legitimacy?"

"You don't know how long probate takes," she responded, an odd thing to say to a man who'd spent whole years of his life testifying in various of the nation's courts.

"But you never asked for the court documents?" he asked. "You know, wills, records, letters testamentary?"

"I'm not experienced in such things," she offered.

Marshall knew Conway was concealing a second monster in her closet. She had earned $1 million in 2000, and it looked as if she'd flushed some of it through the Virtuous Women's International Ministries and some more of it into a bank in Tennessee. Marshall also knew she'd failed to file a tax return. If she'd made a million in one year, she owed the government about a third of it.

Like Baker, Conway was initially indignant that her motives were being questioned. She asked Marshall what crime she could possibly have committed. "The one that comes first to mind," he replied almost casually, "is conspiracy to cause money obtained by fraud to be transported in interstate commerce." Conway asked what sort of sentence such a crime might carry. He said it was up to the judge, but it could be as much as twenty years. That's when Conway lost her smirk and voluntarily offered up numerous boxes of financial records. Marshall elected to drop the tax-evasion bomb on her a little later.

Back in Memphis, Gwen Baker stopped selling cars. Briefly. The lure of quick cash would soon prove too great a temptation. And when she did go back to selling, she wasn't any longer remitting the proceeds to California. She kept the proceeds herself, "for refunds and personal money," as she later put it. But most important, at least to the feds, was this: As of September 1, 2001, both Baker and Conway officially possessed what prosecutors call "guilty knowledge." Both now had reason to believe they were involved in some manner of wrongdoing, and if they continued to dabble in that wrongdoing, well, a judge would take a dim view of it when sentencing rolled around.

After the feds departed, Baker called Conway and told her, "Just hold the incoming checks until we can find out what's going on." Conway stopped showing lists of cars to new buyers. But what she did *not* do was tell any of her clients that federal agents had pointedly questioned her about the estate's existence. Instead, she described her contact with law enforcement as "a private thing that I should not publicly share." She said she didn't want to inform investors "until I knew there was actually something real wrong."

Baker next called the Kemp Avenue office in Carson. She spoke first to Rose, from whom she got another lemon-tree parable, on which subject the woman was evidently a world expert. When Baker finally connected with James, she was surprised to learn he already knew about the trouble brewing in Kansas City.

"I'm aware of people, authorities, who are calling and inquiring," he said, his voice a monotone, his affect flat. Nothing she said surprised him.

"James, I even have the Memphis Better Business Bureau all over me," Baker added, hoping to rouse him to action. "And if I don't do something, they say they're going to write all of this up in the newspaper."

"Don't worry," he replied, "because they'll certainly end up doing a retraction."

Baker wasn't so much interested in editorial retractions as in James's advice on the matter of federal agents aswarm on her doorstep. But on that topic, he was tight-lipped, distant, apparently apathetic.

It wasn't long before Conway noticed that refund checks from the L.A. office had slowed to a crawl. "It would be like just scattered refunds here and there," she described. "Where it used to take seven to ten days, now it took sixteen. And then, no refunds at all."

Conway called Baker to complain. The *last* thing the National Finders wanted to do was stop doling out refunds, especially now that the feds were presumably watching. "But I couldn't get through to her," Conway complained. "It seemed as if Dr. Baker's phone was always busy, and when it wasn't, it was just the answering machine that picked up."

In fact, so much bad news had arrived, in so short a period, that Baker was now following the advice she'd earlier given Kim Krawizcki. She quit answering her phone. Besides, she had a play to produce.

Baker and fifty-one-year-old Alphonso Slater, an L.A.-based writer, were in the final throes of producing a stage play called *Strange Devotions.*

"Dr. Baker was the writer/director, and I was the producer," Slater explained. "I raised half the money. Gwen paid the actors, I paid everything else. Honestly, it was a pretty good play. Strange and different. It ran only two days in October, in San Francisco. It was in a good theater, but it needed better casting and better promotion. Dr. Baker herself didn't act in the play, but I'd lined up a star, of sorts—Todd Bridges, the actor from [the TV show] *Dif-f'rent Strokes.* And then Baker had this car-dealer guy named Randy Lamb appear in a small part. He didn't display obvious talent, but he was new to acting."

Baker was disappointed by the sparse audiences, and Slater was disappointed to learn the playwright had just been interrogated by federal agents. "She described their interviewing techniques as 'very fierce,'" Slater remembered. "I knew she was selling cars from some sort of estate. She even tried to sell some to me, said maybe I could become one of her sales reps. But my motto is 'cash and carry,' so I wasn't going to put down money on something that couldn't be delivered for a year. She told me, 'Alphonso, you don't understand. These cars are a *blessing.*' She was a strong-willed person, very high-minded. She was using her spiritual influence to get people to buy. That was right up her alley. I remember she had this piece of paper from South Bay Toyota that she showed me. I looked at it and thought, I'll bet these two boys are leasing vehicles and reselling the leases."

Slater lost $11,000 on *Strange Devotions* and assumed Baker lost more. But he liked this strong-willed woman from Memphis, and he was in awe of her ability to concentrate so soon after being cross-examined by none-too-gentle feds. "I told her, if it were me, I'd be shaking in my boots," Slater recalled. "Gwen told me, 'God has a plan, Alphonso, God has a plan.' And I said, 'Yeah, well, what if the district attorney has a plan, too?' "

By the fall of 2001, Assistant U.S. Attorney Dan Stewart had officially reached out and "touched" all three National Finders. They knew who he was, and he'd revealed at least some of his suspicions to them. It was interesting to monitor the women's reactions, either via the tap on Kim Krawizcki's phone or via the detailed financial records that Special Agent Gary Marshall was compiling. The women didn't know it, but Marshall was looking at what clothes they were buying, what food they preferred, how much they were giving to husbands or boyfriends, what charities they supported, what houses they'd lived in, what concerts they'd attended, how far they were driving, and what they did on their vacations. He knew every single year they'd fudged their income-tax returns, and he knew the financial histories of their accountants and business associates. He even knew when Baker obtained a cashier's check for $5—a refund for the five Cadillacs that Janice Siglar would have received if she'd continued as a Regional Finder. Instead, Janice had spoken to Dan Stewart, then had abandoned her post as if struck by a bolt of lightning.

"We were swimming in an ocean of records," recalled Stewart, "but when you're preparing for federal court, you're required to have your case ready to go the moment you make an arrest. It's not like filing a civil complaint. We were looking at a massive scheme, just huge. If it was difficult for *us* to get our arms around it, how could a jury? And who were the representative victims—little old Thelma Carnes or the rich football players or businessmen like Randy Lamb? And because this was federal, we'd have to show that the fraud touched the western district of Missouri, via Corinne Conway, of course, but also that it crossed the country, right to Matt Jones in Seattle. Meanwhile, the three of us were still trying to learn how the California casinos worked. That was new to us. And on top of that, we could follow the money only until Gomez converted it into chips. Then it went into the ether. I mean, a bunch had to be coming out the other end, right? Out of the casinos as laundered winnings? But other than a small percentage that he was spending on Lincolns and jewelry, where the heck was it? There weren't any clues. It wasn't as if these two boys were spending millions on yachts, planes, trips to Europe, big houses in Hollywood Hills. And if they weren't spending it, were they investing it? If so, where? With whom? Was there someone helping Gomez, a 'Mr. Big' who was the actual mastermind? We just didn't know. And neither did anyone we talked to."

Stewart grasped that the moment had come. It was time to have a heart-to-heart with the estate's executor.

On August 28, 2001, Special Agent Marshall and Inspector Hamilton flew to L.A. They rented a nondescript sedan, then drove to the Kemp Avenue address and knocked on the door. Sam Nichols answered. He said he hadn't seen James and didn't know where he was but that his son called regularly. Marshall and Hamilton waited a day, then returned. This time, Rose Nichols answered. Her words mimicked her husband's.

"It was one stall after another," Hamilton recalled. "But I could only get so forceful about it, because James was an adult. It wasn't the parents' responsibility to know where he was. But I recall thinking, If this kid is a criminal, he sure lives in a nice house, in a nice neighborhood, with nice folks."

While Hamilton and Marshall waited, they toured the card parlors, learning more about third-party bankers and the intricacies of pai gow poker, all the while keeping an eye peeled for the man most of the gamblers knew only as Buddha. Right then, they weren't positive where Gomez lived. That's because he had an unlisted phone and resided in a condo that was leased in someone else's name.

"We *did* view some interesting video footage of Gomez gambling," Marshall recalled. "It clearly reflected his style of play—very fast. He was in control of the game. Also quite obnoxious. During that trip, we also learned that the casinos filmed their safe-deposit boxes. At the Bike, we viewed Gomez coming and going, taking out and putting in large sums of cash and chips. Unfortunately, each casino filmed on a seven-day loop, so we were only able to see one week's worth."

"The fact is, I wasn't so worried about Robert," Hamilton stated, "because I knew his pattern. This guy always came back to the casinos, *always*. He'd put down such roots there I figured we could pick him up any time. But James? That was different. I had this uneasy feeling that James might be a runner. We found out he didn't have a passport, but you don't need a passport to enter Canada or Mexico."

The agents tracked down Ken Ayers, the San Bernardino detective who'd earlier believed he was interviewing James but was instead talking to Robert. Ayers had subsequently taken a phone call from Gomez, who this time correctly identified himself. Over and over, Gomez had asked, "Now tell me this: If we pay the money back, there's no crime, right?" Ayers was somewhat mystified, wondering why refunds were necessary if the estate cars were real, and he attempted to explain that, legally, it was more complicated than merely returning the money. But Gomez wouldn't listen. "Yes, but if a buyer gets a refund," he'd interrupt, "then everything's okay, right?"

The agents obtained photos of both boys. "I remember thinking, I'll bet relatively few people would have bought cars if they'd seen these guys' faces," Hamilton recalled. "Gomez didn't look like any rich heir, and Nichols didn't look like any executor.

What they looked like were two kids from Carson. I thought, *That*'s why so much of the face-to-face work was performed by the respectable ladies far, far from L.A. And *that*'s why the boys avoided all those awards banquets. They were smart enough to know they didn't look the part, that their strong suit was working the phones."

In a way, it was scary. Hamilton and Marshall had not previously squared off against this brand of juvenile cunning. Here was precocious avarice and youthful manipulation on a scale yet unseen. It was wholly unexpected from a pair of underworld "virgins." Criminals who achieved even moderate success were usually quick to trip over their own egos. Gomez might still, but Hamilton didn't expect Nichols would.

He didn't have too long to think about it. Out of options, Hamilton drove back to Kemp Avenue and "set up" on the Nichols house—law-enforcement slang for a stakeout. For several days, the agents parked themselves halfway down the block in their rental car. After they had remained stationary too long, they'd drive to Christ Christian Home Missionary Baptist Church in Compton, or to the home of Kimberly Hall's mother. They suffered all of the clichéd stakeout indignities—cold French fries, acid coffee, sore butts, and hour after hour of stultifying boredom. But only Sam and Rose Nichols came and went.

"Finally, we ran out of time," recalled Hamilton. "I walked across the street and talked to Sam one last time. I said, 'Mr. Nichols, it looks like we missed your son. But the next time we come out here, there won't be any courteous chitchat. It'll just be an arrest warrant.'" Rose appeared at the door. For her benefit, Hamilton added, "You know what a warrant means, ma'am? It means a whole bunch of cops and cruisers parked on your street and guys with guns instead of suits, and it means handcuffs and a trip downtown for as long as it takes. It's a big production, a big scene, and it draws a lot of attention in a quiet neighborhood like this. So I hope you'll tell James that if he just talks to us, we can avoid it." Hamilton couldn't tell whether Sam and Rose were intimidated, but it didn't look like it.

On August 30, the agents left for the airport at 8:45 A.M. Just fifteen minutes later—as if he'd somehow been watching from heaven above—James Nichols eased his BMW M3 into his parents' meticulously swept driveway. He was calm and relaxed, solemn and quiet, and dressed for a routine day at the office.

"My mother brought me up to speed," he later recounted. "She told me, 'The police were just here to talk about the estate. They spoke to me and your father for a while, but it's not us they want. They want you. Go take care of it.' Then she handed me their business cards."

James knew it wasn't the "police" who were after him. These guys were a hundred times worse than the police. Within the hour, Nichols drove to Torrance, to the office of his attorney, Ron Wasserman.

That's what he *said* he did, and maybe it was true. But James had plans that reached far beyond an office visit with his attorney. He was about to take a sudden, silent sabbatical that would last the next nine months.

THE CASINOS HAVE EYES

On September 11, 2001—the day the towers toppled, the day the Pentagon was punctured, the day America was plunged into its blackest hour since the attack on Pearl Harbor—Robert Gomez felt spunky enough to stroll into the Bicycle Casino for a few hours of gambling fun. As if going out of his way to further disrespect the gruesome events of the moment, he fished from his pocket the smallest check he'd seen in years. It was written in the amount of $169.15, and it had been mailed to his mother's home in Bell. This particular check was not from James Nichols. It was from the United States Treasury, and it was a refund on the woefully understated $4,062 taxable income he'd claimed in 1999. On the one day that no American wanted to be anywhere but home, Buddha cashed his refund check in a casino.

Happy-go-lucky Gomez didn't know it yet, but the check he'd just cashed would soon find its way not only to the U.S. Treasury in Austin, Texas, but also to the fifth floor of the Whittaker Courthouse in Kansas City, where it would be closely scrutinized by Special Agent Gary Marshall. And that was only *one* of Robert's unseen problems. The other was thirty-five-year-old

Elijah Zuniga, a special agent with the Division of Gambling Control, who was himself a habitué of the Bike.

Zuniga was a poster boy for U.S. law enforcement. He had dark brown hair, powerful arms, and the youthful good looks of Ben Stiller. He moved like a bantamweight boxer and was so clean-cut he appeared to be a rookie. Instead, he was the archetype of the undercover cop, having logged fourteen years busting dopers on behalf of the San Diego PD. Then he quit in the face of mountainous paperwork, additional hours of testifying, and the birth of his third child. Now he worked in the L.A. casinos, watching mostly for double-dealing dealers, money launderers, rigged games, and skimming cage managers. He stuck out in the crowds—too much the all-American boy—but compensated with a finely tuned bullshit detector that rarely failed him. What's more, a hundred midnight stakeouts had taught Zuniga to interpret body language like a pro.

Agent Marshall and Inspector Hamilton had asked for Zuniga's help. The card parlors represented a strange world, and they wanted Zuniga to find out what he could about Robert Gomez, aka Bobby "Code Blue," aka "Buddha."

"The Kansas City guys had already tried to talk to the casino owners," Zuniga recalled, "but they always clammed up. California casinos operate under a zillion regulations, both state and municipal, and they've got a lot of detractors. The public perceives their customers as con men and thieves, so they operate in a perpetual mode of paranoia."

Zuniga had no trouble extracting stories about Buddha. "Everyone knew him," he said, "but they knew him mostly as a big fat jerk. A lot of employees sucked up to him in person but despised him behind his back. He told everyone he was the heir to a lot of money—from his dad, his grandpa, a rich industrialist, even from his mother. That made me laugh. I speak Spanish, and

I'd already visited his mother. She lived in this dumpy two-bed-room house, and, meanwhile, Robert apparently has millions and isn't taking care of her. It was sad. After I interviewed her for an hour, she blamed Robert's troubles on James Nichols. Said James was a bad influence. She told me, 'I don't know what's going on, but *please* don't hurt my son.' She was in tears. I felt so bad for the lady that I gave her a hug. Yet in the casinos, Robert was telling people, 'I love my mother so much, I take her to Tahiti.' I'll bet he couldn't find Tahiti on a map. For Robert to allow her to exist like that . . . well, it showed me what he's all about—taking care of himself."

Zuniga learned that Gomez worked ceaselessly at embel-lishing his legend within the "gaming industry," as the gambler pretentiously called it. "There were a bunch of gambling Web sites," Zuniga said, "where Gomez was described as being in the mob, or being pursued by the mob, or being on the periphery of various gangland murders, or being associated with Mexican drug cartels. It was laughable. If you talked to the guy five minutes, you'd pick up his speech pattern, and you could tell that all that Web-site garbage was written by Robert himself. I got the impres-sion he'd watch a cop show one week, then pretend he was one of the characters the next."

As usual, Gomez wasn't afraid to talk to anyone, anytime, anywhere, and Zuniga was no exception. "He'd see me and give this great big greeting, like we were long-lost buds," Zuniga recalled. "Then he'd say, almost as if it were a joke, 'Are you gonna arrest me?' I'd say, 'No, the guys in Kansas City just want to talk.' Then he'd ask, 'Is the Division of Gambling Control investigating me?' I'd say, 'No, it's the attorney general's office and the IRS who are investigating you.' And it would be a big relief to him. If it was the IRS, he couldn't care less, because when the IRS got mad at you, he figured you just paid them what you owed and they'd go away. But getting banned from the casinos, well, that scared him. That scared the *crap* out of him."

Zuniga considered Gomez a "degenerate gambler," so the two never became close. But they sometimes spoke on the phone. "He'd call and say, 'Hey, Eli, my man! I didn't sell any cars, you know? The cars are James's thing. But I occasionally bet on sports with the bookies, sure. Okay, so maybe it's illegal. But you know what? You should go arrest so-and-so, because he's making book.' That was Robert's way of trying to erase his debt—have somebody else arrested. I'd just agree with him, pretend it was what I wanted to hear, like I was writing everything down."

Zuniga watched and waited. Then he called Hamilton and Marshall to confirm their worst fears—that Gomez probably *was* laundering vast sums, and that if he was applying even the barest smidgen of care and common sense, then the outgoing proceeds might well be untraceable. Zuniga recounted the path of a $100,000 check that Gomez had converted into chips at the Bike. It appeared that $35,000 of the chips had been cashed at multiple cage windows, and a further $10,000 got cashed right after a shift change. Zuniga couldn't swear to it, but he didn't think any of that had triggered a cash-transaction report. Then Gomez had driven down the street to the Hustler, where he met a few shoeshiners in the parking lot. For a small fee, those men apparently converted another $25,000 of chips into cash. From the original check, that left Gomez with $30,000 in Bicycle Casino chips, which he then wagered on football games. Win or lose, his bookie pals would convert those remaining chips into cash. *"Voilà!"* said Zuniga. "One hundred grand laundered in just one day, no problem."

Marshall and Hamilton were dismayed, but they pointed out that Gomez could only launder funds if he were winning. Again, Zuniga had bad news for them. "If the point of all this activity isn't really gambling," he explained, "then it doesn't matter. What if his primary goal is hiding money? What if, every time he wins—even if it's rare—he puts that laundered money aside, saves it? Remember, Gomez never worked a day in his life for this loot, so anything he takes out—anything more than a penny— means he's ahead of the game."

Gomez was aware that Zuniga was watching. To get the agent off his back for a few days, he flew to Las Vegas with his pals—roommate Tony Zaldua, partner James Nichols, and James's boyhood friend Steve Finnie.

"Basically, he invited me there to thank me for making it this far," James explained later. "Robert knew I was stressed out. He knew I was trying to make things work with Kim. And he said, 'Just enjoy.'"

But Robert also wanted to see if his luck in Vegas had turned. He tried a new location, the Rio Suite Hotel & Casino, and it worked. Early in September 2001, at 3:45 in the afternoon—an unusual time for Gomez to be gambling—he finally emerged victorious in Nevada. When he cashed in his chips, he was $75,000 richer, although it triggered yet another cash-transaction report. He didn't care. It felt great cruising the strip with that much cash in his pants. He drove over to the Bellagio and purchased a maroon leather jacket for $1,700. He had a game coming up with Larry Flynt, and he wanted to look nice. Larry was his idol, and Gomez was fond of quoting various of the pornographer's maxims. His favorite was, "You can't help a drowning man. You know why? Because he'll pull you under."

19

THE PARTNERSHIP IS DISSOLVED

James Nichols's weekend fling in Vegas helped calm his frayed nerves. But only for the seventy-two hours he was in Nevada. When he returned to Kemp Avenue in Carson, his problems greeted him at the door. Every time he clapped eyes on his mother, he could think of nothing but the five words she'd quoted from Inspector Hamilton: *"a warrant for your arrest."* He stopped enjoying his BMW M3 convertible and began losing sleep. Were they serious about arresting him, or was this merely a form of intimidation?

After a week's contemplation, James still didn't know, but he decided he'd had enough. It was quittin' time. Time for a change in careers. In the early days of September 2001, he wrote a letter of resignation, then phoned Robert. The two met in James's little bedroom office, the apex of their business successes for seven astonishing years.

"When I arrived," recalled Gomez, "James just blurted that he wasn't going to take his $5,000-per-month salary anymore, that he was sick of doling out car refunds, that nobody appreciated the work he'd done, and that he was going to take what was owed him. I knew what he was talking about. He meant whatever was left in the Lakewood account. He had a major attitude, let me tell you."

"I was under the impression that the money was mine," James told his partner. "That I was entitled to it."

Gomez didn't know how much was still in the First Bank & Trust account. Whatever it was, he certainly didn't want Nichols grabbing it. But Robert was not one of the signatories on that account, so he couldn't prevent it.

"When I told him I was quitting," remembered Nichols, "he started nitpicking me, finding fault with everything I'd done. That's what Robert always did to people. He said Dr. Baker was much more efficient than me anyway, and since she had experience running an office and knew how to handle people, he was thinking of giving her my title as executor."

James felt insulted that an underling—the woman his mother had "discovered"—might now replace him. He wadded up his letter of resignation and threw it at Gomez. It bounced off Robert's chest.

"Hey, come on, you're under stress," Robert said. "Why don't you just take it easy? Don't worry, I'm going to take care of you. We're still cool. But your services are no longer needed. And if you think you're gonna get physical with me, I know 'made' men, real muscle on the coast. I'll call my godfamily, I'll call Sam Pellegrino."

Gomez was related to no such family and James knew it. "More Mafia?" he asked sarcastically. "If it were me, I wouldn't be portraying myself as the heir to a $411 million estate who, in addition to problems with drugs and alcohol and gambling, is now dealing with gangsters who are former friends of a rich father who was in the CIA. A little dramatic, know what I mean? Do you ever take two seconds to think about the things coming out of your fat mouth?"

"Well, if you can't take the heat," Robert replied.

"I'll tell you what *you* can take," James said. "Take my letter of resignation, and the next time you're in New York City—as if you've ever *been* to New York City—shove it up Shawn Houston's ass."

"I gave you $50,000 on your twenty-fifth birthday," Robert countered, making cow eyes and looking hurt.

"I don't allow people to forge my name," James said, referring to the checks that Gomez regularly crafted at the casinos. "I'm proud of who I am, because I'm from my parents. I'm proud of what they made. So I don't allow just anybody to take it."

"If you close the account, then *you're* the one who's taking," Robert offered.

"I'm not afraid of any man standing before me," James said, again reciting his mantra, "but I'm often afraid of what I cannot see."

"What you won't be seeing," Robert shot back, "is a monthly statement of a half million or so."

James cursed infrequently, but he called Robert a "fat piece of shit," then added, "I don't want to be on the same side of the planet as you."

"If you come after me, you better be sure you kill me with the first shot, or I'll crush your ass," Robert replied theatrically.

"So that's it?" James said.

"Have a good life," Robert offered.

Bosom buddies for seven moneymaking years, Robert Gomez and James Nichols were officially divorced in September 2001.

James then did precisely what he'd threatened. He drove to First Bank & Trust in Lakewood and asked the clerk to prepare a cashier's check in the amount of $276,851.85—every cent in the account at the time, including recent wire transfers from his increasingly productive National Finder, Pastor Alexander.

Within days of federal agents staking out the Nichols home, and within twenty-four hours of closing the Lakewood account,

James moved to Las Vegas. When he left, he forgot to suggest to his aunts and uncles and the Milligans that they should try to get Miracle Cars refunds, ASAP. It was now James's intention to make a new life for himself, a life that didn't include undercover cops parked outside in nondescript rental cars.

James and his boyhood friend Steve Finnie opened a business account at a Vegas branch of Bank of America, where they deposited the car-sales money, plus $13,066 in cash that, ironically, triggered a cash-transaction report. It was James's first CTR. Robert, right then, was working on number 131. Nichols and Finnie called their new operation "Dream Pursuit, Inc.," doing business as HDP Enterprises on East Flamingo Road. On their business-account application, James listed himself as "treasurer" and Finnie as "president/secretary."

James's plan was to open two retail concerns. The first was to be a hot-rod parts outlet called Black & Brown Motor Sports. Once that was rolling, he and Finnie planned to franchise a series of "super Laundromats" right across the country. The seed money for all of this was $276,851 in Miracle Cars sales.

By virtue of his enthusiasm for fast cars, James had become familiar with the brands of aftermarket parts that sold the quickest and carried the greatest margins. "I felt a mail-order outlet in Vegas would be perfect, because the car-parts market wasn't yet saturated there," he explained. "I wanted Kim to work with me. You know, I could get Sprewells [oversize chrome wheels] for a thousand dollars less than they were selling for in L.A., and I knew everything about Schnitzer shift kits and Dinan superchargers and the most tasteful aerodynamic add-ons." He printed up a brochure touting all manner of accessories for imports and SUVs. The store's motto was "When the competitors' prices aren't down, call Black & Brown."

But neither of his businesses ever got off the ground, largely because James withdrew $193,040 in cash from his seed money and spent it "on rent, lawyers, my debit card, on a baby that Kim was about to have, and on a truck I helped a relative pay off." What's more, he sued his friend Steve Finnie "because he was stealing from me."

Within months of substituting Nevada for California, James Nichols had spent all the money, and his life was flying to pieces. He'd even had to trade in his next-to-last BMW M3, for which he got $45,000. He had been a better manager of Miracle Cars than of real cars. James's mother didn't have a clue where her son had gone, nor did she know what occupation he might now be pursuing. Neither did his father. Neither did the federal agents in Kansas City.

Using what was left over, James mailed a $10,000 retainer to his lawyer, Ronald Wasserman, back in California. Better safe than sorry. One of the things he asked Wasserman to do—a masterful piece of forward thinking, as it turned out—was to investigate whether Shawn Houston and Howard Gaines were registered as attorneys in New York State.

As the year 2001 wound down, the Miracle Cars operation had lost its CFO. James was out. Finis. But it had been a good run. The two boys, plus their nationwide network of finders, had reaped the rewards of hard work. By that point, they had sold between *$18 and $19 million* worth of automobiles. But now the scheme appeared finished.

Robert Gomez, however, was not. Not by a long shot. Robert didn't need the cramped little office on Kemp Avenue, and he didn't need Rose giving him all those dirty looks. And, come to think of it, he didn't need an executor. If James wasn't inclined to manage the Miracle Cars operation, Robert *would*. He didn't want to hijack the con, just reinvent it. It would require a little imagination, that's all. A little verve. Robert had the imagination of Walt Disney, and it wasn't long before he conjured a solution.

From just the three most lucrative car-selling years, James Nichols had converted $777,840 worth of Miracle Cars sales into cash—his very own "go wild" money, roughly half of which he spent on BMWs and Ducatis. He had funneled $59,603 of it to his parents for miscellaneous "office expenses" and for an automobile he'd awarded his mother. Skimming 778 grand was no simple undertaking, even for a boy who'd cofounded the "company" at age nineteen. But it had left a surprisingly intact paper trail that Special Agent Gary Marshall was, by late fall of 2001, reconstructing piece by piece. "And since the two boys had grossed many, many millions," Marshall said, "I was concerned I was glimpsing only the icing on the cake."

Marshall was wrong. What he was glimpsing was more like the tip of an iceberg.

During the same thirty-six months that Nichols had converted $778,000 to personal use, Robert Gomez had converted— on paper at least—only *$2,500,* about what the average middle-class businessman converts into cash *every single month*. It was a forceful feat of fiscal obfuscation, the sort of perfectly opaque accounting that would have landed him a job at Enron. Robert had a knack for keeping everything off the books. He had no bank account, no credit cards, no cars in his name, and no residence in his name. He eschewed receipts and shredded those that were forced on him. He paid cash for everything, and when clerks required his name, he happily became "J. R. Nichols." Even though he'd just about wallpapered one entire room in cash-transaction reports, there was no proof that that money landed in his pockets. He had shoeshiners aplenty who'd swear to it.

"In my career, I try not to be impressed by criminal sleight of hand," noted Assistant U.S. Attorney Dan Stewart, "because it's so much easier to cheat than it is to live life honestly. But when we could only trace $2,500 to Robert personally—a kid who I believe was lucky not to have wound up in a barrio gang—it caught me short, I'll admit. I still believed he had a really huge stash, whether we could see it on paper or not. But that begs the question, Okay, so where is it? And if Gomez doesn't have it, then who? Robert's going around telling his pals, 'Oh, I buried it!' like it's a big joke. But what if he did?"

No one outside California knew the answer to that.

REINVENTING THE CON

Robert Gomez's final meeting with James Nichols had been ugly, filled with personal accusations, threats of violence, nasty recriminations, and a disputed "property settlement." Bridges had been burned. The two had vowed never to speak again. As business partners, they were now kaput.

"James and I were increasingly like two bulldogs in a cage," Gomez recounted. "I'm upbeat and optimistic, he's dark and pessimistic. I see a silver lining, he sees death and destruction. We'd been pals for years, sure, but I don't know how we lasted that long."

Gomez was determined that Miracle Cars sales should proceed, but he was facing what looked like insurmountable challenges. National Finder Kim Krawizcki was out—was cooperating with the feds, in fact. Corinne Conway was making refunds only. Gwen Baker was scoring a few sales here and there but wasn't sharing the proceeds. Unmarked cars piloted by "black suits" were regularly cruising the length of Kemp Avenue. James had fled with the entirety of the Lakewood account—the golden egg that funded Robert's gambling. And Agent Zuniga seemed to be lurking in every dark corner of every casino. "I expected to see him in the goddamn men's room," Gomez complained.

The average young man would have given up. Or at least lain low. Not Robert Gomez. The king of pai gow poker had a plan, and it was a beaut.

First, Robert handed $10,000 in cash to an L.A. law firm. It was comforting to have counsel standing by, just in case. Ironically, the retainer triggered another Cash Transaction Report. Then Robert phoned Pastor John Alexander in Atlanta, who'd already shown signs of becoming an all-star National Finder. He told Alexander about his big blowup with James, how they'd hurt each other's feelings, and how James remained the executor of the estate "but only on paper." Gomez said, "I want you to become my official estate representative." To Alexander, it sounded like a promotion.

Then it got complicated. Gomez explained that he, the heir, was taking as much flak as anyone regarding delayed deliveries of cars. Robert said he couldn't stand it anymore, that he was embarrassed and frustrated and was prepared to take drastic action. "In order to bring probate to a swift conclusion," he told Alexander, "what I did was buy all of the remaining estate cars myself." He said he'd purchased those final five-hundred-some vehicles using his own funds. This meant he could now go to Judge Jack Lomeli and the estate's lawyers and say, "All the cars are finally sold. Now we've got the money we need to cover the tax liabilities they represent. So let's wind this up!"

What he wanted Alexander to do was sell those last vehicles —which now were owned by Gomez personally, rather than the estate—for approximately $6,500 apiece. That, he said, would allow him to recoup what he'd had to pay into John Bowers's estate. And Gomez added that he wanted the money soon, because this scheme had really lit a fire under the lawyers, and probate was now hurtling along at breakneck speed.

Alexander apparently didn't question the circular logic of this plan. Why should cars in an estate—cars that would momentarily be transferred to Robert Gomez for free—be purchased by Robert Gomez beforehand? But maybe he was distracted when Gomez promised him a 15 percent commission on every sale he made. That commission would be a monster, Robert promised, totaling $450,000, maybe more.

There was one final instruction. Henceforth, Alexander was to forward car-sales proceeds—preferably by wire—directly to Gomez himself, not to the estate account in Lakewood. That account, he said, "had been closed by James when he realized all the cars had been sold." Which was, in small part, true. "What you're doing now, technically, is wiring car *refunds* to me," Robert explained, "because I bought these cars and obviously don't need them. So it's easier if I just give you the names of my banks." The "banks" that Gomez specified were HPC Services and Eldorado Enterprises. He did not mention that those entities were, in fact, the parent companies of Hollywood Park Casino and Larry Flynt's Hustler Casino. But it might not have mattered anyway. Robert avowed that HPC and Eldorado were merely "flow-through accounts." That is, the money landed there briefly, then was swiftly transferred to Gomez's actual savings and checking accounts. It was a major pain in the butt, he allowed, but it was the lawyers' method of protecting him from thieves and con artists who preyed on rich trust-fund babies like himself.

It was a complex story, and it took some explaining. But Gomez had taken the advice that James had so recently and rudely offered. This time, there was no mention of the Mafia, of the CIA, or of gambling addictions. No evil-doers in Buicks, no gold bullion in the trunks of black limos.

Pastor Alexander leapt at this new opportunity. He immediately printed up official "Contractual Agreements" in which he referred to himself as "Estate Representative." From now on, all buyers had to sign this contract, and it was a document that proved the pastor had been paying attention. For one thing, it clearly stated that no finder's fees would be charged—a previous sticking point in Miracle Cars sales. It further stated that the contract itself would simultaneously serve as a receipt, thus reducing paperwork by half. And it boldly pronounced that buyers absolutely would *not* be permitted to see or touch their cars "until vehicles have been delivered to their distribution point and an appointment made for pickup." Alexander had attended the Smoke House meeting and had witnessed firsthand the chaos caused by investors demanding to see their cars. He had no desire to open *that* particular can of worms again.

Now, all that was left was to flog the final five hundred Miracle Cars. Alexander felt certain—as did Robert—that he would experience not the slightest difficulty in this endeavor. After all, he was the towering head of the John Alexander Ministries, and God's blessings sold like hotcakes when you, personally, were in charge of the flock, when you, personally, were promising to keep the wolves at bay. By November 19, 2001—only sixty days into his new deal with Robert Gomez—Alexander had already chalked up $333,931 in sales, and he was just warming up. He wired the funds to the casinos, as instructed, with each transfer carrying the notation, "Refund Money, Purpose Rt. Gomez."

Not even Baker or Conway had come out of the blocks as explosively. Moreover, this new arrangement meant that Robert didn't have to beg James for his weekly allowance. He didn't have to drive anywhere to pick up the cash—it was coming to him electronically. He didn't have to worry about infighting among the women. With just one National Finder, there was no jealousy. He didn't have to hand out any more $50,000 birthday gifts to cheer up sulking partners. And best of all, he didn't have to worry about doling out refunds—now *he* was the customer being refunded.

It was such a perfect plan that Robert could have kicked himself for not thinking of it sooner.

The Miracle Cars operation was back on track, as profitable as ever. Potentially *more* profitable, given the significant reduction in employees. Robert's downsized company was lean and mean, and he was again Numero Uno. Now he could concentrate on gambling rather than fund-raising. It was now Gomez & Alexander, Inc., at least until the good pastor sold all five hundred cars. But that would be three million laundered dollars down the road, and Robert could decide what to do then. Since the scheme's conception seven years prior, no buyer, no civil judge, and no business partner had come close to derailing the locomotive that pulled the Miracle Cars train.

Buddha celebrated with three dogs at the Wienerschnitzel, then ate dessert at Arnie Morton's. He felt wonderful. He felt invincible.

When Robert Gomez entered a casino, he became accustomed to hearing this refrain: "Buddha, you have another wire." It was music to his ears. Forty-two-year-old Pastor Alexander had become the Robert E. Lee of car sales in the South. It was as if the man never rested. Even forty-eight hours after Christmas—when most men of the cloth were overwhelmed by church services, choir recitals, extra sermons, charity events, and family dinners— the good pastor somehow found time to wire $125,000 to Eldorado Enterprises, followed by $174,985 the day after.

Robert was gleeful, and so were the casinos. "When Gomez played," explained Robert Turner, then the player-development director at the Hustler, "he could double our revenue for the day. The drop from a table where Gomez played was anywhere from $30,000 to $75,000. Just huge. For all the Hustler's glory, Larry [Flynt] had spent $30 million renovating the place, and we had months when we didn't make a profit. So we pursued Gomez. I went so far as to offer him a thousand dollars a day for each day he'd stay at my casino. He'd always say, 'I'll think about it,' but he'd never commit. He liked playing the field, so all the casinos would fight over his business and shower him with gifts."

Turner frequently observed Gomez win staggering sums from banking groups, only to stand abruptly and abandon the game. "You could see it gave him enjoyment when he punished people like that," he said. Bookies fell into the habit of calling Turner as the night wore on, asking, "How's Buddha doing?" If he was on a winning streak, they'd ring Robert's cell phone to remind him of various big sports games the next day. If it was a game featuring one of Gomez's favorite teams, he'd sometimes bet as much as $50,000.

Turner recalled an incoming wire for $225,000, again from Alexander. There had been so many similar wires that he began to wonder if the real secret to Gomez's success wasn't so much Lady Luck as a sugar daddy with an agenda. Robert's former roommate, Richie "Fingers" Sklar, wondered, too. By that point, Fingers claimed to have watched Buddha rake in roughly $14 million. Gomez had told him it represented $2 million in sports winnings and $12 million from pai gow poker. But Gomez famously kept no records, and he was quick to exaggerate his skill. All anyone knew for sure was that his luck, real or perceived, had become the stuff of legends.

"I once saw him win for six straight weeks," said Ray Garcia, a thirty-six-year-old third-party banker for Network Management Group. "We lost over $1 million to the guy. Gomez would often call me between one and three in the morning and say, 'Hey, Ray, I'm hot, I want to set up a private game.' To get back some of our money, we'd never refuse him. He favored young Asian male dealers, and the games would last from six to twenty-four hours. I don't recall ever seeing him convert his chips to cash."

So frequently did Network Management lose to Gomez that something seemed fishy. At intervals, the company would assign employees to monitor the action. Gomez resented the surveillance and began referring to the company's owner as "that Asian Jew." One night, with Network Management employees hovering like buzzards, Gomez reached into his winnings and counted out twenty individual chips, each worth $5,000. Then he leaned over the table and placed them in Ray Garcia's hand. He said, "There, now you don't have to work for them anymore." The men surrounding the table were stunned into silence.

Garcia walked away, almost in a daze. He was holding $100,000 in his right hand. He thought about it for a minute, then walked back. "I can't keep this," he said. "I can't accept." He placed the chips back in the tray.

Gomez grinned. Not only did he get his hundred-grand "toke" refunded, but he then proceeded to win an additional $200,000 before the night was out. "It was a bad evening for Network Management," admitted Garcia, but it was the sort of war story that traveled like wildfire, and Gomez's reputation, for better or worse, now preceded him. He had become the biggest gambler in California. He wasn't a whale. He was bigger than a whale. He was the ocean the whale swam in.

"Whether he was truly skilled or just reckless and lucky, I don't know," said his pal Linda Janowski. "But as soon as too many people would show admiration for his play, he'd fly off the rails again." She was right. Before the year was out, Gomez had once again thrown a tantrum at the Hollywood Park Casino.

"He called the shift manager a 'little fuck,'" recalled a policeman who filed a report. "So the shift manager called him a 'fat fuck.' Then Gomez said, 'I hope you and your mother die of cancer.' The shift manager replied, 'Yeah, well, you're excluded.' Gomez came back with, 'I'm not going anywhere, you little Jew,' and then, when he turned to leave, he added, 'Why don't you meet me across the street at the Chevron station, and we'll see what will happen to you.' "

"Sometimes he was like a third-grader having a fight during recess," said Janowski. "It was funny. Well, funny a week or so later. But it just rolled off Robert's back. He could be happy and smiling and hugging everybody twenty minutes later. He'd just climb into his Lincoln and say, 'Oh, well. Come on, let's drive over to the Hustler, have a Baileys or two, see if Big Larry's playing,' and he'd have that grin plastered on his face, the class clown. He lived in his own little world, and in that world, boy, you'd better believe, Robert wasn't a clown, he was the king."

Unfortunately, Janowski was about to stop smiling at the king's antics. Forever.

21

GOOD COP/BAD COP

In January and February of 2002, Special Agent Gary Marshall and Inspector Steve Hamilton began noticing some odd coincidences. With Agent Zuniga's help, they'd already discovered that Robert Gomez held a joint player's account at the Bike with a woman named Linda Janowski. On her application, the woman had listed her occupation as finance director at South Bay Toyota. That name rang a bell. Wasn't there a July 17, 2001, fax from South Bay suggesting the dealership was maintaining some three hundred Miracle Cars? Wasn't it the same fax that the finders had used to stimulate sales?

Marshall made a few phone calls and tapped a few computer keys, looking into Janowski's background. She was making $200,000 annually and owned several properties. She had even signed a lease for a fancy condo on a golf course in Long Beach. Funny thing was, her mail wasn't going there. It appeared that this woman was inextricably linked to Gomez's affairs, which meant she was likely an accomplice. Marshall and Hamilton jetted to L.A. to have a little chat.

"When two federal agents walked into the dealership, I about fainted," Janowski recalled. "They said, 'How do we know you're not involved in this?' And I said, 'Well, that's a good question, because I don't have a clue how I can prove it.' But I honestly didn't know a thing about any estate cars, about James Nichols, about pastors and reverends selling cars across the country. I kept saying, *'What?* What are you *talking* about?' like some sort of big dope. I must have sounded guilty as hell.

"The agents played good cop/bad cop," Janowski recalled. "I didn't know they were doing it at first. Hamilton was so nice. He'd say, 'I know this is hard for you, honey, but it will be a learning experience, and you can call me any time of the day or night if you want to talk.' And then Marshall came on like a hard-ass. He'd bait me, provoke me, and I'd get mad and lash out, which I guess is what they wanted. I said, 'Listen, I didn't fax *any*-thing, but I did give Robert a couple pieces of South Bay letter-head.' He said, *'You gave him letterhead?'* I asked, 'So now it's a crime to give someone letterhead?' And he said, 'Well, yes.' Then he asked, 'Have you ever used a towing company?' I'm like, 'Are you kidding, I was formerly a used-car manager. I'm around cars day and night. *Of course* I use towing companies.' And then he holds up another fax, this one on Payless letterhead. Well, my heart sank, because my coworker Val Morella used Payless all the time. I was getting deeper and deeper. They were looking at me like *I* might be Mr. Big."

The agents told Janowski that she better recall what she was doing on the day the letter was faxed. They didn't say it in so many words, but they made it clear she might want to come up with a few witnesses while she was at it.

"My life just stopped as I tried to remember," she said. "I looked at the ceiling all night. I felt certain my phone was bugged. Why was this happening to me? I'm a nice person, I do nice things, I live by the Golden Rule. And now I wake up and it's *Alice in Wonderland.* My ex-husband is like, 'How do you get into these messes?' I played it over and over in my mind, a million times. Where was I that day? My boss kept saying, 'Linda, *think*. What day did you go to lunch with that guy?' "

The agents instructed Janowski not to speak to Gomez, but she wanted some answers. "So I phoned," she remembered, "but Robert said he had no idea what day we'd had lunch, and he didn't care. He said, 'Linda, Linda, just calm down. It's not me they want. It's this friend of mine, a financial adviser named James. Don't worry. They'll never be able to prove anything if you were out to lunch, will they?' That was the extent of his compassion for my predicament. He added, 'When you talked to the agents, did you tell them I always win?' He wanted me to tell them how great a gambler he was. Then he asked me, 'So, you wanna zip over to Vegas this weekend?' "

Janowski didn't think she'd ever gamble again, certainly not with Robert. But he had jogged her memory, quite by accident. Now she remembered they'd gone to a Mexican restaurant, and, while they were eating, she had noticed two young women who'd just quit their jobs at South Bay that same day. "I ran back to the dealership, and we pulled their employment files," Janowski recalled, "and there it was. *The day*. Now I had a reference. And then I realized I had the manager's meeting every Tuesday, from one to three P.M., and I'd left Robert and Val in my office, alone. It clicked. I was so happy. I called Steve Hamilton in Kansas City and said, 'Oh, my God, I remember!' They began treating me better after that."

But Janowski's problems were far from over. South Bay's general manager was irked to learn that one of his most vital employees—the one who handled the big money—was being investigated by two branches of the United States government. The agents' appearance in his showroom suggested that criminal activities were taking place, the sort of thing that would reliably spook customers. No one at South Bay believed Janowski herself had faxed the letter, but she *had* given Gomez the run of her office for two whole hours. That was irresponsible.

The feds had shown up at South Bay on a Friday in late February 2002. On Monday, Janowski was fired from her $200,000-a-year job—a job that had taken her twenty years to land—and her coworker Val Morella was fired from his $150,000-a-year job. Janowski cried for a week. Morella sold his house and temporarily took off for parts unknown.

"I was suddenly divorced from something that truly gave me pleasure," she said. "It's like a husband who cheats on you, and you suddenly realize, Oh, my God, I can't go there anymore. Such a huge chunk of my life flew out the window. I was so mad. Robert had put me in harm's way."

Now it dawned on Janowski that it might be wise to drive over to the Bike to look at her player's account. That's when she learned Robert had somehow secretly signed on to the account and had run it $20,000 *beyond* her $30,000 credit limit. Janowski was responsible for the overage, exactly as if she'd been Robert's wife, and her previously perfect credit record was in jeopardy. When she asked a casino employee why Robert's name was on the account, "he went silent," she said, "and then he called Robert on his cell phone to report that a weird woman had shown up asking strange questions."

When Janowski got home, her lawyer was asking for a $15,000 retainer, and the federal agents were calling back with *more* questions, and, well . . . "When I realized everything I was facing, I became physically ill," she said. "Had all the jewelry and free trips to Vegas been Robert's way of buying me off? If so, why? I'm forty-four years old, he's twenty-something and rich. What do I have he could possibly want?"

Janowski had befriended Gomez merely to have someone

who could show her the casinos and let her watch the action. She had barely brushed up against the kid, much as a hiker nonchalantly brushes up against a sprig of poison ivy. But in that moment, he had infected every aspect of her life. She described him as "an evil life-form that eats you from the inside out." She changed her phone number and scanned the parking lot before walking to her car. She carried all the jewelry he'd given her to an appraiser in Los Angeles. One bracelet was valued at $4,000, and the remainder was worth between $30,000 and $40,000.

Within ten days of Janowski's contact with the agents, Robert sent her an e-mail describing an underground Web site he promised "will make you laugh." He was wrong about that. "It was an online magazine, badly written," Janowski recalled, "and it more or less said Robert had been involved in a murder. I assumed it was his way of saying, 'See, Linda, I'm dangerous, so keep your mouth shut.'"

She was afraid to be in the same room with Robert again, so she called one last time. "I said, 'My *God*, Robert, I really don't know who you are. Does anybody? What did you get yourself into? You told me you were an orphan, now you have a brother, a family? There's nothing I know to be real about you.' And I was praying he wouldn't say to me, 'Well, Linda, sorry to tell you this, but I'm in the Mafia.' Because here I was talking to the feds, which he obviously knew, and I was sure someone would show up at my door. You know, lights out for Linda."

But Robert didn't claim to be in the Mafia, even though, ironically, this was his big chance. What he said instead was, "Linda, I'm just back from the Bellagio. You should see the leather coat I bought."

In the fifth-floor "war room" in Kansas City, Special Agent Gary Marshall was listening to a tape-recorded phone call between superinvestor Matt Jones, in Seattle, and National Finder Corinne Conway, in Higginsville.

Matt Jones: Can you give us a date this deal can't go past?

Corinne Conway: I can't give the exact date, because of new businesses that the IRS found in the inheritance. So when Dr. Baker came here, with the mayor and dignitaries, she did say they cannot prolong it. I don't see it going longer than six months, and that's going to the extreme of it. My inside feeling is maybe in the next three months. [But] the discovery of these new corporations they have to access for the inheritance tax for the IRS, that will take a little more time. If there are people who can't wait, they can get their money back. We do not have a lot of people who do this. I only know of two professors who had to get their money back, because of loans they'd received from credit unions. It's never a problem of your money being tied up. Thank God for that.

MJ: If I can't see the vehicles because of the gag order, can I receive a letter stating what vehicles I *will* receive?

CC: There is a gag order. The young man who inherited the estate is only twenty-three years old. It's a high-powered estate, and they're keeping a low profile on it. They want to protect him and the assets. When you request a car, I take it from a listing, and your receipt is given to you. Those are the cars you will receive. We are accountable for those cars in good condition. Even when you go to the compound to pick up your vehicle, if for any reason you do not want your vehicle, you can get your money back.

MJ: Does the gag order stop you from giving out the VINs?

CC: Yes, it does. They will not allow anyone to go into the compounds to see the vehicles. If they allow everyone to go into the compound to get VINs, it would be crazy. The judge will not allow it.

MJ: How could all the vehicles be 1998 models with about five hundred miles?

CC: I do not know where that five-hundred-mile figure came from. There are none that are older than that. There are some cars with 112 miles, [but I know all are] less than ten thousand miles. The cars are in excellent condition.

During their various conversations with the president and founder of the Virtuous Women's International Ministries, Agent Marshall and Inspector Hamilton began to wonder if Conway genuinely *did* believe the estate existed and that all of the cars were parked in some top-secret location in Los Angeles. At the same time, Conway, like Baker, was suspiciously adept at answering direct questions with impressive-sounding irrelevancies that arrowed off in dead-end tangents or were cleverly fashioned to deflect follow-up questions. As a politician, she would have been a natural.

"What we wanted to hear her say," said Assistant U.S. Attorney Dan Stewart, "was, 'Matt, the government has been talking to me, and I may be in big trouble, and there might not be any cars, and you might lose every cent you've invested, and if I were you, I'd bail right this instant.' But she didn't say that."

22

DIVERGENT PATHS

Robert Gomez didn't need any lowlife PR guys offering him a puny $1,000 per day to play in their casinos. It was almost insulting. In the first few months of 2002, Pastor Alexander had wired *$1,272,000* to the Hustler Casino *alone,* which had increasingly replaced the Bike as Robert's "home."

Exactly as Gomez had predicted, Pastor Alexander was on a heavenly roll. Word had spread to fellow Southern pastors, who were now doing much of the selling for him. The senior pastor of the Breakthrough Christian Center in St. Petersburg, Florida, for instance, told his congregation that the cars were "an uncommon harvest" of blessings. He singled out a $6,500 Cadillac Escalade as a particularly persuasive example of the Lord's graciousness, and he suggested to his flock, "You ought to tell somebody!" They did. He urged them not to gossip or fight over the cars, pointing out that purchases could be made for merely "a little piece of money." Then he added, "Pray, and don't get impatient. Prayer keeps the river flowing. God's got millions in store for you!" It was, almost word for word, a speech that Baker and Conway had frequently delivered in the preceding years. There was no script, yet church leaders coast to coast somehow knew the text verbatim.

In virtually every case, the pastors and reverends intimated that purchases of cars indirectly supported the church itself, that it was the pious thing to do. They made faith in God synonymous with the investment. As a result, buyers were loath to back out. Giving up on the cars would indicate a shaky Christian core. Even those who ran out of patience—or perceived they were being conned—rarely talked about it, and none went to the authorities. To deal in rumors was "an attack of the enemy," because only Satan would pooh-pooh a deal that had emanated from the pulpit.

Church members who were less devout and more skeptical were eventually persuaded to jump on board when they witnessed fellow members receiving refunds. "If they were refunding buyers, it's *got* to be on the up-and-up," rationalized Wayne Herman of Duluth, Georgia. He bought a '99 Cadillac Seville.

Mark Grissom, of Atlanta, initially purchased a Toyota Camry, then later upgraded to a GMC Yukon. He was told his vehicle and all the others had been wrapped in protective plastic and that each was started at least once a month to keep the engines limber. Grissom was impressed and told twenty of his friends. Then he borrowed from his father-in-law to purchase a Ford Expedition.

And so it went. It was a scene that Gwen Baker, Corinne Conway, and Kim Krawizcki had witnessed roughly six thousand times previously, but it was still a thrilling new experience for Pastor Alexander. So far, ironically, his only setback had been Krawizcki herself, up in Philadelphia. The former National Finder was refunding buyers left and right, and her attorney had mailed warnings to investors who hadn't even requested refunds. Because Krawizcki had shared some of her car lists with Alexander, there erupted a small overlap of buyers asking thorny questions.

Pastor Alexander soothed them. "He said, 'Kim doesn't know what she's talking about,'" recalled Krawizcki. "He told them,

'I'm dealing with the actual heir, with Gomez himself. I'm not dealing with a bunch of women intermediaries. If you knew what *I* know, you'd stay in.' That was his favorite phrase, 'If you knew what *I* know.' Well, one thing he *did* know was that I was up north, talking to the feds. He knew that. His joke was, 'Ignore the government, ignore the IRS, ignore the FBI, because soon we're gonna get the cars, and all the detractors will have pie on their faces.' And it worked. Boy, did it ever. And when he ran out of his own parishioners, he went to other churches."

Krawizcki felt sorry for John Alexander's wife and phoned her several times. "She'd tell me, 'Oh, God, if this falls apart, what are we going to do, Kim?' She wondered how she could walk to the grocery store with something like that hanging over her head. She had kids in school. I said to her once, 'Janie, get out of this thing, *get out*.' But John wasn't going to have that."

When the feds questioned Krawizcki about Alexander, she nevertheless defended him. "I don't think he knows the money's going to a casino," she told them.

"Maybe it's time to let him know," suggested Special Agent Gary Marshall.

"When I reached Alexander at his residence in Georgia, he was very cordial," Marshall recalled. "I told him, 'Sir, the government has no evidence of an estate, and we can find no trace of even one car, much less thousands of them.' And then I added, 'We're aware you've been wiring money to California. If I were you, I'd take two minutes to look up what HPC Services and Eldorado Enterprises actually are. And then, frankly, I'd think very seriously about selling any more cars.' "

Pastor Alexander followed none of that advice.

James Nichols's fresh start in Las Vegas had fizzled before it got started. In the desert, he had spent a quarter-million dollars in four months and had nothing to show for it, save the $45,000 he'd earned by trading in a BMW M3. In late January 2002, he ventured back to California and stopped at his parents' house on Kemp Avenue. He told his mother, "I want to sift through the remnants of my office."

Rose Nichols adored her handsome son and was glad to see him, but James was sullen, morose, and uncommunicative. Throughout his life, James had been a person who was easily depressed, but he forced his black moods on no one else. He simply became quieter than usual. Once again, Rose asked her son why Robert Gomez would possess a business card identifying himself as an FBI agent. "I saw six letters mailed from this house," she told James, "with no return address, to the Federal Bureau of Investigation in Sacramento."

James couldn't imagine what Robert was up to now, but he predicted it would soon blow up, and then everybody would know.

Rose asked what Robert had meant when he said, "The settlement of the estate was being delayed by IRS investigations and their wanting more tax dollars." She asked if James had talked to Inspector Hamilton, as he'd promised. She asked why mail addressed to Gwen Baker was still arriving at the house. She asked whether, as Robert had represented, James was making numerous trips to New York. She asked whether James had ever truly worked for John Bowers. And she asked what would be done about the "gifts" that Robert had promised various members of Christ Christian Home Missionary Baptist Church. One such cash promise had been made way back in 1998, to Gary Collins, who was wheelchair-bound. The man had since died. She wanted James to inform Robert that "Mr. Collins is no longer a recipient."

James sighed. Now he felt even worse. The Kemp Avenue office, the scene of so many triumphs, now represented only toil and trouble. He began sifting through two bins of office items. He halfheartedly riffled through some leftover paperwork. Then he dismantled the office computer, which he was afraid Robert would commandeer. At the bottom of a stack of papers he found a cardboard FedEx box that his father, Sam, had signed for while James was in Las Vegas. The box was almost four months old. In his previous role as executor, James had received many such boxes. He assumed it contained receipts and sales contracts and lists of cars that had been sold and, worse, numerous requests for refunds accompanied by snarky letters and veiled threats. Along with the computer, James carried the FedEx box over to the residence he had begun to call his "safe house," a modest ranch on Bankers Drive rented by Kimberly Hall, five minutes from his parents' house. He unceremoniously flung it onto the top shelf of the front closet and forgot about it. He never opened the box, never so much as peeked inside. Given his financial situation right then, he probably should have. It might have cheered him up. Inside the FedEx box was $239,800 in car-sales proceeds.

By April 2002, Gwen Baker had become as sullen, silent, and sour as James Nichols. She was a desperate woman. Investors weren't calling for cars any longer. They were calling for refunds and for a pound of flesh. Baker laid off her Auto Emporium staff and cut corners wherever possible. Irate customers were calling at all hours, leveling threats that weren't so subtle. Hoping for advice on how she should process refunds when there was so little cash on hand, Baker called James at the Kemp Avenue office. The phone rang and rang, but no one picked up. Not even Rose.

Seamstress Thelma Carnes wrote to get her money back. A lawyer in Norman, Oklahoma, was threatening to contact "appropriate federal and state agencies" if Baker didn't wire $60,000 to a Dr. Cranmer there. Theater owner Fran Schwarzer, in Higginsville, wrote: "It has been well over two years with very little communication—*I need to know.*" Impoverished Rosie Ingram in Gladstone, Missouri, had been reduced to begging for her $8,000. A woman in Montgomery, Alabama, chastised: "This is no way to do business. My next step is to see my attorney." And a man named Donald Bell, in Kansas, had requested a refund for $31,500 for ten vehicles, and he'd coincidentally forwarded a copy of this request to the U.S. attorney's office in Kansas City.

Baker cringed. That last one was likely to wind up on Dan Stewart's desk. It was nerve-racking, because she was trying to keep a low profile until she understood what the feds planned next. Now she momentarily expected another call from a special agent in charge of God-only-knew-what. Undercover cops seemed to be crawling out of the woodwork.

And then, real disaster. On April 15, 2002—income-tax day—Baker discovered that superinvestor Matt Jones and ten of his partners were demanding their money back, too. Scrounging up an $8,000 refund for Rosie Ingram was one thing. But Matt Jones wanted the whole shebang back, and the total—including finder's fees and extra cars—now amounted to $443,500.

Baker was out of choices. On April 23, she sat down to compose what would thereafter be known as the "For the Love of God" letter, which she mailed to James. She wrote:

> Some of these people are really good God-fearing people who trusted me with their money the same as I trusted you and Robert. They have no answers, and I have no answers to give them. You just can't keep on ignoring these good people. Please give us some kind of hope. The people really need it. I think they would forget about suing if they knew they were getting cars. God is watching, and I know He is not pleased with how His people have been treated. I pray I can receive some encouraging words from you. To be honest, this has

nearly taken its toll on me. I can't take any more at this point. Please do the right thing, the Godly thing.

Waiting,

Dr. Gwendolyn Baker

It was a touching plea—also an exculpatory plea—but James never read a single word of it. His mail was piling up, unopened, at the Kemp Avenue office, and he had no interest in collecting it. In fact, his main interest that month was attending a "Fabulous Fords" show at Knott's Berry Farm, where he wanted to study customized Mustangs and have his picture taken in front of a Ferrari. Ironically, if he'd only opened the FedEx box in his own front-hall closet, he could have *purchased* the Ferrari.

But there was another reason James wouldn't see Baker's letter. That's because Postal Inspector Steve Hamilton would shortly fly to L.A. and ask Rose Nichols to hand over all the office mail. She complied. Among the confiscated materials, Hamilton found copies of letters from the attorney in Oklahoma, plus two Better Business Bureau complaints, not to mention the Donald Bell letter that had already landed on the U.S. attorney's desk in Kansas City, just as Baker had feared. Moreover, Hamilton found Matt Jones's request for a refund—at $443,500, it was a whopper among whoppers—as well as Baker's heartfelt "For the Love of God" letter, mixed in with two dozen other missives stipulating general outrage and threatening all manner of legal retribution. Hamilton didn't know where James was, but he could see why the boy was spending so little time at his parents' home. There was nothing there but bad news.

When Baker's epistolary pleading failed to elicit so much as a peep, she did the next best thing. She called Robert Gomez. "I told him I'd been through a very rough time," Baker remembered. "Robert told me he was sorry for all the trouble they'd put me through, and that James had gone to Washington, D.C.—his third trip there—to talk to the government about what he was doing concerning the cars and how he did it, and for me not to worry, that they were going to have the agents in Kansas City clear me. He also stated that his mom had been ill and that he himself had been in a car accident and injured his chest. He said, 'It's going to work out. Cars will be delivered.' His voice was very husky, as if he were sick."

Robert further advised Baker not to trouble herself over Matt Jones's refund, that it would be forgotten the instant a freight train full of shiny cars rolled into Memphis. "Everyone will be so happy," he said. In fact, he told Baker almost everything she most wanted to hear in soothing and comforting tones, proving he was as adroit as James when it came to deflecting the former National Finders' various crises.

Baker was pleased that Robert had a plan. Still, she needed to put her hands on some cash. Her $30,000-per-month Miracle Cars salary was history, and she'd long since quit her job at Primerica. Mainstream America wasn't in a big rush to hire middle-aged black women. But, like Robert Gomez, Gwen Baker was imaginative. She called Kansas car dealer Randy Lamb, who'd acted in her play, *Strange Devotions*. Lamb had invested close to $218,000 in 102 cars that he hoped to resell at auctions. Lamb was one of the few investors still wildly enthusiastic about the deal, and he'd even snapped up 20 cars that had been described on Baker's list as "slightly damaged." At only $500 per, he considered them shrewd purchases.

Baker told Lamb her problems. She asked if he could find it in his heart to lend her $20,000. "Remember," she comforted, "I've *seen* the cars, and what a beautiful sight it is!" Then she typed up a brief note. She promised: "It is my understanding that if the vehicles are distributed before the loan is due, you would prefer me to purchase for you, in your name, the following cars in place of repaying you the cash: five 1998 Ford Explorers, five 1998 Jeep Cherokees, five 1998 Ford F-150 trucks, five 1998 Ford Expedition XLTs."

In a heartbeat, Lamb wired the $20,000, inflating his investment by an additional 20 cars. Baker was relieved. It was enough money to put out at least a few of the smaller fires.

Unfortunately for Baker, Postal Inspector Hamilton and Special Agent Marshall were silently, patiently watching. It wasn't long before Hamilton held in his hands a photocopy of Baker's "promise." He and Marshall had interrogated Baker seven months earlier. Back then, they had warned her that no estate cars had been located, and they had explained, in lurid detail, the meaning of the term "guilty knowledge." Hamilton showed Baker's "promise" to Marshall. "Gary," he said, "read this and tell me how you interpret it."

Marshall studied it, then said: "What it looks like to me is she's still selling cars."

The two men looked at each other, then carried the letter to Assistant U.S. Attorney Stewart. Together, they asked, "Dan, what does this look like to you?"

Stewart didn't hesitate. He said, "What it looks like to me is she's still selling cars."

The prosecutor was dismayed, and he was feeling the first stirrings of anger. He'd gone out of his way to let these people demonstrate their innocence, and, except for Kim Krawizcki, they'd instead demonstrated arrogance and defiance. Their pious declarations of carrying out "His will" lasted for as long as it took to reach the nearest bank. If it was true that God had set forth various commandments for mankind's behavior, well, so too had the U.S. penal code, among them about thirteen counts under the heading of conspiracy to defraud.

At the time, Gwen Baker was fifty-one years old. She didn't know it yet, but never in those fifty-one years had she committed a costlier mistake.

23

THE WORLD ACCORDING TO ROBERT

Robert Gomez was in the groove. His life was humming along on cruise control, and he'd pretty much passed everyone in the gambling fast lane. Money wasn't just flowing in, it was *gushing* in. He had a warm and easy relationship with "Estate Representative" Pastor John Alexander, who was considerate about not asking pointed questions. He had no further communication with anyone in the dour and pessimistic Nichols family. The casinos were treating him like the king he believed he was. He'd just bought another Lincoln Town Car, which was registered in a fellow gambler's name. And his friendship with thirty-four-year-old Tony Zaldua was in full bloom.

Zaldua was an artisan who built wheels for racing bikes, painstakingly cutting them out of costly alloy billets in all manner of zoomy shapes. He'd met Gomez by accident at the Bicycle Casino the year prior. "I was an amateur player," Zaldua recalled, "and I'd just lost $200, which was all the cash I had. So I was holding my head in my hands, feeling sorry for myself. And up walks Robert, and he says, 'Hey, what's the problem?' So I told him. He says, 'Don't sweat it. You want me to spot you?' So he saved me. He saved my night. But I soon learned that a couple hundred bucks to Robert was like a nickel to the rest of us. I once saw him lose $200,000 at pai gow—*bam!*—just like that. It really fascinated me, you know, to meet someone with such a crazy life. It was very thrilling. His life was a big amusement-park ride."

Gomez told his new friend that his money derived from gambling alone, that he'd been on a winning streak for more than three years. Zaldua didn't press for details, and Gomez didn't offer any. He never heard Robert utter the name John Bowers or Pastor Alexander. Zaldua had earlier caught a glimpse or two of James Nichols in the casinos, but James never lingered, and he often appeared to get into arguments with Robert, albeit in hushed tones.

For those days when Robert didn't feel like driving his big Lincoln, he purchased a Chrysler PT Cruiser. He asked Tony to put the car in his name. Tony agreed, understanding that major gamblers—at least those who were successful—had to keep their names off the books. In January 2002, when his Long Beach condo was burglarized, Robert had simply said, "See what I mean? In the gaming industry, there are people who are jealous of me."

"I didn't dig into his private business," Zaldua conceded, "but I considered him a truthful person."

He might have thought otherwise if he'd right then been perusing Robert's pseudonymous contributions to various gambling Web sites. Gomez had written of himself: "This young man broke into the Los Angeles gambling scene back in the spring of 1997, with millions in financial backing from some of the world's biggest dope lords. Buddha is financed by the Arellano-Felix family of Mexico, under the control of the Medellin [and] Ochoa brothers drug cartels. He has been seen at many Miami drug lords' personal estates, [riding] on six-figure speed boats. Buddha was disowned by his father back in 1995, when there was a legal battle over his grandfather's estate. His mother is a well-respected woman with 'old school' views. This woman has been given many awards by the Catholic Archdiocese of Los Angeles and is said to have had the great opportunity of meeting the holy one himself, Pope John Paul. She lives in a nice 3500-square-foot home in the West Covina hills. She also has quite a bit of real estate and one of the largest homes in Calban, Colombia. She has had two major surgeries within the past 45 days. Buddha is by her side almost every hour of the day."

Robert was only warming up. "Believe it or not," he continued, "Buddha, the King of Pai Gow Poker, is a money launderer for many different dope lords and has close ties to the Miami and New York City mobs. Buddha was financially backing a small-time thief by the name of Richard 'Fingers' Sklar, both in cards and golf. One day, Fingers got his car blown to pieces in front of his own home. Buddha's friends and close associates had done this to silence him. You see, Fingers was going around town spreading a lot of false representations. He even went so far as to call Buddha a homosexual who had a fetish for young Asian men. BOOM!!!"

Gomez went on to suggest he'd recently beaten up a seventy-five-year-old man, had flown by private jet to Mexico to meet with "narcos," and had arranged the slaying of an Inglewood man who'd earlier stolen Robert's gambling winnings. "Buddha's connections to drug cartels and the Mafia make him a very dangerous individual," he added, in case readers had somehow missed his point. "Is Buddha a gambler, gangster, or both?"

At the same time, Gomez was boasting to friends that he was "mentoring" an underprivileged fifteen-year-old African American boy and stood ready to subsidize the youth's tuition at the University of San Diego. And he continued to forge a series of $20,000 checks made out to the Hollywood Park Casino, never mastering even the barest rudiments of James Nichols's signature. But it hardly mattered. What made the forgeries so brazen was that the First Bank & Trust account had been closed for nine months, and James's whereabouts were largely unknown.

"It meant he was absolutely, positively certain he could buy back those checks at the end of each night's gambling," noted Agent Elijah Zuniga, who was still monitoring Robert's flamboyant actions. "I guess you develop courage when someone else is wiring millions from the opposite side of the country."

In April 2002, Gomez and freelance gambling writer Max Shapiro went to dinner at Arnie Morton's steakhouse. Again, the bill was close to $300. "Robert told me the government was after him," Shapiro remembered, "and that they wanted dirt on Larry Flynt and the Hustler, and also on another casino. He said, 'I can expose them if I want,' like he had a load of insider stuff. I mentioned it to the owner of the other casino, and he shrugged like it was just another load of Robert's bullshit. Robert was a compelling figure, but it was hard to separate fact from fiction. It was difficult to peel away the layers and get to the core. He was like a Chinese puzzle."

On May 3, 2002, the Chinese puzzle's infamy truly peaked. That was the day the record-setting cashier's check arrived at the Hustler. It was for $518,731.22, and it was the check that cage manager Eleanor Gonzales said "took my breath away." It came, of course, from Pastor John Alexander, and was attached to a handwritten note that said, "The enclosed reflects the balance of my account that has been used to collect refunds owed to Robert Gomez, per instruction of James R. Nichols." The cage manager had never seen a check so large, and she forwarded it for approval to two supervisors, then to Larry Flynt himself. It took two days, but when the check proved to be legit, the casino doled out half a million dollars' worth of chips to their most extravagant customer.

James Nichols later swore he'd never instructed Alexander to wire cash from Atlanta to L.A., and he certainly wasn't around when the big transfers arrived.

The significance of the monster check was not lost on Special Agent Gary Marshall, back in Kansas City. "Between January and April 2002," he said, "we had watched Alexander wire about $2.5 million, so this brought the total to more than $3 million. This was May 2002. By then, the guy *had* to know that the money was going to casinos. How could he not?"

By the end of May 2002, Special Agent Gary Marshall had collected thousands of canceled checks, receipts, bank records, and payment vouchers. It had been an accountant's nightmare, but he'd been patient and methodical. Everything was filed chronologically and cross-referenced. Now it was time to total the sums. Cage manager Eleanor Gonzales may have lost her breath looking at a half-million-dollar check in the Hustler, but now Inspector Hamilton and Assistant U.S. Attorney Stewart had an identical reaction as they stood in the war room in Kansas City.

What they'd been observing represented the largest retail automotive fraud in U.S. history. The three feds had never seen anything like it. To date, the sale of Miracle Cars had generated $21.1 million.

It was God's gravy train.

From the gross, $8.6 million had been refunded to unhappy customers. The remainder—$12.5 million—was what Nichols, Gomez, Baker, and Conway had netted. The profit. The cream. The "back end."

Marshall, one of the U.S. Treasury's most dogged criminal investigators, had lived up to his reputation as a "silent strangler." By following canceled checks, he knew Baker had converted $313,000 of the take into cash, but she'd been generous about spreading it around. She'd given $182,200 to her daughters, had purchased a new Camaro, and had acquired two juicy pieces of subdivision real estate.

James Nichols had done a lot better. He'd stuffed $777,840 of the booty into his pockets and now, presumably, was still kicking around somewhere in the Southwest. But no one was sure. He might also have run to Mexico or Canada.

The rest of the loot had been filtered through Robert Gomez's favorite California casinos. The Crystal Park Hotel and Casino had taken in $3.2 million; the Bicycle Casino, $828,000; the Hollywood Park Casino, $1.08 million; the Club Caribe, $447,000; and the Hustler Casino, $3.03 million. There was likely more—no one even speculated how much might have found its way to Las Vegas or Atlantic City, for example—but that was what Marshall could confidently track on paper.

The three feds stared in disbelief. They called in Todd Graves, the U.S. attorney for the Western District of Missouri. Here before them, in black-and-white, was evidence that Robert Gomez had carried *at least* $8,694,098 into the California card parlors, funds he and James had continually been misappropriating since 1997. What Gomez may have won or lost in the casinos was not known—was not known, in fact, even to Gomez. But everyone agreed the kid had won more than he'd lost.

For a few minutes, the feds remained silent. Stewart was the first to break the silence. "I hesitate to ask this," he said, drawing out his words, "but where's the $8.7 million?"

"I hesitate to tell you," said Marshall, "but it's gone."

"You mean gone as in *lost* gone?" he asked.

"I doubt it," said Marshall.

"You mean gone as in hidden?"

"Might be," said Marshall.

"You mean gone as in stashed in an offshore account?"

"Might be," Marshall repeated.

"Well, who do we talk to to get it back?"

There was another long silence. Then Marshall said: "That's the twenty-one-million-dollar question. As a car-selling operation, this was a success. And as a money-laundering operation, this was a success. What's more, the money's not in the casinos' safe-deposit boxes, because we looked. What I'm telling you is, the funds are untraceable. That means the government can't tax them. And, for now at least, it means I can't find them."

In Kansas City, Dan Stewart was known for his patience and compassion, the Fred Rogers of assistant U.S. attorneys. But now he turned red in the face and clenched his fists. Until this moment, he hadn't been certain he even wanted this case. Why weren't his counterparts in Los Angeles or Memphis pursuing it instead? Neither Nichols nor Gomez had ever set foot in the state of Missouri. Why had it taken a five-foot-tall lady cop in tiny Higginsville, for God's sake, to bring matters to a head?

Now it didn't matter. Dan Stewart was steaming mad.

"So, what do you want to do?" asked his boss, Todd Graves.

"Well," Stewart replied, "I guess it's time we get their attention."

24

THE FEEL OF STEEL

E arly in June 2002, a federal grand jury in Kansas City returned sealed indictments alleging twenty-three counts of interstate fraud and money laundering. Warrants were issued for the arrest of James R. Nichols, twenty-six, of Carson, California; Robert Gomez, twenty-seven, of Bell, California; and Gwendolyn Baker, fifty-one, of Memphis, Tennessee. If found guilty on all counts, the trio faced more than two hundred years in federal prison. For the time being, the feds opted to let Corinne Conway stew in her own tax-evasion juices. What's more, they were keen to observe her reaction upon seeing her compatriots in cuffs. She'd cop a plea for sure, they felt.

Then the U.S. attorney installed a toll-free hotline so Miracle Cars victims could phone in their tales of woe. Within a week, the switchboard lit up like Times Square.

Now it was time to make some arrests. James Nichols remained missing in action, and the feds knew it might take a while to bring him to ground. But Gomez, they figured, would be a cinch. They figured wrong.

Inspector Steve Hamilton and Agent Elijah Zuniga were already camped out in the California casinos, methodically cruising the poker galleries. Both men stuck out like sore thumbs. Anyone could see they weren't gamblers. But when the indictments were unsealed, both were ready and eager to drop Bobby "Code Blue" Gomez. Unfortunately, Robert had suddenly and inexplicably stopped bellying up to the pai gow tables. There were brief "Buddha sightings," but the two feds were never in the house when it happened, and it was making them nervous. Gomez possessed enough cash to move to Monaco if he wanted. Hamilton nosed around, leaving his business card with dozens of casino denizens. Zuniga called all his contacts, telling them that he just wanted to talk to Robert "about getting the IRS off his ass." When that produced nothing, Zuniga began calling Gomez's cell phone, to tell him directly. "I actually reached him a couple of times," Zuniga recalled, "but he told me he was in Las Vegas and planned to be there a month. I knew it was a lie, because other sources had seen him the same day in L.A."

Hamilton and Zuniga spent another night roaming the Hustler. "I figured he'd be there for sure," recalled Zuniga, "because he hadn't gambled in a few days, and the Hustler had become his latest, favorite place. That night, the casino was packed, because there was a pay-per-view fight on TV. Larry Flynt was also there, playing poker. I knew Flynt would act as 'Gomez bait.' But nothing."

The next morning, the two agents "set up" outside the Kemp Avenue house. Maybe Gomez had moved back into James's boyhood bedroom. Hamilton and Zuniga even followed Sam and Rose Nichols to Christ Christian Home Missionary Baptist Church, somewhat suspicious that the couple had taken separate cars. "While we surveilled the church, other investigators set up outside Gomez's mom's house," recalled Zuniga. "It was incredibly boring. Steve was preparing to be in a community-theater play, so, at one point, I passed the time by helping him practice his lines." Still, no Gomez.

The agents were about to give up for the night. Then, at four in the morning, as Zuniga was driving on the freeway, his cell phone rang. A casino employee said, "Your boy is here. The Hustler. He's playing against [third-party banker] Network M." Zuniga called Hamilton, who contacted the Gardena Police Department—mostly as a courtesy, but it was always reassuring to have backup—then everyone met in the parking lot. At six A.M. on June 10, 2002, the two undercover agents and two uniformed cops walked into the Hustler. "The place was practically empty," remembered Zuniga, "except for potbellied Robert playing pai gow. He had a rack of chips in front of him, and a pile of cash. I asked the dealer not to touch anything. It looked like a whole lot of five-thousand-dollar chips, but I couldn't count it until we got a photograph of everything."

Gomez casually remarked, "Hey, guys, what's happenin'?" still thinking the men were there—at dawn, no less—to help him fix discrepancies on his income-tax returns.

Instead, Inspector Hamilton instructed Gomez to stand, and when he did, he clicked handcuffs around Robert's doughy wrists. "He was very docile," recalled Hamilton, "and while I read him his Miranda rights, he was silent. I asked, 'Do you own any firearms?' and he told me he didn't, that they'd been stolen. Then I asked, 'Where's James Nichols?' He said, 'Well, I'm sure I have no idea.' I said, 'Where do you live?' and he gave me his mother's address in Bell." Robert had answered three out of three questions with lies.

But no one really made a note of it, and here's why: At the time of his arrest, Robert Gomez was holding $818,120.

"Really, it about blew us away," said Zuniga. "You know, just to happen to have it *on you* at the time we showed up. I had to assume there were times when he was carrying more. It was like busting a drug kingpin or something. Then I thought, Oh, *no,* maybe that's what he *wants* us to believe, more of his Mafia bullshit."

The agents returned to the parking lot to search the 2002 Lincoln Town Car Gomez had driven to the Hustler. "It turned out to be registered to a professional gambler who'd once won Binion's World Championship of poker in Vegas," Zuniga learned. "Gomez held a joint account with the guy at the Bike, sometimes sharing as much as $175,000. The man admitted to us that Gomez sometimes gave him money to purchase automobiles and put them in his name. But beyond that, I couldn't turn him into an informant."

When he was arrested, Gomez hadn't recognized Inspector Hamilton, but he certainly recognized his old pal "Eli." "When I asked him about the con," Zuniga recalled, "he told me, 'Hey, man, it was James's idea. He's all mixed up with those women, Baker and Conway.' His whole explanation was, during any given week, Nichols would sometimes owe as much as $1 million in refunds but didn't have it. So he went to Gomez, who then purchased Miracle Cars to keep James afloat. In that manner, he said, he'd eventually bought $620,000 in cars and was now as pissed off as anyone to learn they didn't exist. Then he said he was deathly afraid of James, because James had people following him, and James was allegedly involved with drug dealers, and James had broken into his house. Blah, blah, blah. Laid everything on James. I said, 'Well, that's funny, Robert, because we've got copies of all these checks going from James to you, and none going from you to James.' He said to me, 'Well, *of course,* Eli, sure, but that's because I deal in cash only. Cash is king.' "

Zuniga replied, "I thought *you* were king."

Gomez's arrest caused quite a stir—the foremost topic of discussion among gamblers from Los Angeles to Las Vegas. He appeared before U.S. Magistrate Paul Game Jr., where he didn't say much, just that he had attended Canyon Verde High School in El Segundo and now made "$15,500 per month as a professional gambler," even though he had never admitted to so handsome an income on his tax returns. Robert was held without bail, and his tale traveled at the speed of sound.

In a story for the *Los Angeles New Times,* reporters Michael Gougis and Traci Jai Isaacs wrote: "On the night of June 10, Robert Gomez was in the zone, sitting at the pai gow table at the Hustler, $818,000 in front of him and in his pockets. He was in his element, and on a typical night he'd be at the tables for hours. But this night wasn't typical. State gaming agents and U.S. Postal Inspectors cut Gomez's play short. They slapped handcuffs on him and hauled him out of the casino where he'd once gone toe to toe in private, high-stakes games with card aficionado, porn king, and First Amendment activist Larry Flynt. There weren't many people in L.A.'s small community of high rollers who didn't know Buddha. He would play for up to 12 hours at a time, moving tens of thousands of dollars in and out of his player accounts. He had safe-deposit boxes at several casinos and thought little of cashing checks for $50,000. Prosecutors say he was trying to make the money harder to trace. But it gave him a reputation as a 'whale.' One person who knew Gomez said he dropped so much money at the tables that he lived rent-free in a ninth-floor suite of the Crystal Park Hotel."

Ten days after Robert appeared before Judge Game, United States Marshals transferred him to a place in Kansas he'd heard about but never seen. It was a place with no ninth-floor suite and no custom-made pai gow tables. It was the federal correctional institution called Leavenworth.

Within hours of Robert Gomez's arrest, Gwen Baker, in Memphis, knew all about it. She called Special Agent Gary Marshall in Kansas City and asked, "Are you coming for me next?"

"As a matter of fact," he replied, *"today."* Baker was distraught. She begged Marshall not to arrest her at her home in front of all her neighbors. "She said, 'Can I turn myself in to someone by myself, maybe tomorrow?'" Marshall replied, "Yes, you can self-surrender to the FBI, but if you don't show up, the consequences are pretty awful. You understand what I'm saying? Let me clearly hear you say you do."

"The night before my mom was to surrender, someone tried to break into our house," reported Baker's daughter Angela Arnold. "So she came to stay with me, she was so scared. Someone had tried to cut the burglar alarm, but it went off anyway. I assumed it was someone in law enforcement trying to retrieve documents. I *do* know they'd already tapped the phones."

When Baker surrendered the next morning, the agents let her know she was in big trouble for selling cars after they'd warned her to stop. "But it wasn't true," protested Angela Arnold. "It was Randy Lamb just trying to help. My mom needed money for refunds, because James and Robert had been her only means of support. So now they're gone, and she's strapped. She thought her godsons would come through for her, because she was their employee. So she tells Randy, and he lends her some money that he himself had borrowed. And when he borrowed it, he didn't tell the lenders truthfully what he was using it for, that it was just a personal loan to my mother. Instead, he told them he was buying more cars, so they wouldn't pester him about it. That's why, to the government, it looked like she was selling more cars. My mom could have left the country weeks before she was arrested, but she didn't. She told me she was willing to face the consequences."

Agent Marshall wasn't particularly moved by Baker's explanation. In his day, he'd heard plenty of con men blame their victims. "But I called Randy Lamb anyway, to hear his side of the story," Marshall said, "and I found out he'd borrowed against his house to invest in those cars. He believed the loan he gave Baker was an option to buy more cars—cars that James Nichols didn't want anymore. Overall, you know, Lamb had invested $218,000. I didn't tell him at the time, but I felt certain he was never gonna see a nickel of it. I felt bad for the guy."

"Those two boys ruined a lot of lives," said Arnold after her mother was booked. "I don't trust people anymore. People who say they're good Christians, well, you have to go out and investigate claims like that. You can't just go with your gut. You have to find out."

When Robert Gomez was arrested, he refused to tell anyone where he was living. "He'd just recite his mother's address," recalled Agent Elijah Zuniga, "and I already knew that was a fib. So four days passed while I was trying to figure it out." Zuniga checked with the Crystal Park Hotel, with a hotel in Compton, even with Richie "Fingers" Sklar. Then, on the very day Gwen Baker was to be bailed out of jail, Zuniga received an anonymous phone call: "The caller said, 'Listen, that black lady, the one from the Midwest, she just took a plane to Long Beach, and she's going to Robert's house to clear out all the evidence.' I said, 'Yeah, well, if you know so much, what's the address?' And darned if the caller didn't give it to me: 4455 Country Club Lane. Now I knew where Buddha slept during the day. So I called the Long Beach police and had a unit rush over there, see if there's a female removing household items. They called a half hour later and said, 'Hey, it isn't a black woman, it's a white *male*, and he's hauling stuff to his car. We ran his name and guess what? He's on probation, so we're entering the house right now.' As they did, I asked what they were seeing, and the cop says, 'Well, a whole bunch of sports memorabilia and a whole bunch of casino chips.' That's all I needed to hear. I went tearing over there, and when I arrived, it turned out that it was little Tony Zaldua who was trying to empty the place."

Inside the "Ferris Bueller condo," as everyone now called it, Zuniga was intrigued by what he found. "Gomez had about a hundred Buddha statues," he discovered, "plus his 'King of Pai Gow' license-plate frames, a lot of male-oriented pornography, and as many shoes as Imelda Marcos. He had a huge bowl of casino chips at the base of a Buddha statue in front of the fireplace, almost like a religious offering or something. There was cash lying around, six hundred dollars or so, plus discarded wrapping bands in five-thousand-dollar denominations. There was a lamp whose base was a rack of gambling chips. There were big-screen TVs, stereos, and sports memorabilia that appeared to be worth a fortune. He had jerseys from Michael Jordan and Kobe Bryant, both autographed. Baseball bats signed by Willie Mays, Ted Williams, and Pete Rose. Boxing gloves signed by Ali. Super Bowl helmets signed by John Elway and Brett Favre. There were certificates of authenticity for everything, and the Long Beach cops told me it was all stuff that would appreciate. There was antique currency from the 1800s. And there was jewelry everywhere, some of it still with price tags. It was mostly gaudy stuff, with big stones, way more than the average man would have. Watches, bracelets, diamonds, at least thirty rings."

Zuniga kept searching. He found four handguns registered to Gomez—a Smith & Wesson .357 Magnum, a Glock .45, a Browning 9mm, and a Beretta .32. These were the weapons Gomez had told Inspector Hamilton he didn't have. Zuniga also found an address book in which the very first name listed was James Nichols's. And he uncovered a secret floor safe, in the closet of Gomez's bedroom. "When I saw that, I was rubbing my hands," said Zuniga. "I thought, Hot damn, the mother lode, the missing millions!" But after a locksmith drilled it open, all that was stashed inside was a diamond-encrusted platinum bracelet worth $4,000 to $5,000.

What most interested the agents was a strange handwritten letter—an original—that had been signed by James R. Nichols. It was addressed to John Bowers and was the letter James claimed to have written in 1994, in which he'd agreed to take care of Robert. In it, he told Bowers he'd be "honored and privileged" to work for him. He then added: "Robert and I go out very often, and we always have a great time. He has been there for me so many times, I can't count them all. That is why I refuse the extra pay, out of respect for my dear friend, Robert."

That amused the feds. The boys clearly weren't "dear friends" anymore. Zuniga wondered why Gomez would have held the letter for eight years. Had it been recently manufactured by Nichols to demonstrate his belief in Bowers's existence? And if so, wasn't it in Gomez's best interest to burn it? When asked, Robert said he had no idea how the letter had wound up in his home. "Maybe it was meant for some other guy named Robert," he posited. Again, Zuniga laughed.

As far as the agents could tell, no middle-aged African American woman ever showed up at 4455 Country Club Lane. "If she did," said Zuniga, "she'd have seen a zillion police cars and would have kept right on truckin'. But to this day, I don't know who that caller was. Over and over I've asked myself, Who would have knowledge of Robert's address *and* my phone number? I still can't answer that."

Gomez's former roommate, Fingers Sklar, wasn't at all surprised to hear Robert had been busted. "If he was involved in a moneymaking scheme, I don't know how he carried it off for so long," Fingers offered. "Robert was just the *dumbest* person. He used to sit in front of the fireplace and fall asleep, and he'd leave the fire screen open. I said, 'Robert, don't do that, embers will fly out and burn down the house.' He said, 'Yes, but I'll get more heat that way.' That's how dumb he was."

If the two had argued over fires, it was more than a little ironic. Fingers couldn't swear that it was Gomez who torched his car, but he *did* imply it might have been one of Robert's shady compatriots, "laying out Buddha's legend a little bit."

"Because of Robert's imagination," said Zuniga, "I double-checked with the Los Angeles County Fire Department, to see if there even *was* a car fire. But, wouldn't you know, that story was apparently true."

Robert's more recent roommate, Tony Zaldua, also found himself the object of unwanted scrutiny. He'd been on probation and was living in a house full of handguns. Only a few days passed before the L.A. district attorney issued a warrant for Zaldua's arrest. Because the case involved firearms, it was standard proce-dure to call the Violence Suppression Team, whose members located Zaldua in a parking lot across from the Bicycle Casino, mysteriously sitting in a car belonging to one of Robert Gomez's former attorneys. Wearing bulletproof vests and armed with MP-5 submachine guns and M-16s—overkill, to be sure—the cops took little Tony into custody without a hiccup.

"After they cuffed him," Zuniga recalled, "I put my hands on his shoulders and said, 'Come on, Tony, don't you want to tell me what the heck Robert's been up to all these years?' Tony asked, 'How much time am I facing?' I told him it wasn't up to me, that I had no idea. So then he stared off into the distance for a minute or so, just contemplating. Finally, he said to me, 'I guess I'd rather go to jail.' "

The evening after Robert Gomez was arrested, Inspector Steve Hamilton and Agent Elijah Zuniga drove back to the Kemp Avenue house in Carson.

"I warned Rose and Sam that I had an arrest warrant for James and that a lot of people were now looking for him," Hamilton recalled. "I told her it would be safer for their son if he just turned himself in. I said, 'If this thing comes to a head, I don't want Kimberly Hall and her baby involved in a high-speed chase or something worse, like a shooting. Why should anybody get injured, you know?' And it *did* worry me. We knew Gomez had firearms when his house was searched, but we didn't know about James. Neither of the boys was a felon, so there was no prohibition against their owning guns. Anyway, Rose thanked me and promised to call if she heard from James. Then we drove over to Kimberly Hall's mother's house and gave her the same warning."

Two weeks passed and still no James. "We'd get messages from time to time, via his attorney," remembered Assistant U.S. Attorney Curt Bohling. "James made a big show of saying he wanted to talk to us in L.A. But when a meeting was scheduled, he'd abruptly cancel it." Inspector Hamilton became all too familiar with the scheduled flights from Kansas City to L.A. Finally, the Kansas City feds instructed Zuniga to interview Kimberly Hall, adding that it was time to apply more pressure.

Zuniga drove back to Carson. "Kimberly told me, 'Well, when I see James—*if* I see James—what we do is go to a safe house,' " he reported. "I thought, Oh, no, here's another one who's watching too many movies. I said, 'What's the address of this safe house?' She said, 'I can't tell you, because then it wouldn't be safe.' It was comical, actually. She didn't want me to know the address because she was afraid Robert Gomez would somehow hire someone to hurt her family. Frankly, I got annoyed, felt she was lying or obstructing. I made a few calls, and it turns out she was on probation, just like Tony Zaldua. So I drove back to Carson, and this time I wasn't her friend anymore. I said, 'Kim, that BMW you're driving, I believe it was paid for with stolen money, and you're living with a guy apparently involved in an ongoing criminal enterprise. Know what that means? If your probation officer finds out, he'll revoke you so fast your head will spin.' "

It had the intended effect. She led Zuniga to the house on Bankers Drive, just five minutes from the Kemp Avenue address. "When I asked if there was anything inside related to the Miracle Cars scheme, she told me, 'Oh, yeah, he has a whole office of that stuff.' So I got a search warrant. The house was messy, clothes piled in mounds so high you had to walk around them. All in disarray, almost like it had been tossed. I wondered if James had just taken his stuff and run. In the kitchen was hardly any food, because they ate out every night. They had a lot of electronics— big-screen TVs, sound systems, cell phones, digital cameras, and close to two hundred DVDs. I found a $5,000 Rolex, a receipt for a $28,000 BMW, brochures for Black & Brown Motor Sports, and computer disks listing various stock-market accounts and mutual funds. And he had a little office, with pictures of Porsches and Lamborghinis on the wall."

Zuniga walked next door to talk to the neighbors. "They told me, 'We *knew* the cops would raid this house someday.' When I asked why, they said, 'Well, he never had a job, but he always drove expensive BMWs, and everyone who visited had fancy cars, too. We assumed he was a drug dealer.' I showed them a picture of Gomez, but no one had seen that face before. So then I went back and said to Kimberly, 'Hey, your neighbors all knew something was funny, and you're telling me you *lived* with this guy but never had a clue?' She goes, 'Well, see, I knew James was selling some cars and had made some enemies, but that's about all.' My eight-year-old would have known as much."

The house on Bankers Drive was rented, so the government had nothing to seize except a white BMW and a yellow $17,608 Ducati motorcycle in the garage. From the agents' standpoint, the fancy machinery meant nothing. What interested them far more was a single piece of paper that Kimberly Hall had viewed as totally innocuous. Zuniga discovered the document in a night-stand beside James's bed. It was a forged invoice on the letterhead of Payless Towing and Storage. "I said out loud, 'Oooh, mama, I wonder if James is gonna regret stickin' *that* baby in there,'" Zuniga recalled. "I wondered if it was a smoking gun."

Someone besides Zuniga wondered, too.

On June 23, 2002—thirteen days after the grand jury indict-ment was unsealed—James Nichols surrendered to authorities through his lawyer, Ronald Wasserman.

"I was curious where he'd been," recalled Assistant U.S. Attorney Dan Stewart, "so I asked. James's only response was, 'Nowhere, sir. Just been doing my normal stuff. You guys didn't look for me.'" It made Stewart laugh. Then he asked James what he had to say about the Payless invoice.

"My father boxed all that stuff up for me, from the home office," he replied. "I thought Robert had taken those materials with him. I believe [the receipt] came from Mr. Robert Gomez."

Stewart remembered being almost disappointed. "I thought, That's *it*, your defense is 'Robert did it,' and Robert's defense is 'James did it'? These boys ran this operation like two geniuses for more than seven years, and that's all they can come up with when they're busted?"

But it wasn't going to be that simple.

James's days of camel-hair coats and racy BMWs appeared to be over. Like Robert before him, he was awarded a one-way air-line ticket to the Midwest. He found that Leavenworth was bru-tally hot in July. He wasn't there long before he met a fellow prisoner named Enrique Perez, who knew Robert and could relay messages. James said to Perez, "Tell that fat bitch Buddha that he's never getting his money *or* his cars back."

25

STONEWALLING IN THE MIDWEST

Even as the agents were cuffing James Nichols, the U.S. attorney's office in Kansas City was chatting with Corinne Conway in little Higginsville. Her resolve, surprisingly, was not notably shaken when the "executor" and the "heir" were transferred to Leavenworth, only seventy-five miles from her home. As it happened, she had found quite a persuasive ally in Kansas City.

"When I first met Corinne," said Robin Fowler, her attorney, "I told her, 'You're looking at a minimum of 120 months in prison. If you were part of this, just say that. They [the government] are fair people, they'll give you a break. Tell them you met with James, you talked with Robert, you planned it with Gwen Baker.' Without hesitating, she said to me: 'I didn't know there were no cars. *I did not know.*' Here's a sixty-two-year-old woman willing to risk what could well be the last ten years of her life. She would not say she was guilty, couldn't form those words in her mouth."

Fowler liked Conway and her husband, Wilbur, calling them "salt-of-the-earth types." He said, "Corinne's involvement in this was like a hurricane that finally meets warm water and blows up. And she was the warm water. Through her reputation in churches, her contacts, she really caused the scheme to explode across the country. She helped spread it, but she was not a knowing part. She was first approached by another minister, Pastor Holt. That's not the typical way someone gets involved in a scam, and Holt has never been charged. Corinne offered to sell cars to a policeman in Higginsville, to the mayor, to every public official, her banker, her neighbors. Who would perpetrate a fraud on the very people you have to face every day of your life? I think she sold twenty-five hundred cars, but after she was initially approached by law enforcement, she never sold another. She told everyone, 'I *still* think this deal is valid.' Then she gave the agents four boxes of alphabetized records. Someone committing a fraud doesn't keep records like that."

Fowler couldn't find a single year, prior to the scam, in which Conway made more than $20,000. "Then, all of a sudden, she makes a million," he pointed out. "She didn't know how to take care of it, and I think she adopted an ostrich approach—put her head in the sand, hoped it would go away. With the money she made, she didn't buy a Ferrari. Just some clothes for herself and the building on the hill, for the ministry, overlooking land her husband, Wilbur, was raised on. You know, with the smartest agents in this nation working on the Miracle Cars case, it took them way more than a year to put the indictment together, to figure out the scheme. It's easy for them to say she was willfully blind, but when they first approached her, all they could tell her was, 'There's a high probability that the [South Bay and Payless] faxes are fraudulent.' A *high probability*. Even law enforcement was having a hard time putting this together. Corinne couldn't run John Bowers's name through the IRS indices like the agents did. I don't know if she would even have *tried* to call every county in New York and say, 'Hi, this is a private citizen in Missouri, would you please take an hour or two and look for a John Bowers in your county?' A private person isn't able to call every registrar of deeds, like Inspector Hamilton did. Many, many months into the investigation, the government was still saying, 'We *think* it's a scam, but we can't tell for sure.' If *they* couldn't tell, how could Corinne? She's religious and believes that miracles *do* occur, and she thought this was one of them. She believed that Gwen Baker was a writer, an actress, and a playwright, and had been a powerful executive at American Express. When all of this came out, Corinne's hometown newspaper essentially called her a thief, and she felt vilified. All she wants is to live in little Higginsville and spend the rest of her life trying to get her name back."

It was a defense that a lot of people in Missouri wanted to believe, Miracle Car victims not among them. "But the fact is, we negotiated back and forth with her as best we could," recalled Inspector Steve Hamilton, "and we weren't getting anywhere. I didn't believe she was simply an unwitting dupe. Conway employed real forethought in this—turning all the finders into 'doctors,' holding shindigs to elevate Baker's profile in front of potential buyers, disguising some of her earnings as contributions to her own tax-exempt church. Then she paid herself expenses out of the Virtuous Women's account. Did all that happen by accident? And what adult human being in America just happens to *forget* to pay income taxes? That doesn't fly. Conway needed to come to an agreement with us, but we couldn't make it happen."

"Conway was in her own world," added Assistant U.S. Attorney Bohling. "She wouldn't really acknowledge that there was even a problem."

Two days after James Nichols was arrested in California, Corinne Conway became the fourth name added to the U.S. attorney's indictment. It wasn't exactly what the agents wanted, but neither could it be avoided. They were now charging a sixty-two-year-old woman of color with selling $6 million worth of nonexistent cars out of a $21 million con from which she'd skimmed $1,171,000 in commissions and fees on which she paid not a penny in taxes. Still, when the U.S. attorney added up the counts, it appeared Conway was in slightly less hot water than her colleagues. She was facing "only" $3.5 million in fines and 135 years in prison without parole.

Just on the other side of town—in Independence, Missouri—Gwen Baker had also retained counsel. Her attorney, Lance Sandage, was likewise putting the best face on things, and he, too, genuinely liked his client. "My impression of Gwen when we first met was that she had a high character, was very caring about the people near her, especially her daughters," he claimed. "And she was very articulate and well educated—an education that was self-learned through her readings and through Bible studies. It was always her intention, from day one, to plead *not* guilty. She had no criminal history, and when she started selling cars, she absolutely, positively believed the estate existed. Obviously, she admitted to making some bad decisions. The worst was selling cars to Randy Lamb after the government had already talked to her. But she was honest about that and admitted she had no intention of repaying those so-called loans. And there were other things that weren't too serious but just looked bad—the promise of cars in return for a degree from Friends University, for example. But she was basically a good person who was aware of the painful dichotomy of her victims. Some of the victims had very little and lost everything, people who just wanted a little status or a car for their kids. Then there were others who invested hundreds of thousands, who never asked for any verification that this was legit, people who should have known better and were acting out of greed. I felt Gwen was 'upper middle management' in this scheme—lower than the boys but higher than Conway or Krawizcki. I asked her, 'Is there someone you believe was controlling Nichols and Gomez?' She thought about it. She said, 'Maybe.' It was always a rumor."

Sandage showed Baker some of the evidence he knew the government would trot out at trial, and a list of witnesses who were sure to testify. Some were Baker's customers, some were personal friends, and a few were reverends and pastors of churches she'd helped bilk. "She looked at those witnesses," recalled Sandage, "and I could see it weighed heavily on her mind. Heavily."

By then, the *Kansas City Star* had seen the press releases emanating from the U.S. attorney's office. A few juicy newspaper stories had appeared, mostly about the "local woman," Corinne Conway, and the details of the Miracle Cars scheme were now spreading nationally. For the citizens of Kansas City, a trial was an alluring prospect. It wasn't O.J., but it had the potential to become a minor media circus: *Here, on our stage downtown, for a multiweek tour, James "the Executor" Nichols and Robert "the Heir" Gomez, live and in person!*

"I'll tell you, this whole scheme, it was one of the craziest things I'd ever heard or seen," said Baker's attorney, neatly summing up his fellow Missourians' take. "I've always been amazed by what a little religion and a few fraudulent pieces of paper could get accomplished. But this one took the cake."

In Leavenworth, James and Robert had no further contact, and they spoke to no one except their lawyers. The feds were left to develop their own pet theories on how the scam had evolved.

"Right then," said Agent Gary Marshall, "the big thing in my mind was whether the two of them actually split the money—the unaccounted-for money that went through the casinos. I mean, they *had* to have split it, right? They're partners, yet up to this point there's been this huge disparity in their incomes—Robert is getting millions, James is getting a few hundred thousand. At least that's what they had to tell people, because Robert is the supposed heir and James is only the executor. But that's just a made-up story. In reality, they're partners in this thing, and I always thought that their agreement was that Gomez would launder it, then they'd split his winnings fifty-fifty at a later date. And the later date suddenly arrived when *we* entered the picture. Maybe that's when Nichols said to Gomez, 'It's over, it's time to divvy it up.' But Gomez shocked him with, 'Good luck, it's been real, you're on your own,' and walked out the door. *Surprise!* And that's why, from that point on, they don't talk to each other and Nichols wasn't involved in the sale of cars. The next $3.5 million comes from John Alexander and goes directly to Gomez. Nichols grabs all he can— the quarter-million in the Lakewood account—and flees. But I don't think James ever got his share of the laundered loot. If he had, he might not have run out of cash in Las Vegas so fast."

Assistant U.S. Attorney Dan Stewart was fascinated that Nichols had the foresight to ask Ronald Wasserman to search for the invisible estate attorneys. "We looked carefully at Mr. Wasserman's billing records," Stewart said, "but all they proved was that James *asked* him to search, not that he did." Then Stewart contemplated the meaning of the handwritten note found in Gomez's condo—the letter from James to the phantom John Bowers. "My feeling was that it was a communication to help prove he believed the estate existed," Stewart speculated. "We couldn't find a witness who'd seen the document ever before, and there was no date on it. It could have been written at any time, and then James tells Robert, 'Hey, put this in storage for later, as my cover.' His defense then becomes, 'I believed Bowers existed and thus believed in the estate and the cars.' And Robert's defense becomes, 'I never sold any cars, I just gambled with the money that James gave me, and I don't know how he got it.' "

Stewart knew it was a defense that wouldn't hold water legally or logically, but it might diminish each boy's culpability in the eyes of a compassionate jury.

"Right when the boys had their blowup, the scheme was looking a little raggedy," noted Marshall, "but it actually ran like a well-oiled machine. They started the con at James's church, where they told everyone Robert was an alcoholic who needed help. The smart thing they did was take their time. They rolled out the con slowly, one piece at a time. They established credibility that way, so the congregation would buy into it. Once they sucked all they could out of those small-time buyers, they moved the operation out of state. That's when Baker and Conway became the front men, with emphasis on fat investors, not individual buyers. When you look at how it worked, you see that everybody had his own specific role. Conway was spreading the word through the churches. Baker was the clearinghouse, collecting and recording funds and forwarding them to California. James was the CEO, arbitrating disputes and monitoring the operation back at headquarters. And Robert was the laundry man, scrubbing the profits for a big payday later. Four specialties: marketing, sales, administration, laundering. It didn't seem like a casual plan, you know? They plugged professionals into the key leadership roles, like a business would do. Pretty amazing, really. Not the work of your average teenage boys."

Of course, the feds had yet to prove any of this.

In Kansas City, the U.S. attorney set up a special fund to reimburse victims, a fund that was growing rapidly. The government would shortly grab the $818,000 found in Gomez's pockets, plus his jewelry. They had the BMW and Ducati that belonged to James. It looked like Conway would shortly lose her white church on the hill. And a warrant was issued to seize the two Cole Farms properties that Baker had purchased in Tennessee.

"But we had boxes and boxes of claims from victims," Dan Stewart pointed out. "Unless we found the missing $8.7 million, we were only going to be returning pennies on every dollar."

Special Agent Elijah Zuniga's investigation of Robert Gomez had more or less concluded, but at least one element of the case still gnawed at his gut. "After I searched Gomez's place in Long Beach," he admitted, "I should have performed follow-up searches at the parents' houses—Mercedes Flores's place and at Kemp Avenue. I'll probably go to my grave wondering if I'd have found millions in chips there. The boys trusted those locations and the owners. I can't recall how many casino employees came up to me and said, 'Eli, dig up the old lady's back yard, see if you find some treasure.' It's my one big regret."

By July 2002, Dan Stewart, Curt Bohling, Gary Marshall, and Steve Hamilton had already devoted seventeen months of their public-service lives to untangling the Miracle Cars affair. They had twelve to go.

In May 2003, just days before the much-anticipated Miracle Cars trial in Kansas City, the predicted four-ring circus was suddenly reduced to two. That's because Gwen Baker and Corinne Conway—the National Finders who would never, *ever* admit their guilt—both copped pleas.

Sixty-two-year-old Conway agreed to plead guilty to felony income-tax evasion. In return, the government would drop the conspiracy-to-defraud charges. It was, by anyone's lights, a sweetheart deal. Her attorney, Robin Fowler, was ecstatic.

Gwen Baker's deal wasn't a whole lot more complicated. Her counsel, Lance Sandage, had been correct about victims' testimony "weighing heavily" on her mind, and she had folded, too. The government was willing to forgive all of Baker's many fraudulent car sales, save two—the so-called loans she'd solicited from

Randy Lamb, after having been warned there were no cars. She'd made those two final transactions, totaling a mere $33,000, with guilty knowledge, and it was not forgivable. The feds had bent over backward to set her on the path of righteousness, and she had willfully declined. Now Baker faced two counts of interstate transportation of stolen property and would likewise be obligated to testify against her "beloved godsons," James and Robert, on whom, right then, she wasn't expending much affection.

Baker was fifty-two years old. Before she copped a plea, she was realistically facing as much as two decades in prison without the possibility of parole. Assistant U.S. Attorney Dan Stewart asked her, "Aren't you concerned that if you're convicted on all counts you might never see the outside of a prison again?"

Baker replied, "No, that did not cross my mind."

She was as feisty and defiant as ever, and Inspector Steve Hamilton wondered whether she'd make it through her testimony without an explosive tirade or two. It was fine with Hamilton if she suffered an entertaining meltdown on the stand. He found it distasteful that Baker constantly referred to herself as a doctor, and he refused to use that honorific in her presence. "Those two women," noted the inspector, "were by themselves responsible for $15.6 million in fraudulent sales, and I wasn't convinced they knew how lucky they were."

"Two down, two to go," said Agent Elijah Zuniga, who was still searching for casino informants who "might be willing to work for consideration." As the trial approached, Zuniga felt certain Nichols or Gomez would agree to testify against the other. They had a real hatred brewing, and a ton of money was missing. "Gomez would always tell me how innocent he was, just a victim of Nichols's shenanigans," recalled Zuniga. "He'd brag that he had several voice recordings of Nichols incriminating himself, plus documentation to prove James was the *real* bad guy. He'd tell me he was gonna turn over the evidence and 'cooperate soon.' But soon never came."

In the casinos, Zuniga was surprised—almost a little offended—that no one came forward with information. "But one thing I've learned," he said, "is if a casino has one thousand employees, they act more like one thousand independent contractors, and they're all after one thing: the tip. They're like waitresses, they *need* that tip. And I believe many of them had at one time or another accepted money or chips or tokes from Gomez, and now they felt embarrassed about having to admit it in public. And then Gomez's personal friends, they were just hostile toward me. I remember serving a subpoena on [former South Bay employee] Val Morella. I set up appointments with him, but he'd never show. So I called him on my cell phone, pretending to be a customer, and kept him on the phone until I could walk right into his office. He was furious that I'd tricked him. He said he wouldn't cooperate with the government no matter what. He said, 'I'll enjoy the trip to Kansas City, but I'm not gonna say *nothin',*' and then he disappeared. At the time, though, I wasn't worried. In fact, I called Gary Marshall and Steve Hamilton the Friday before the trial and said, 'You watch, one of those guys, James or Robert, will flip, and the whole house of cards will collapse.' But it didn't happen. I was surprised, and now we were facing a long trial where the defendants were saying, '*He* did it!' then, 'No, I didn't, *he* did it!' I told Gary, 'Well, maybe a fistfight will break out.' "

PART III

Doubtless the pleasure is as great

Of being cheated, as to cheat.

As lookers-on feel most delight,

That least perceive a juggler's sleight,

And still the less they understand,

The more th' admire his sleight of hand.

—Samuel Butler

26

KANSAS CITY, MISSOURI

I've written magazine stories for thirty years. In that time, I've accepted some colorful assignments. I've ridden with the U.S. Army on gun patrols around Kosovo. I've driven a Land Cruiser from Lhasa, Tibet, to Kathmandu, Nepal. I've slept on the ground in the jungles of Borneo for thirty consecutive days. And I once spent two weeks aboard a Russian icebreaker in the High Arctic. But I'd never been asked to cover a criminal trial.

The offer came from *Car and Driver,* in Ann Arbor, Michigan, the largest-circulation car-enthusiast magazine in the world. The editors there had seen Internet snippets of the Miracle Cars story, and a California subscriber had mailed in a small item from the *Los Angeles Times.*

I wanted to write that story. I wrote a breathless pitch, hoping to land the assignment:

> Pick any consumer product you can imagine—baseball bats, beer, or bonds. Now sell $21 million worth. Tough? Now make those sales without ever showing the product to the buyers, not even once. Tougher? Now do it without ever delivering one single product for seven years. Impossible? Now do

it with two 19-year-old salesmen with no training and a business plan they concocted in their shared bedroom. Incredible? Now plan it so, in the end, you're left with $8.7 million in profit that the government cannot find and therefore cannot tax. You'd need a miracle, right?

As pitches go, it was over the top, a Journalism 101 reject. But it worked. At the time, I remember that the editors' reactions pretty much matched my own. We thought the Miracle Cars tale was about 50 percent urban myth, fabrication, an Internet exaggeration. In an era of instant communication and widespread consumer cynicism, it didn't seem feasible that two boys could sell 7,000 cars to 4,000 U.S. citizens and never deliver on a single promise for seven years. It was absurd. No such thing could happen in hard-bitten seen-it-all misanthropic America.

My assignment was to live in Kansas City for as long as the trial lasted and to write 3,000 *humorous* words chronicling the con. Apart from living alone in a downtown hotel for a month, it would be easy, I thought. I'd feast every night on the town's famous barbecued pork and chicken. My father, a trial lawyer in Ohio, had advised: "If the trial's boring, befriend the bailiffs. They'll have hundreds of stories."

I checked into Kansas City's turn-of-the-century Historic Suites hotel, which offered three perks. I could walk to the courthouse every morning. The room included a small kitchen. And the sympathetic desk clerk booked me into a suite with a spacious desk on which I could spread hundreds of pages of notes.

The night before the trial, I sat down to read every jot and tittle of the twenty-three-count indictment in the matter of the United States versus James R. Nichols and Robert Gomez. When I finished, I felt certain my assignment would have to be revised. For one thing, the Miracle Cars tale was not only true but also more fantastic than anyone had so far reported. The government's list of James Nichols's BMWs alone, for instance, proved I wouldn't have to elicit any stories from grizzled bailiffs. And I'd never heard of anyone on the planet proffering a hundred-thousand-dollar tip. On the other hand, the story wasn't particularly funny. The scheme had derailed too many lives, and U.S. attorneys are not given to bouts of fantasy or humor.

I didn't know it yet, but I was in for the most entertaining month of my life.

The Charles Evans Whittaker U.S. Courthouse affords its occupants a gorgeous view of downtown Kansas City. Built in 1998, it is a gray marble sanctuary—clean, open, airy, cool. Behind the building runs the caramel-colored Missouri River, carrying all sorts of moldy debris, including tires and trees. The courthouse is fronted by a neatly manicured, block-long park that features a reflecting pool that shimmers and sparkles in the hot Missouri sun. The U.S. Department of Justice occupies the entire fifth floor, including the Miracle Cars "war room"—base camp for Assistant U.S. Attorneys Dan Stewart and Curt Bohling, who were prosecuting case number 02–00114.

The matter was to be tried in U.S. District Court 7A. There were no windows in that pie-shaped room, but six huge overhead circular lights—covered in a brown Art Deco latticework—lent a credible simile of sunlight. The walls were paneled in rich walnut, and there was an austere and imposing slab of battleship-gray marble behind the judge's bench. The floors were expensively carpeted to muffle noise. Even though the courtroom was essentially sealed to prevent defendants from escaping, it was a pleasant and contemplative place, like sitting in a new college library. Apart from the rock-hard spectators' pews, I liked being there. I fell into an easy daily banter with the bailiffs, whose first order of business every morning was to confiscate cell phones and the reporters' tape recorders.

The king of Courtroom 7A wasn't a king at all but a queen: Judge Nanette K. Laughrey—pronounced "*law*-ree." She was in her mid-fifties, with short brown hair, dark glasses, red finger-nails, thin lips. She wore little makeup, was stern, sometimes severe. She controlled the room from the nanosecond she entered, peering at the occupants as a hawk might study a pasture full of unruly rabbits. Tina, her court clerk, never had to ask for silence when Judge Laughrey entered. Silence descended unbidden. Judge Laughrey was the kind of grade-school teacher you hoped you'd never have. More than a few Kansas City attorneys referred to her as "No Nonsense" Laughrey.

A few months prior to the trial, both Nichols and Gomez had been released from Leavenworth on $100,000 bonds. Gomez quickly squandered his freedom by asking a professional gambler if he could "back his play" on a poker cruise, violating a key con-dition of his bail. But James had returned to Carson, to the "safe house" on Bankers Drive, where he and his wife, Kimberly, stayed busy with a second baby girl. Relatives and friends helped with expenses. James spoke to no one about his troubles, not even to his mother.

At 8:30 A.M. on Monday, May 19, 2003, "No Nonsense" Laughrey scanned her courtroom and made an unhappy dis-covery. James Nichols was not present. Her face turned black.

"Where is your client?" she asked Nichols's attorney, Tom Bradshaw. There was venom in her voice.

"Your Honor," Bradshaw began sheepishly, "Mr. Nichols missed his flight from Los Angeles and is now arriving on another flight. From Chicago, I believe. Soon."

"Did you call the airlines to ensure he was on that flight?" she asked.

Bradshaw looked to his legal assistant for help. It was the worst possible way to begin the trial. "I did not, Your Honor," he finally mumbled. "Should have, but didn't."

"Well, here's what we're going to do," Laughrey said. But then she went silent for at least a minute, perhaps regaining control of her temper. The only sound in the courtroom was cold air whumping out of the ventilators. "I'm going to instruct the U.S. Marshals to greet Mr. Nichols at the airport," she finally intoned, "to give him a nice, warm handshake, have them explain things to him face-to-face. I want someone more reliable than a taxi driver to deliver him to us. Do you understand?"

Robert Gomez, along with his attorney, Bruce Simon, sat mutely at a table to the right of Bradshaw's. Each defendant had been allocated a separate working area, and their tables were separated by five feet of no-man's-land. It was obvious they weren't pals anymore. Gomez killed time by working his crossword puzzles. In front of him sat a stack of papers, atop which he'd placed a Buddha statue paperweight. He was clearly pleased that James was already in hot water. He wore a smirk that lasted the entire day.

At 10:40, more than two hours after his trial was to have started, James burst breathless into Courtroom 7A, flanked by U.S. Marshals holding him by the armpits. His hair was arranged in tight corn rows that concluded in a neatly bunched four-inch ponytail—a coiffure no Miracle Cars victim had ever seen. He was wearing a beautiful light green, summer-weight suit with matching socks, and he looked like a handsome black businessman from anywhere but blue-collar Carson.

Judge Laughrey gave him a look that would have killed livestock, but she said nothing, preferring to move immediately to jury selection, which consumed the day. She waited until quitting time before instructing Nichols to stand before her. Attorney Bradshaw knew what was coming. James, apparently, did not.

"Where were you this morning?" she began. "A thinking person, for his own out-of-state trial, would have been here yesterday, the day before, at a minimum."

"Well, see, what happened," Nichols began, booming away in his sonorous Barry White voice, "was I had a funeral to attend, then my wife booked my tickets on a *very* late flight, and when I got to the airport, the security guards saw I was wearing an electronic tether. They thought I was a fugitive." He did not sound contrite. "And when we got *that* particular hassle sorted out, well, the plane had left. I had to find another way to get here."

"Oh, I see now," said the judge. "It's your *wife*'s fault. Is that correct?"

"He doesn't get it, Your Honor," chirped prosecutor Dan Stewart.

"Your Honor, I am very responsible about being irresponsible about my own flight plans," Nichols gushed, having suddenly realized he was engaged in an argument he absolutely, positively could not win. His admission didn't sound heartfelt, but at least he said it loudly.

"No Nonsense" wasn't won over. She ordered Nichols to be jailed at nights, at least for the first week of the trial, and the marshals led him away. It caused Robert Gomez to smile broadly, but it also had the effect Laughrey intended. James Nichols thereafter became a model defendant—silent but polite, alert yet noncombative. He would say little to his lawyer throughout the trial, and he would retain his tombstone expression in the face of all testimony, good or bad.

Not so Robert Gomez. From day one, Robert squirmed in his seat, cracked his knuckles, smiled at everyone who made eye contact, whispered endless instructions to his lawyer, and fussed over the expensive Cross and Montblanc pens that he'd arrayed in neat rows for his crossword puzzles. When he heard unfavorable testimony, he contorted his face into a billboard-size frown and sighed deeply, and he'd sometimes guffaw through his nose or make small pig snorts. To show that he believed a witness was lying, he'd stage a coughing fit that could last minutes, until he actually made himself purple in the face. If that didn't work, he'd get the jury's attention by shaking a packet of Tic Tacs, resting only to eat four or five at a time. Unlike James, he never wore a sport coat. Robert preferred polo shirts with a palm-tree motif, a Ralph Lauren windbreaker, and baggy khaki trousers that hid the electronic tether attached to his ankle. He was Mr. Hyde to Nichols's Dr. Jekyll, the flamboyant class clown to the end. For some reason, he always made me smile.

On Tuesday, May 20, the twenty-three charges were read before the jury. It took forever, and each charge was tangled in so much legalese that several jurors zoned out. Essentially, the charges fell into two categories: interstate fraud and money laundering. Fifteen jurors had been impaneled, twelve to hear the case, with three alternates on hand if needed. In protracted cases, jurors had a habit of "getting sick" or being removed for other reasons.

Seated closest to the jury were Assistant U.S. Attorneys Dan Stewart and Curt Bohling, and sharing their table, for every minute of the trial, were Agent Gary Marshall of the U.S. Department of Treasury and Inspector Steve Hamilton of the U.S. Postal Inspection Service. Having already worked on the Miracle Cars con for twenty-nine months, the four men had long since coalesced into an efficient and unified team, communicating in nods and eye movements and supplying documents before anyone had asked for them. And there were plenty of documents—cart after cart after cart overflowing with canceled checks and phone-tap transcripts and casino records, a miniature freight train that was wheeled into court every morning.

Only minutes into the government's opening statements, it

was clear the jury was disarmed by Assistant U.S. Attorney Dan Stewart. He was neat and trim, bookish, innocently awkward, never mean-spirited, a guy you'd like to have as a father if you couldn't get Fred Rogers. In laying out the elements of the scheme, he was almost a reluctant accuser.

"James Nichols portrayed himself to be an executor of a fictional estate," he began, introducing the curious cast of characters to jurors already relieved this wouldn't be a dry recitation of bank statements. "Robert Gomez pretended to be the adopted son of a man named John Bowers—said he was the heir to that man's estate. Corinne Conway was a so-called National Finder in Higginsville, Missouri. And Gwen Baker was a National Finder, too, who turned into more—turned into the manager of the scam's Midwest office. They funneled millions and millions to Mr. Gomez, who skillfully laundered those funds while playing poker in any of five California casinos, where the money was turned into untraceable chips. The cars were offered to persons of Christian faith as a gesture of good will—a blessing, if you will, a kind of miracle. When Mr. Gomez was arrested, he had more than $800,000 in front of him. When Corinne Conway was arrested, she had made $1 million in finder's fees in one year, without paying any income tax. When Gwen Baker was arrested, she was paying herself $30,000 a month in salary."

For the jurors—and for me—it already sounded like a made-for-TV movie. We couldn't wait to hear more. Even the bailiffs in the lobby began asking for updates.

Throughout the opening statement, Robert adopted an F. Lee Bailey pose—the palm of his left hand held under his puffy chin, with one temple bar of his tinted eyeglasses gripped firmly between his teeth. The Thinker. And he remained in that affected posture all morning.

Months before, Nichols had informed the court that he was

penniless. Whether he was or not remained unclear, but it turned out to be a lucky stroke. It meant he qualified for a court-appointed lawyer, and the lawyer assigned to his case was Tom Bradshaw. Bradshaw was no rookie. In his mid-fifties, with a distinguished-looking crop of gray hair, he was a full-fledged Kansas City heavyweight with the powerful Armstrong-Teasdale firm. He accepted Nichols's case because he liked a good fight, and he certainly looked the part: compact, fierce, as taut as a compressed spring, with the craggy nose of a street-fighting Irishman. Even if James had had millions to spend, it was unlikely he could have obtained better counsel.

"Ladies and gentlemen," Bradshaw began, "Mr. James R. Nichols was just like Gwen Baker and Corinne Conway. He *believed* the estate existed, *believed* what Robert Gomez told him, *believed* that there were cars. When he found out otherwise, he ceased to be the executor of the estate. He quit. His father is a truck driver, his mother a former nurse. He belongs to Christ Christian Home Missionary Baptist Church, which he still attends. He believes that miracles include miracles of financial benefit. You will hear many years of evidence, dating back to 1994, when Mr. Nichols first met Mr. Gomez. You will hear that James purchased cars and motorcycles for himself. It's true, but it was with money that he believed he'd earned while acting as the executor. What you should know is this: Mr. Robert Gomez concocted this scheme to feed his gambling appetite."

At that, Robert sighed heavily—making sure his chest heaved—then emitted a pig snort. The jurors noticed. So did the judge.

Gomez had retained a heavy hitter, too: Bruce Simon, also of Kansas City. Simon was rotund, sixtyish, with thinning blond hair, gold-rimmed spectacles, and a florid complexion. He wore pin-striped black suits, was quick to smile, and—despite his size—was lively and engaging on his feet, with a decidedly British mastery of the language. He was Rumpole of the Bailey, uttering sentences such as, "It is of little moment for the nonce." He was also the only lawyer in the room who always preceded a comment with, "If it please the court and counsel," and when his objections were overruled, he'd politely reply, "Very well, Your Honor." But Simon's wisdom came at a price. The rumor was that Gomez had already shelled out a $150,000 retainer. It got the prosecutors' attention. If the money could be proved to have been derived from Miracle Cars sales, there was a chance they could seize it.

Simon's opening statement for Gomez was brief. "I don't dispute the facts," he said, "but I dispute their interpretation. Mr. Gomez was a gambler at very high stakes, a 'whale' who gambled in the hundreds of thousands. He would play seven hands of poker at a time, and a casino, on a long, hard day, could make as much as $40,000 on the drop alone. But the truth is, it was Mr. Nichols who controlled the bank account in this matter. At no time was Mr. Gomez's name added to that account. It was Mr. Nichols who represented that he wanted to become Mr. Gomez's backer. And it was Mr. Nichols, not Mr. Gomez, who was sued in civil court in California by unhappy car buyers. Mr. Gomez merely gambled with funds Mr. Nichols provided. Maybe Mr. Gomez suspected they were from a fraudulent source, or maybe he didn't. But in any event, all he did was gamble with money that Mr. Nichols supplied."

So there it was. Agent Zuniga had been right. The two boys were pointing the finger at each other. With mutually exclusive defenses, it seemed a certainty that at least one defendant would go down in smoke and flames. The question was, Which one?

After the opening statements had been offered, the media—apart from me—mysteriously cleared out, as if they'd been gassed.

"Everybody comes for the first day," explained a reporter named Tanya Samuels, from the *Kansas City Star.* "But after that, all they care about is the last day—the verdict. It's stupid, I agree, but that's how it works." She said she envied my assignment, attending every minute of the trial, no matter its duration. However, in the courtroom next door, there was a judge being tried for attempted murder. "See you in a few weeks," she said. "Keep good notes and you can update me later."

The exodus meant I suddenly had my pick of seats. I parked myself in the first row behind Robert Gomez's defense table because it allowed me to view his computer screen and listen to private comments he uttered to attorney Bruce Simon. What he usually said was, "Ask the witness if I ever sold any cars." Given his strategy in the case, it wasn't a bad question, and Simon asked it often.

On the trial's third day, during a short recess, Robert Gomez leaned over the railing that separates the spectators from the lawyers, then offered his hand to me. "How ya doin'?" he said with a huge grin on his face. "Welcome to Missouri." He asked who I was writing for, then said: "Well, that sounds interesting, but I'm a professional gambler, which is even more interesting. This is the highest-stakes game I've ever played. At least when I lost in the casinos, they'd let me go home at the end of the night. I already did five months in Leavenworth, did they tell you that? It was tough, sure, but the guys loved me there. I was giving gambling seminars. I know Steve Wynn and Larry Flynt, did you know that? They're both eager to clear my reputation. They said they're standing by, willing to help, be here in a sec if I call. But I told them, 'Guys, guys, I don't *need* help right now, I'm doin' fine.' "

His words came in a torrent. His eyes twinkled, his grin appeared genuine, and his body language indicated openness and ease. He was engaging, amicable, and gregarious, the nicest young man on earth. At a stodgy cocktail party, Robert would have been the guy I'd have sought out first.

"We're only three days into the trial," I mentioned. "How do you know you don't need help?"

"There's tons of stuff that won't come out in open court," he said. "I think the government is just chasing organized crime in the casinos, you know? They don't want me, except as a snitch." He put his hand on my shoulder, as if we'd been friends for years. "There was bad stuff going on in there, I admit—guys getting killed, cars getting blown up—but it's nothing to do with me. I can't rat those guys out. I'd lose my authority in the industry. They'd never let me back in. All of this," he said, making a sweeping gesture with both arms, "is a charade." Then he laughed so hard his breasts jiggled.

During the lunch break, on the same day, James Nichols and his wife approached me in the courthouse lobby. He shook my hand—an absolute bone crusher of a shake—and said, "My name is James Nichols, and I believe you are Mr. Phillips. I subscribe to *Car and Driver*."

"That's great," I said, "but you can call me John."

"No, I can't," he replied. "Where I grew up, our elders were strictly 'Mr.' or 'Mrs.,' and it's a habit I'm not able to break." He went on to describe cars that he loved, including a 1965 six-cylinder Mustang that had belonged to his mother.

"A six?" I asked. "That's a secretary's car."

"*Tell* me about it," he said, rolling his eyes. "The only six that's ever been any good is BMW's. That's my car, the M3. I was about to compete in my first autocross. But then, well, I was in jail."

During this exchange, Nichols stood ramrod straight but did so without appearing stiff. He stood like a professional athlete. At his side, his wife remained silent. James was formal but polite, exuded steely confidence, was meticulously groomed, and spoke in whole sentences, with no "ums" or "uhs" or "you knows." He reminded me of a navy officer I'd once met on a ballistic-missile submarine.

"Robert says the government's only after the Mafia," I said.

Nichols shook his head in disgust, then replied, "See what I'm dealing with? Imagine slaving your guts out and having to stand up to that type of thing. Robert once told me he went to military school. But it was more like special ed."

Meeting Nichols felt like some sort of privilege, like having a charismatic celebrity cross the room to shake my hand. For some reason, I hoped everyone was watching.

The next morning, as I was walking to the courthouse, a Chevy Impala zoomed up beside me, and a horn honked. It was Robert in his rental car. Every morning, he drove into the city from the $3,600-per-month apartment he'd rented in the suburbs. "I don't like hotels," he explained, "because I like to cook in the middle of the night." In the passenger seat sat his lawyer, looking sheepish. "Come on, get in," Robert insisted. "Ride with us. I *love* to drive, sure."

From the back seat I asked attorney Bruce Simon, "Do you mind if I talk to your client during the trial?"

"It doesn't matter whether I mind," Simon said. "I can't stop him." It caused Robert to pound the steering wheel and roar. He seemed to be having a terrific time.

Gwen Baker and Corinne Conway testified early in the trial, helping to explain the scheme's basic parameters. Because they were swapping testimony for reduced sentences, the two were responsive and truthful if a little mechanical. Their deals had already been struck. There was no need to obfuscate.

Conway testified first. Even though she was then sixty-two, she cut an imposing figure. She was bold and assertive in an expensive black suit, with her hair piled up every which way, making her look more than six feet tall. When she was sworn in, she told Judge Laughrey that she couldn't "swear" to tell the truth but would, because of her faith, instead "affirm" to tell the truth. Laughrey smiled and agreed.

Conway informed the court that her pretentiously named Virtuous Women's International Ministries was intended to "train and empower and support women in their purposes," and she asserted she was more or less unwillingly drawn into charging big finder's fees when Baker's "godsons" failed to deliver the $100,000 they'd promised at the outset. Conway recalled that, in March 2000, she, Gwen Baker, and Robert Gomez had engaged in a three-way phone call. "Mr. Gomez asked that I not charge the finder's fees," Conway said, "that it was going to make it difficult to pay the people back their refunds. He didn't seem upset. He just said to stop, but he wanted me to continue selling, to help his godmother [Baker] with the cars. He said that probate was just about over and he'd call back with a list of more cars."

That piece of testimony did damage to Gomez's defense. Apparently, he hadn't merely gambled with car-sales proceeds. He had assisted in the sales enterprise itself. Gomez's lawyer, Bruce Simon, scored points only when Conway admitted under cross-examination that she'd never met Gomez face-to-face.

While Conway was on the stand, Assistant U.S. Attorney Curt Bohling, forty-four, played the videotape of the "Millennium Conference" at the Doubletree Hotel in Kansas City, where the women had awarded blazers to the football stars. When Baker said, "God wants you to prosper, *God wants you to roll,*" Judge Laughrey evinced a wry smile. She seemed to be enjoying the performance as much as the rest of us.

The jury loved hearing how Conway had been snubbed during her first meeting with James Nichols, who introduced himself as

"Sam." And they were fascinated by the story of Conway's "Mandela Award" to Gwen Baker, an award she implied was from the South African statesman himself. They snickered at her admission she might "possibly have made $1 million in finder's fees in the first four months of 2000." And they clucked at her initial interview with federal agents, which she self-servingly described as "a private thing I shouldn't share publicly."

"I never investigated where the car-sales proceeds were actually going," Conway admitted under oath. "I didn't know the money was for anything other than the cars, didn't know it was being spent. I feel bad that people lost their money. Very bad."

But she didn't sound like she felt bad. Conway wasn't a compassionate witness. Sometimes she sounded like a woman reciting a confession written by someone else, and sometimes she sounded like *she'd* been the victim.

Stewart knew it. After Conway's testimony, he wisely interrogated a trio of elderly buyers who truly *had* been duped, who truly *had* suffered. It was quite a contrast. One such witness was seamstress Thelma Carnes, who had sewn the Miracle Cars blazers, and another was Rosie Ingram. Ingram spoke slowly, haltingly, and appeared close to breaking down. She had purchased cars for her husband, who had been in an accident. "We requested our money back," she testified, "but we never heard back. My husband and I were praying for a financial blessing, and we thought Corinne was believable. I thought it was real. I thought it was God Himself blessing us."

Then seventy-three-year-old Elijah Buggs testified. He was soft-spoken and visibly frightened to be on display in U.S. District Court. Buggs recalled James once saying he'd "already been fined by a judge for trying to expedite the release of cars." Buggs appeared exactly like the gentle and withdrawn soul he was, and his testimony was moving.

Stewart then put mega-investor Randy Lamb on the stand. Lamb, an accomplished car dealer who resembled actor James Garner, was educated and white. The point was clear. The con hadn't damaged only impoverished minorities who couldn't fend for themselves. Lamb had invested $218,000. "I lost every cent," he testified. "Baker told me, 'This is the real deal, Randy, good things *do* happen.' I lost the majority of my friends, I'm nearly bankrupt, and it meant that my mom couldn't retire as she'd planned."

"So it's been hard on you?" Stewart asked.

"It's about ruined my life," he replied. He looked like he might cry, and no one in the courtroom would have blamed him if he had.

In fact, Lamb was the perfect witness to precede Gwen Baker on the stand. It was Baker's final few car sales to Lamb that had doomed her to an as-yet-unspecified stay in Club Fed. But if Baker had a notion to lash out at him, she wisely overcame the impulse. Her testimony pretty much mirrored Conway's.

Baker wore bright red lipstick and a light green suit with a frilly blouse, looking a little as if she were on her way to a faculty cocktail party. She spoke confidently but slowly and was no longer the brassy huckster she'd so damagingly resembled on the Millennium Conference videotape. She described her initial meetings with the Nichols family in Carson, how comfortable she'd felt in the Kemp Avenue home, and how she'd attended the family's church in Compton. She said that James told her "many times" he had worked for John Bowers and that, as the estate's executor, he "reported to a board of directors." She testified she'd been told Robert had been adopted at age five, that Robert's mother lived in Bogotá, Colombia, and had a brain tumor, and that Robert's natural father was dead. She claimed James told her he'd personally met with the probate judge for the estate and that he once had to fly to Miami to pick up an alcohol-sodden Robert.

Sitting solemnly at the center desk in the courtroom, James pretended to study the contents of a manila envelope. He heard her comments but never looked up.

"And you never saw legal documents that could prove any of this was true?" asked Assistant U.S. Attorney Stewart

"I never saw any court documents," she replied. "I never saw a will for John Bowers. I was told he died without one. I never saw a document appointing James executor. I never saw an escrow account. I never saw a gag order. When I asked, James and Robert said the gag order even prevented telling people there was a gag order."

"So there was a gag order on the gag order instructing that you couldn't even show the gag order?" Stewart repeated, clearly amused.

He then showed the jury a series of photos—James in Baker's home in Memphis, picking up a packet bulging with cashier's checks; Robert sitting inside Baker's daughter's house in L.A.; and Robert and the Bakers in front of the *Queen Mary* in Long Beach, during an obviously happy social outing.

Stewart asked if it wasn't misleading for Baker to refer to the boys as her godsons.

"They called me 'godmother,' sometimes 'auntie,' " she countered, sounding curt. "I have done that many times in the past. The term 'godson' is common where I come from. I loved them both like sons."

She went on to describe setting up the Memphis office, and how she eventually came to pay herself $30,000 per month. She recalled James's visit to her Temple of Blessings Church, where he promised the congregation $50,000. She recalled the finders' meeting in Las Vegas, which she had vigorously cohosted with Robert. She remembered withdrawing $200,000 from the Lakewood account for Gomez, for which she earned an $8,000 bonus.

She offered damning details of the Smoke House meeting in Burbank, at which it was revealed that Robert "probably had liver cancer." And she admitted to instructing Kim Krawizcki to "destroy her records" to keep everyone out of trouble. The jury was mesmerized. Several jurors were taking notes.

"Didn't you ever think you might need some sort of license to sell automobiles?" Stewart probed.

"I never asked," she replied.

"And when Mr. Gomez said he was purchasing extra cars at auctions and from liquidators," Stewart asked, "didn't you think it was peculiar to be selling estate cars that weren't part of an estate?"

"I wasn't familiar with the workings of estates," Baker replied, a line that every Miracle Cars defendant would utter often as the trial progressed.

Baker's testimony did more damage to Gomez than to Nichols. She made it clear that many instructions had come from Robert, as had lists of cars and the South Bay fax. His participation went beyond gambling. Way beyond.

As Baker answered questions, Robert searched the back pages of the *Kansas City Star,* hoping for a word jumble or two, and he occasionally downed a Tic Tac. He'd relax now and then by cracking his knuckles—left fingers first, in order, then the right fingers. Each pop sounded like a pencil being snapped in half.

Like Conway, Gwen Baker was not a sympathetic witness. She had not lost her temper or become openly combative, as Inspector Steve Hamilton had predicted. But neither did she act remorseful or ashamed. She seemed a little sick of telling her story, in fact. What she resembled was a hard-bitten saleswoman who'd already struck her deal and was eager to move on.

"She was impassive and dismissive when she was first arrested," Assistant U.S. Attorney Bohling remarked in the hall that day, "and that hasn't changed."

Toward evening, the bailiff in the lobby asked, "That one boy, the handsome black kid? He's so polite. I heard the figure $21 million. He stole $21 million? That can't be right."

"He may have had some help," I replied.

THEY'LL NEVER FIND MY MONEY

Only one week into the trial, Robert Gomez and I had become pals. He sometimes sat with me at a table in the hallway just outside Courtroom 7A, and he'd smile and say hello to passersby, shaking hands, acting like a celebrity, and looking like the happiest guy on earth.

"You know, one of the charges against me is for money laundering in Missouri," he said, slapping a meaty hand on the table. "I've never even *been* to Missouri!" It was a line he repeated often, a chestnut in his standup repertoire, and it always amused him. He told me his favorite snack was a couple of hot dogs from the Wienerschnitzel and that his favorite TV shows were *Monday Night Football, The Tonight Show,* and *The Man Show.* Every other day, he shaved his head so closely that his skull glistened under the courtroom lights. He often asked me where the heck the media had gone. "You're *it?*" he'd ask, obviously disappointed.

"If the trial goes bad," Robert confidently asserted, "I'll be out in a couple years, no problem. Back in California, I have friends who are organizing my household and personal effects. The government seized all my jewelry, you know, plus the $818,000. But I didn't have any bank accounts they could get, and they never will.

I'm one of the smartest people in the industry, so I'll always have a piece of cake for a rainy day. As I sit here, I'm clearly a millionaire. Dan Stewart told me in jail, 'You're gonna run out of money.' I told him, 'Dan, I'll *never* run out.' They'll never find my money. It will always be a mystery to them. I won a lot over the years, sure. They can't prove it's all from fraud. Okay, part of it was fraud, but not all. They said they were gonna subpoena casino execs to find out more, but they won't. The casino execs *like* me."

Talking with Robert reliably wore me down. He spoke so quickly, and the subjects came and went with such rapidity, that I'd often forget the question I'd originally asked. If I failed to concentrate, then a query about missing funds quickly morphed into a discussion about Larry Flynt, "the greatest man I've ever met," or he'd suddenly be talking about Donald Trump's "recent phone queries regarding Asian card games." In all the days and weeks I eventually spent conversing with Robert, he never asked a question about me personally, except for once wanting to know the names of other magazines I wrote for. I'd never met anyone like him. Not even close.

"When the agents searched my house," he continued, "there was a lot of stuff they didn't get. I'm a collector of fine art, for instance, plus some other items I shouldn't even be talking about. Some of it I shipped out of the country. I put it away, sure."

"During all those years you claim James was your financial backer," I asked, "you never questioned where he was getting the money?"

"James is conniving about this," Robert replied. "He isn't a victim. He has such an active mind, he should write a book. I didn't know about the car-sales end of this until it was ninety percent over and the authorities contacted me. I had car-related receipts in my house, sure, but it was because I was buying cars to help James pay refunds. But I can't complain, because I'm only out about one hundred and forty grand, is all. I could win that back easily. You know, I hardly lose. Pai gow poker, also pai gow tiles, I was a master at both for many years. I once made $500,000 in six hours. Although one night, it was October 2001, I did lose $3 million. Boy, was I depressed."

I quickly learned you could ask Robert anything, no matter how personal or raw, and he'd reply in a flash, although he'd often fashion an answer to a question you hadn't asked.

"In 2000, you were making huge money," I said, "so why didn't you pay any income taxes?"

"Oh, I did," he replied, contradicting the IRS's records. "But no one files an honest return, right? Not even the DA. I filed what I could, what I could keep track of. The volumes were large. I can't remember. I had an accountant who did them, but he's deathly ill now, out of circulation, probably can't be found. His name was Jim Smith, from northern California. He'd fly down to do my returns."

"*Jim Smith?*" I replied sarcastically. But it didn't faze Robert. In fact, he smiled broadly. I asked if he believed the jury would buy a defense in which he claimed it was all James's fault.

"I'll tell you who should be on trial here," Robert immediately suggested. "Rose. Plus her whole family. Even their church was selling cars. Her family is sitting on plenty of money right this instant and driving nice cars. It's amazing they weren't indicted. The government targeted me to get info on the casinos. If I'd given it to them, it would have been James sitting alone in this courtroom, trust me. I loved and trusted James, a boyhood friend, sure. But he became bitter. When we first went to Leavenworth, we got into a shoving match. They had to separate us. What a guy. He's a womanizer, you know. Then he impregnated Kim right after he was indicted. With two other kids already, that's crazy. What was he thinking? James is intelligent in a street-smart way, but in life's other lessons, you know, he can sometimes be a slow learner."

As I tried to record this rant in my notebook, I said, "Robert, you're every reporter's dream come true."

"Oh, I know," he replied. "Sure. I'm quite a character."

The witnesses came and went, and each contributed a gem or two. The two football players and their wives all testified, briefly drawing a nice-size crowd. Together, the NFL celebs had invested close to $703,000. Ricky Siglar, who clearly *did* wear a size 50 blazer, admitted he wanted "to start a car dealership and maybe a trucking company" with the Miracle Cars he'd bought. Siglar barely fit on the witness stand. His wife, Janice, confirmed Baker had told them she'd "peeked inside one of the Freightliner trucks for sale," a statement Baker denied. Instead, Baker claimed only to have seen the "estate cars parked in the driveway on Kemp Avenue"—that is, James's various BMWs and Robert's various Lincolns.

Seattle superinvestor Matt Jones testified. He wore a brown suit that rivaled James's in its European cut and silky texture. Jones impressed the jurors. As the scam was playing out, he had hired two private detectives, had been in informal contact with the FBI, and had retained attorneys to determine whether the deal was legit. And *still* nothing overtly negative surfaced. As a result, University of Washington graduate Jones and ten of his cronies invested $223,250, plus an additional $100,000 in finder's fees.

Jones was asked to identify James Nichols in the courtroom. He did, then remarked: "Mr. Nichols's hair was groomed better than it is now. Right now, in this courtroom, it's hard looking at him. I get choked up." His display of emotion was real, and the jury knew it.

Car salesman and journalism grad Greg Ross recounted the tale of his nerve-racking weekend, hoping to track down Bob

Burrows, the banker who sounded African American one week and British the next. And he described his fury when he first realized he'd been tricked. After he had testified, Ross spoke to me in the hall. "I don't think Nichols and Gomez ever thought the con would get this big," he said. "They were never equipped with proper receipts and computer printouts to make it look credible. When the scam started, I think they may have sold cars to their neighbors just to see if it would work. Word traveled quicker than they thought, and the thing grew out of control, like a fire. And I think when James realized he couldn't put it out, he just ran, you know, like to save himself."

"Do you still feel like doing violence to him?" I asked.

"Let me get back to you on that," Ross replied.

George Denton, the pastor who replaced Houston Buggs at Christ Christian Home Missionary Baptist Church, recalled Gomez's speech from the discipleship pulpit, in which he'd promised congregants everything from cash to free horses to fireworks. "The church was in an uproar," Denton said, a comment that caused Gomez to laugh out loud.

And Pastor Leo Holt, of Grace Christian Fellowship Church in Memphis, recalled Gwen Baker telling him, "The heir will fly in later on his private jet if the doctors will allow it." Gomez responded with a coughing fit designed to display his disdain for so ludicrous a comment.

Wearing a tight black sweater, notary public Juliet Lozano described how James had hired her to notarize dozens of documents. She had affirmed only that his signature was true, whereas buyers widely assumed her seal ensured the letters' *content* was true. Lozano admitted to dating James "on and off for over a year," but when she left the courtroom, she didn't so much as glance in his direction. James's wife, on the other hand, glared murderously at both.

In fact, it wasn't long before Kimberly Hall Nichols herself took the stand, although no one expected she'd have anything new or controversial to say. Short and stout, with blond highlights in her long dreadlocks, she again described her marriage to James as "a work in progress," and it wasn't said with a smile. Her testimony was laced with a caustic, not-happy-to-be-here tone. She described first meeting James at a video-rental store. She related—to a truly curious room of onlookers—how she was "*secretly* married to James in October of 1998." After that, the two had lived apart for nearly a year. She didn't explain why, nor would she explain it to me in the hall when I later asked. After James had been arrested, it was Kimberly who discovered the long-forgotten FedEx box in a dusty closet in the couple's rented home on Bankers Drive in Carson. She pried open one corner of the cardboard box, peeked inside, saw $239,800 in car-sales proceeds, and promptly hustled the package over to James's lawyer. Jurors were astonished that anyone could possess a box containing a fortune and not know a thing about it. It was the sort of detail not even a fiction writer would conjure.

Sporting a goatee and long black ponytail, Robert Gomez's stepbrother, Michael, took the stand. "Robert never told me he was adopted," Michael said, making it clear such an assertion was patently absurd. "I never knew him to say such a thing, and I never knew him to have a problem with drugs or alcohol." Michael Gomez spoke with a thick, almost impenetrable Hispanic accent—the unmistakable patois of L.A. street gangs. The significance of his dialect was not lost on the jury. At some stage in his life, Robert must have spoken similarly, yet not a trace of that accent existed today. How could a young man with a rudimentary education contrive to lose a speech pattern so thoroughly ingrained? Who had taught Robert the verbal mannerisms of white Midwestern businessmen?

Michael Gomez's appearance on the stand produced one other reaction. His testimony had been purely factual, neither sad nor sentimental, yet it caused Robert to bawl like a baby. Heavy teardrops rained down on his Buddha paperweight. Strangely enough, when Michael Gomez exited the courtroom, Robert's tears stopped as if a petcock had been twisted. Dabbing at his eyes while popping a few Tic Tacs, Robert then turned to his lawyer and described why cheating was so prevalent in the game of pai gow tiles.

28

LYING FOR PROFIT AND PLEASURE

I n the second week of the trial, during a recess, I noticed James Nichols and Kimberly sunning themselves on the front steps of the courthouse. James was wearing his tortoiseshell Foster Grants, a black knit pullover, and a tailored black sport coat. He looked like Denzel Washington standing outside a Hollywood nightclub. I gave him a small wave, and he beckoned me over. I asked what he thought of Matt Jones's testimony.

"I think he put a little extra mustard on his hot dog," James replied, "and it wasn't good for me."

Then I asked how he felt the trial was going.

"Nothing in this business is as it seems," he said, as solemn as ever. He'd said the same thing the day before. "You'll see the real story in a few days. I've seen you talking to Robert, taking notes, so I know you're getting an idea of what he's like, how full of himself, how full of lies. My big mistake was to befriend him. You already know how easy that is. Seems like a nice guy, right? Let me warn you, Robert only acquires friends for monetary purposes. If he talks to you, he's working an angle."

James spoke slowly, selecting his words, and what he said always had about it a full measure of cautious deliberation and credibility. "Was Robert 'working an angle' when you first met him?" I asked.

"Maybe not at first," he replied. "But I was only eighteen, and I'd led a pretty sheltered life. My friends were sort of arranged for me, by the church or by my parents. So meeting Robert was very thrilling. He was my age but wasn't afraid of adults, didn't care what older people thought. He was very wild and didn't live by the rules I'd learned in church. He had adventures all the time, blowups at home, and he always had fantastic stories, so I was drawn to that. He'd mislead you, lie to your face, then suddenly blurt out the truth and laugh. He could shock you like that. He'd say things like, 'Oh, my God, James, on the way over here I hit a woman in a crosswalk and I think I killed her, but I was afraid to stop. James, you have to *help* me. Should we call your parents or get a lawyer or make a run for it? What should I *do*?' And he'd look like he was going to cry—in fact, he *might* cry—then he'd put an arm around you and say, *'Whoa, just kidding!'* As I got older, I began to believe he was a person who made himself up out of characters he'd seen on TV. Two, four, six of them, who knows? And those characters would say crazy things, stories and lies, but Robert was pretty good about remembering it all. He could keep the stories straight in his head. But if there was one *real* Robert, I don't think I knew him, except maybe just at first. He could wear you down. You'd eventually say to him, 'Robert, don't force your crazy life on me anymore,' and that's when he'd do something really nice, something lavish or generous, like a gift [of $50,000 cash] on your birthday, or a new motorcycle, and you'd be sucked back in. I got sucked back in about twenty times. Now I'm paying for it."

"He's ruined our lives," added Kimberly Hall Nichols, who'd previously eyed me with palpable distrust. "Robert told me he lived in an estate in Rancho Palos Verdes that had a heliport, and his house was featured on TV. I'm serious when I tell you, Robert has some sort of mental thing, some sort of condition, and it's very destructive and scary. What's funny is, he does all this damage, but everyone likes him."

I began to wonder if James Nichols, like four thousand other U.S. citizens, was just another Miracle Cars dupe. After I'd talked to him for ten minutes, it seemed possible he'd been tricked, too. In any event, James and Kimberly's creepy description of Robert couldn't have been more timely. That's because the next witness was Robert's former pal Linda Janowski.

Like Matt Jones and Randy Lamb, Janowski's personal finances had been comprehensively swept to sea by the indiscriminate Hispanic hurricane that was Robert Gomez. She described how she'd lost her $200,000 job at South Bay Toyota, how he'd lured her into straw purchases of automobiles, how he'd seduced her into signing his lease and paying his rent for a year, and how he'd weaseled his way into her player's account, almost doubling her debt.

Janowski told me it wasn't until authorities had Robert in jail that she started to feel safe again. "And even then, he called one day," she remembered, "and he said, 'Linda, honey, they're looking for James, but they'll never find him. Know why? Because he's in Argentina getting plastic surgery.' I thought, Oh, God, here we go again. Will it ever stop?"

The jury heard how innocently Janowski had met Robert, yet how lastingly and irreparably he'd damaged her. It was like visiting a relative in the hospital and inadvertently being exposed to bubonic plague—not what was supposed to happen in return for a good deed. But even as Janowski strode toward the courtroom exit, she turned fully to face Gomez, then smiled and winked—a gesture of friendship and intimacy. In return, he laughed and waved. It reminded me of what Nichols had said, about getting "sucked back in."

The testimony of San Bernardino County Detective Kenneth Ayers should have been played on *Court TV* during prime time. It was Ayers who had repeatedly called James on the phone, only to connect with Robert. Ayers never knew he was being tricked, but he had recorded the calls, and now Assistant U.S. Attorney Stewart played them in open court. The jurors heard how easily Gomez slipped into Nichols's persona, casually offering information about "my sick aunt" and "my mother, Rose."

Pretending to be James, Robert had informed the detective that he was a movie-set builder who had worked on *Titanic,* and he went on to inform Ayers that Mr. Gomez hung out with celebrities and had nothing to do with the con. "It stops with me [meaning Nichols]," he had declared. "It never went beyond me." As the tapes played, a couple of jurors actually scooted to the edges of their seats, fearful of missing a single word.

Here was an eerie demonstration of Robert's acting ability and of his skill at conjuring fictions at the drop of a hat. It actually gave me goose bumps. Robert required no preparation and could fib persuasively even as he was under pressure from a cynical member of law enforcement who'd spent decades listening to criminals lie. It left the jurors slack-jawed. They studied Gomez as a herpetologist would study a new species of poisonous snake.

It had been damning testimony, and, for the first time, Robert knew it. At day's end, I rode down in the elevator with him. As we descended, attorney Simon said, "Robert, we have to go right now to interview a witness."

"I'm too fucking busy," replied Gomez, who knew no one in Kansas City and lived alone in his $3,600-per-month flat.

"Now, Robert," Simon remonstrated, trying to soothe him, "you have the right to question this witness, to face your accusers, and you must."

"I'm not fucking going," he said.

"James will be there," Simon admonished, sounding like a father who was dealing with an overtired child, "and so should you. It won't take long."

"Go by yourself," he said. "I'm leaving."

In all my dealings with Robert, rarely did I witness him rattled, shaken, or looking guilty. This was the first instance. There would be one more.

As I departed the courthouse, I described those brief but bizarre tableaux—the snit in the elevator and the unexpected wink from Linda Janowski—to the bailiff operating the metal detector in the lobby. We'd established a minor friendship based on our mutual love of antique cars. He looked me in the eye and said, "I've worked in the courts a long time. A word of advice: When you talk to that kid, don't reveal where you live, don't tell him who you know, don't buy anything in front of him with a credit card, and stick your wallet in your underpants."

I laughed, but the bailiff did not.

When Rose Nichols was called to testify, spectators and jurors alike assumed she'd defend the actions of her son, but her testimony was objective and balanced rather than defensive. Although she was a gray-haired sexagenarian who spoke in a weak voice, she was also occasionally bitter, as her daughter-in-law, Kimberly, had been. Throughout his mother's testimony, James Nichols held his head in his hands. At one point, he asked his attorney for some aspirin.

Rose explained that she and her husband and her seven children attended church three times a week, sometimes four, and that James had been a faithful usher, a talented drummer, and a precocious Bible-school student. She remembered when James, in his nineteenth year, moved back into the family home, along with his newfound friend, Robert, and how the two boys had transformed

James's bedroom into a busy little office. She remembered the day that John Bowers was allegedly stricken with a heart attack and how Robert had cried. She recalled the first sixteen Miracle Cars that had been offered to the three hundred members of Christ Christian Home Missionary Baptist Church, where she was a deaconess. She claimed to have seen estate cars with her own eyes, although they turned out to be the cars Robert was driving—"a black-and-white Lincoln Town Car, a black Buick Riviera, a white Cadillac Sedan de Ville, a 1997 Mercury sedan, and a red Chevy Suburban." And she made the jurors chuckle with her suspicion that Robert Gomez was a member of the FBI.

True to her reputation as an iron-willed woman, Rose was fearless in the face of questions that sometimes made her look like a coconspirator. She didn't hesitate to admit she'd eventually sold $1 million worth of nonexistent cars to church members who had trusted her for forty years. Bruce Simon asked, "Considering that Mr. Gomez had represented himself to be a drug addict and abuser of alcohol, did you think it was prudent to give hundreds of thousands of dollars to him?" Rose admitted she had used poor judgment.

On at least three counts, her raw truthfulness did damage to James, too. Simon asked, "When you gave cash to your son or Mr. Gomez, did you ever ask for a receipt?" Rose replied, "No, I did not, for I was told that the money was not to make a paper trail." She further admitted that neither she nor her husband had ever clapped eyes on the con's principal characters—John Bowers, Howard Gaines, Shawn Houston, and Vince McNeil. And her testimony included the tale of the $59,000 second mortgage she'd been forced to acquire in order to pay refunds to impatient buyers. James had never offered to assist, even as he was enjoying $343,000 worth of fancy BMWs and motorcycles.

On the other hand, Rose raised at least one question that

would eventually trouble the jurors. If James knew this was a scam, for what earthly reason would he enlist his own mother as the first salesperson? Rose was selling cars to James's aunts and uncles and neighbors. And that was while both boys were living under her roof. In fact, $4,000 worth of estate cars were sold to James's own mother-in-law. Only the most self-destructive con artist would perpetrate a fraud on the very persons who loved, adored, protected, and housed him.

Perhaps Rose wondered the same thing, but it was hard to tell. When she strode out of the courtroom, she held her head defiantly upright and never once glanced at her son. In the hall, Inspector Steve Hamilton said to me, "Did you hear his own mother mention not leaving a paper trail? She fried him with that."

I wasn't so sure.

On May 29, halfway through the Miracle Cars trial, the jurors spent an hour or so locked in an anteroom while Judge Laughrey undertook some housecleaning.

Already, one of the jurors had been excused for "a hygiene issue." And a second had run afoul of the judge's daily instructions not to discuss the trial with anyone, for any purpose. Earlier at lunch, the court clerk had heard a male juror say, "Any chance they'll change their minds and plead guilty?" It seemed an innocuous utterance, but "No Nonsense" felt otherwise. She summoned the man to stand alone before the bench, where he somewhat reluctantly confessed to his thoughtless remark.

"Well," said Judge Laughrey, taking her time, "you've taken it upon yourself to disobey this court's crystal-clear instructions. As a result, I have no choice but to excuse you from these proceedings."

To cover his embarrassment, the man made the grievous error of responding, "Good, I wanted to get out of here anyway."

I could see the four lawyers in the room shrink in their chairs. It would have been safer to poke a bare toe at a coiled rattlesnake than to provoke this particular judge.

Laughrey locked her twin black laser beams on the man's forehead for a few seconds, with her jaw jutting forward. Then she said: "Good? Did you say, *'Good'*? I wonder how good you're going to think it is when the bailiff accompanies you downstairs while the court decides whether to charge you with contempt." The man looked like he'd been kicked in the groin, and there descended on the courtroom the sort of stony silence experienced only in vaults and morgues. Everyone was afraid to look up. Unfortunately, it meant the jury was now down to one alternate, and the trial had yet to enter its third week.

There was another matter to sort out. Gomez's various reactionary snorts and heaves had finally unnerved Nichols's attorney, Tom Bradshaw. "Your Honor, I don't know if the court has observed," he began, "but Mr. Gomez continues to make verbal responses and facial expressions when he doesn't like some testimony, to indicate his disbelief to the jury. Sometimes he throws his pen down on the table. I've asked that his counsel be instructed to restrain him. I don't know what else to ask for."

"I heard the last one," chimed in Assistant U.S. Attorney Dan Stewart, "a kind of exasperated sigh when testimony indicated Mr. Nichols gave $777,000 in cash to Mr. Gomez."

At that, Gomez slammed his hand on the table and emitted the biggest sigh to date.

"I'll speak with him, if you like, tell him to cease," offered Gomez's attorney, Bruce Simon. It was clear by Simon's expression that all he could do was try.

And that was the first time Robert Gomez spoke in Courtroom 7A. He said, "It's an instant thing, not planned, Your Honor. I'm not doing it on purpose, and I'll get it under control.

It won't happen again." But, of course, it happened again and often.

Then the lawyers turned to a more serious matter. During Rose Nichols's testimony, Tom Bradshaw had objected to a minor matter, and Judge Laughrey had casually responded, "Well, we can let the Court of Appeals deal with this issue." Again, it seemed innocuous, and no juror picked up on it, but it left Bradshaw seething.

"I'm concerned the jury will take that as an indication that [you believe] there will be a conviction in this case," Bradshaw said. "And so, on that basis, Your Honor, I move for a mistrial." Gomez's lawyer added, "If it please the court, we would join that motion."

Laughrey mulled it over. She said she regretted the comment and offered to "take the error." But, she added, "I can't think of a curative instruction that would not, in fact, create more problems. I'm going to deny the motion for a mistrial."

The spectators heaved a sigh of relief as audible as any in Gomez's repertoire. We were in too deep to quit now. Gomez turned in his seat and saw me scribbling notes. I thought he was going to complain about Laughrey's decision. Instead, he said, "I take a lot of notes, too, during poker games. Helps me remember competitors' habits. Usually it freaks them out, though."

After court that night, I caught up with Robert as he climbed into his rental car to drive the two blocks to his lawyer's office. I never observed him make that five-minute trek on foot. He had returned to his old, jovial self and immediately waded thigh-deep into further fictions. "In the fall of '98," he said, looking both directions to indicate this was top-secret stuff, "James came to me and asked if I'd help him launder car-sales proceeds. I said, 'No way, that's a federal crime. I'd be barred from the casinos. The casinos are wise to that sort of stuff, and they can lose their licenses.' Then James said, 'Come on, I'll pay you ten percent to flush some cash—I've got a few hundred thousand to liquidate.' I was already making astronomical sums gambling, like two hundred grand a month, and I was driving new cars, had moved my mother into a better home. People saw I was a winner and started backing my play."

"So it was all James's fault?" I asked.

"You underestimate James," he replied. "There was always weird stuff going on at his house. They had a safe with $50,000 in it, the Nicholses did, and it was stolen in 1998. There were family fistfights on the front yard. It was an inside job, that's for sure."

I had again made the mistake of taking notes in front of Robert, an action that spurred him to previously unexplored flights of fancy. "You're not telling fairy tales, are you?" I asked.

"Know what else?" he replied. "James was having sex with Gwen Baker."

"Robert," I said, "I'm not writing that down. Look at me. I'm putting my pen away. That's absurd."

"Yes, it is," he replied, laughing. "Yes, it is."

29

THE MAIN EVENT

On June 2, 2003, James Nichols came to court wearing a black camel-hair sport coat, a silk baby-blue tie, and gray slacks. His hair was still in corn rows, leading to a small ponytail. It was time for the main event, and the jurors knew it.

James Randall Nichols, age twenty-seven, was taking the stand in his own defense. And he did so without the slightest fear or trepidation. He took the oath like a man eager to set the record straight, and he sat upright and rigid in the witness chair like an aggrieved Amish elder. As always, he was painfully, formally polite, even under the most withering interrogation. It was "yes, sir" and "no, sir" for every response, and he steadfastly referred to his nemesis not as "Robert" but as "*Mr.* Gomez." He had obviously memorized dozens of dates and scores of names. His answers—at least to questions asked by his own counsel— occasionally sounded rehearsed. But his charisma and confidence had a powerful effect on the jurors. He appeared to be a serious young man who was making his way through life by dint of Christian values and God-given intelligence.

Tom Bradshaw took time to establish his client's core decency. The jury paid attention when James said, "I was taught all my life to take in a stranger, because you never know if you're entertaining an angel. I had no choice but to babysit Mr. Gomez. As Christians, we aren't supposed to take pay for something we do from the heart."

For hours on end, James held the jurors hypnotized. For one thing, they had assumed the never-seen lawyers were nothing but the residue of adolescent imagination. Yet James swore he'd actually *met* these men. He described the physical traits of estate attorneys Houston and Gaines, as well as John Bowers himself, who, at the Virginia Country Club in Long Beach, showed up sunburned and sporting hair plugs. James credibly related the otherwise farcical tale of delivering gold bullion in the black Lincoln limo driven by a 350-pound Samoan with a German submachine gun. He was nonchalant about the close call he'd endured in the Lonnie Wall civil suit. And he was believable in recalling the day he rode with Robert to a pier in Long Beach, where he viewed "hundreds of estate cars" while Robert waved merrily to passing longshoremen.

Bradshaw asked if James could describe a typical Miracle Cars day. "Yes, sir, I'd be glad to," he said. "Usually, the money would come into the Lakewood account, then there would be people requesting refunds. And I had to be given an authorization from Mr. Gomez, then I could refund people in ten to fifteen days. And if the refunds were really huge, it was somewhere around thirty to forty-five days. I usually had a long list to deal with. Then Mr. Gomez would show me a stack of papers sitting on the desk, and those papers had typed on them only the words 'Sincerely, James R. Nichols.' And Mr. Gomez would tell me he had to send out progress reports, updating people about the vehicles, and that he needed me to sign those [otherwise blank] letters. I never saw the content of the letters. Then Mr. Gomez would ask me to write him a check or give him cash so he could go have his fun, or go shopping, or take Dr. Baker out for a night on the town, or take care of investors, as he liked to call them. Or, in some instances, gambling."

James described Robert's moods, his incomprehensible rants, and his tendency to fixate on irrelevant matters. "He could nitpick you to death," James declared. The jury laughed when James described Robert as "basically a hazard to himself," and laughed again when James claimed, "I would have done *anything* just to hear him be quiet." It was a sentiment that, by then, I could understand.

Assistant U.S. Attorney Dan Stewart asked, "Mr. Nichols, as you sit here today, you know there's no estate, don't you?"

"I know now, sir," James replied.

"And you know the alleged Mr. Bowers is nonexistent, right?"

"Or the person that I met wasn't really Mr. Bowers."

"You talk as if he might be real. Is that just Hollywood drama?"

"I was told what I was told, sir."

"The money that came in went to the casinos, didn't it?"

"I thought it was forwarded to a noninterest-bearing account in the Chase Manhattan Bank, sir."

"And many of the checks were for your personal expenditures, your BMWs and so forth?"

"Mr. Gomez told me I was authorized to have that, yes, sir."

"As the sole executor of the estate, you never had a copy of the last will and testament of Mr. Bowers?"

"Mr. Gomez said it had to go, because of the gag order."

"You never saw a copy of the gag order, you just trusted his word?"

"Yes, sir."

"You had no court order appointing you executor?"

"No, sir."

"There were no reports to the court about the financial condition of the estate?"

"No, sir."

"Robert Gomez's will came from an 'E-Z Legal Form,' and it's handwritten, and this was for the heir to a $411 million estate, and you thought it was a real will?"

"Yes, sir."

"You knew your mother took out a second mortgage to pay car refunds, and you never paid her back?"

"Sir, you're trying to make this my responsibility. The agreement she had with Mr. Gomez was that the estate would reimburse her."

"When you resigned as executor of the estate, did you submit a letter of resignation?"

"Yes, sir, the one I threw at Mr. Gomez."

"But you did not keep a copy of that letter?"

"No, sir."

"You recall closing out the Lakewood account and leaving for Las Vegas shortly after?"

"Within a day or so, had to get ready to go, yes, sir. Mr. Gomez said I was entitled to the money, for all my work."

"And that was three days after Inspector Hamilton left a message with your mother that the agents wanted to talk to you? Do you recall receiving that message?"

"No, sir. What number did he call?"

This was one of only two instances during which James lost his cool under questioning. He'd answered a question with a question, sounding insolent, and it provoked the usually mild-mannered Stewart. "*I'm* not testifying here, sir," he snapped. "No Nonsense" Laughrey wasn't amused, either. She did not countenance impertinent responses. She glared at James and arched an eyebrow. It was a look we'd all seen before: Cross the line *one more time,* buddy, and see what happens.

During lunch recess, James regretted his churlishness. "That was stupid of me," he admitted in the hall. "Lost my temper." He'd also earlier answered a question, "Hell, no," which he now regretted. "I'm going to ask the judge if I can apologize for that," he said.

Whether he did or not was unclear, but I noticed during the next day's testimony that he throttled back, was far more contrite. James had often previously antagonized his interrogators with the line "What you're failing to understand, sir, is . . . ," a remark he no longer uttered, and he had ceased turning his head toward the jury as he answered questions, a Perry Mason mannerism that was far too affected.

Throughout James's cross-examination—where some of his answers still sounded overly practiced—his attorney, Tom Bradshaw, objected at every opportunity, disrupting crucial exchanges and making it easier for his client to collect his thoughts and regain his composure. Bradshaw was truly the "Irish street fighter" he'd earlier described himself as, and he pecked away relentlessly to protect James Nichols. There were times when he'd engage in minor legal debates with Judge Laughrey, testy exchanges that almost certainly pained him personally. He'd pick at something she'd done— failing to grant a motion or overruling an objection—and he'd push the matter just far enough that "No Nonsense" would begin to boil, and then he'd back off. But he'd reliably raise the subject later, when she was again receptive. Time after time, Bradshaw would be slumped in his chair, his nose buried in documents, and he'd suddenly blurt, "Objection, hearsay!" and it would be sustained. He was a courtroom all-star, working tirelessly for minimal pay.

Under cross-examination, James was asked, "You are testifying that you are not particularly aware of wills, estates, or probate matters?"

"Sir, this was the first time I had dealt with them," he replied, as poised as ever.

"As your mother began to sell cars in 1997, and as you began to sell cars, you had never up to that point seen a will of any type?"

"No, sir."

"You made no effort to seek counsel in connection with a $411 million estate?"

"No, sir," James ventured, "because I was always assured I was doing a good job."

"Assured by whom?"

"By Mr. Gomez, Mr. Gaines, and Mr. Houston."

James had spoken so often and so persuasively about the unseen lawyers that they had come to develop material existence, at least in the minds of the jurors and spectators.

The star defendant had been on the witness stand for a day and a half, nine hours of grueling interrogation, and he had made points. Many points. Was it possible this whole thing was the brainchild of Robert Gomez? James had made it sound that way. It was at least plausible.

"I'll say one thing for his testimony," said a surprised Agent Marshall. "He was confident and composed. He played the victim role quite well."

After James stepped down, I spoke to Richard Gil, the president of a biotech company and a victim who'd attended the Smoke House meeting where James had been such an eloquent master of ceremonies. "I saw James on the courthouse steps," Gil told me. "And at first I felt a bitterness that he'd ruined so many lives. And I don't know if you're religious, but you know Saint Paul said that a man who harmed you should be forgiven seven times seventy, and I think he was right. But I didn't do it. I didn't say, 'James, I forgive you.' I missed that opportunity, and it was in front of his mama and all, and I didn't speak to him. I felt like I was being tested by God, right there on the steps."

"I'm not religious," I told Gil, "but that was generous of you. Very Christian. Do you think James is a Christian?"

"It doesn't matter," he replied. "I've forgiven him, and I'll bet most of the victims have, too."

James Nichols's testimony had played well. Bradshaw had cleverly teased out every element that might sow seeds of doubt. For one thing, James had sold cars to his own family and to his mother-in-law. Then there was the handwritten letter to John Bowers, thanking him for his assignment to chaperone Robert Gomez and refusing payment. It could have been written at any time, but it was found in Gomez's house long after the two boys had stopped communicating. It was thus at least ten months old. There was an invoice from October 2001 showing that Nichols had paid Ronald Wasserman to search for attorneys Gaines, Houston, and McNeil. What's more, James swore he'd personally viewed what were purportedly estate cars, that he'd seen a mansion that was said to have belonged to John Bowers, and that he'd briefly examined a will—however badly composed—that clearly appointed him Gomez's "personal representative." He explained that when he told people he'd worked for John Bowers, what he meant was that he'd merely looked out for Robert's general well-being. And he had logically explained that if a few hundred grand had been injudiciously squandered on some fancy BMWs, well, it was Robert who always told him not to worry, and it was Robert who said he'd soon inherit $411 million and then it would be easy to fulfill any number of Miracle Cars refunds.

Moreover, it was in James's favor that he'd emerged from the scam destitute—had even required a court-appointed lawyer—whereas Robert had emerged filthy rich.

To the jurors, James had demonstrated that he was religious, well-groomed, polite, intelligent, attentive, hardworking, and had even wanted to be a policeman. In addition, he had come from a decent home. "Rose Nichols is a strong, fine woman," claimed Bradshaw in his closing argument. "She reminds me of my own mother, who came here from Ireland during the Depression." If James had met Bowers, Gaines, Houston, and McNeil, then they had to have been actors. That much was clear. "However," Bradshaw pointed out, "it's not a crime to be fooled by actors." In fact, Bradshaw went on to wonder aloud whether two of those actors might have been Rouben Kandilian, the former owner of the Crystal Park Casino, and Val Morella, the former salesman at South Bay Toyota. It was an easy assertion to make; neither man would ever appear in Courtroom 7A.

"Remember the tape recording made by Detective Ayers?" Bradshaw asked the jurors. "If James was a coconspirator, why not have *James* call Ayers back? Why did Gomez feel he had to do it under a false name? Second, if they were partners in this crime, why did Mr. Gomez forge check after check in the casinos? Why not just *ask* James for the money? Third, when James got wind of the scam, he quit. He threw documents at Gomez, resigned, walked out the door, then tried to start a new life. Ladies and gentlemen," Bradshaw concluded, "there should be money judgments against Mr. Nichols. He was careless with other people's money and with their investments. But that should be handled in another court."

Bradshaw seemed like such an honest, diligent straight shooter. If *he* believed in James—and he certainly acted as if he did—then shouldn't the rest of us?

I phoned my trial-attorney father in Columbus that night and told him that James had at least *sounded* like a man who'd been tricked. "I don't know what to think, all of a sudden," I told him.

"What if James really *did* believe in the existence of the estate, at least at first? What if he believed in it long enough that big money began rolling in, and then he was overcome by greed or perhaps felt it was pointless to quit when he was in so deep?" I predicted the jury would find James guilty on some of the counts of fraud but on none of the counts of money laundering. And I predicted Robert would be found guilty on all the counts of money laundering but on few of the counts of fraud.

"It was quite a few decades ago," my father replied, "that I gave up predicting what juries will do."

During a recess the next day, Robert Gomez draped a pudgy arm around my shoulder. "I think my defense is going well," he said, even though I hadn't asked. "You know, when they said it was *me* talking to Ayers, did you notice they had no voice spectrogram, no proof?"

"I know your voice, Robert," I replied. "It was you on that recording."

He chuckled, then said, "I talk to my mother every day, and she thinks I'll be out of here soon. I'd have flown her to the trial, sure, but she's a big crier. Cries all the time, very emotional. But my defense is going so well I don't think I'll take the stand. I once had a friend with an IRS problem. He took the stand and was convicted. See, there's a lesson there, I think."

So Robert had waived his right to testify in his own defense and thereby lost his chance to present his version of events. Here, suddenly, was the most persuasive indication that James Nichols might be innocent, yet it was the one piece of evidence that "No Nonsense" correctly forbade the jurors to consider.

In his closing argument for Gomez, attorney Bruce Simon performed his charming Rumpole of the Bailey impersonation, but he didn't have much to work with. For one thing, Gomez, like Gwen Baker, had continued the fraud *after* federal agents had entered the picture, lifting an additional $3,496,937 from Pastor John Alexander.

Still, Simon gave it his best shot. "Mr. Gomez never controlled the money in Mr. Nichols's account," he began. "He was merely a pro gambler who was successful—all the witnesses here testified to that. Mr. Gomez's position all the way back to his first contact with Agent Elijah Zuniga was that he was a gambler backed by Mr. Nichols, and that he had nothing to do with representing himself as an heir to any estate. Third-party bankers testified they lost as much as $1 million to Mr. Gomez in a short time. So why does he need the grief of a scam? He succeeded at gambling for five years. Why jeopardize his career in that way? Remember, after the football players got their red blazers, there was a third blazer that was prepared, and it was prepared for Mr. Gomez. That's because he was an investor, too."

Robert and I ate lunch alone that day, in a restaurant he frequented a few blocks from the courthouse. As usual, he drove and was as happy as a clam. He studied the menu for ages, then ordered two patty-melt sandwiches and two orders of fries. He'd eaten there often enough that the waitress knew him by name. Robert called her "honey" and bummed two cigarettes off her, but she didn't seem to mind.

"I'm confident of a hung jury," he said between mouthfuls. "If I walk away today, I'll take a year off—from the casinos, from everything. Go to Catalina Island, maybe, and relax. I'm a big believer in karma. I've had great luck. It's been more important to me than my skill at gambling. I haven't had a losing year since 1997. Casinos nationwide recognize me by name and want to hire me to stimulate play among their customers. I could get a job at any casino in the country right now, sure. The casino lifestyle has made me fat, though. I didn't used to be like this."

I didn't want to mention that he'd just ordered two entire lunches. Instead, I asked, "But what if you *do* go to prison?"

"I already did five and a half months in Leavenworth," he said. "It's not that hard. I got between twenty and thirty letters from friends every week. I'm not afraid of prison. I view it as an adventure. Frankly, James's case is worse than mine. Mine is all circumstance and innuendo."

One of the last wire transfers that Gomez received had curiously emanated from a Barclays Bank. I asked, "Did you hide the missing money out of the country?"

"Maybe I did, maybe I didn't," he replied. "Let's just say this: The government will never get their hands on it, okay? Never."

"So you didn't lose it gambling?"

"You heard the witnesses. I win more than I lose. I'm the king of pai gow poker, and I'll always be the king."

"Do you regret losing your friendship with James?"

"James is a talented guy, but life goes on. He's gone one direction, I've gone the other. He has to let go of his anger. He'll see that as he grows up." It was always amusing to hear Robert offer psychological advice, and he did it often. During lunch that day, he related at least six tidbits of philosophical wisdom that had been passed on to him by his "close personal friends" Larry Flynt, Donald Trump, Steve Wynn, and Jay Leno.

I sometimes tried to call him on his name-dropping but always failed. "Why don't you introduce me to Leno?" I suggested.

"Oh, sure, no problem," he replied. Then he wrote down an address on West Thirty-first Street in West Covina, where he said he was building a new home he'd be moving into immediately after the trial. "Look me up there," he said. "But I don't have a phone yet."

In the trial's concluding days, the final details of the Miracle Cars scheme fell into place, although many had been presented out of chronological order. There had been whole days when it was easy to believe James Nichols or Robert Gomez might be guilty of little more than bad judgment. Nichols said he believed the estate existed; Gomez said he was merely a gambler backed by James's mysterious income. The origins of the scheme were frequently obscured. Sometimes, so too were the victims' fiscal sufferings. Twenty-one million dollars had been stolen, but days passed when it was never mentioned. Both defendants were intelligent, worldly in their own peculiar ways, articulate, observant, cynical of the motives of persons around them, able to remember the smallest details, adept at following the Byzantine twists and turns of the law, yet *both* professed total ignorance and naïveté regarding the other's perfidious motives in the largest retail automotive fraud in U.S. history.

Among the spectators, the most common utterance was, "I simply *cannot* believe these two boys pulled this off."

For three weeks, the government had worked steadily through 118 groups of documents—some 18,000 pages of background material and evidence collected during 29 months of tenacious investigation, plenty of it logged after hours and on weekends. In front of the jury, Dan Stewart, Curt Bohling, Gary Marshall, and Steve Hamilton performed without emotion or ego. It was their stated intention to put Nichols and Gomez in prison, yet no personal grudge, no vendetta, no particular anger seemed to motivate them.

After all the witnesses had testified and all the lawyers had made their many and varied arguments, there remained only two questions that were never asked. The first was, "Who initially came up with the scam, James or Robert?" And the second was, "Where's the missing $8.7 million?"

30

DELIBERATION AND DECISION

T he jury consisted of three men and nine women. On Wednesday, June 4, 2003, they retired to a locked anteroom to begin their deliberations, where they remained incommunicado and under the watch of a rosy-cheeked bailiff. Robert Gomez promptly disappeared from the courthouse—perhaps again on the patty-melt trail—but James Nichols paced the hallways with his wife. He would talk to me at intervals, then suddenly break off the conversation in mid-sentence. He told me he believed John Bowers and the estate lawyers had been actors hired by Robert—men who may actually have been *controlling* Robert, he said—although he couldn't otherwise explain their role in the scheme.

"I'll tell you, I was extremely afraid of those people," he added. "Vince McNeil, or whoever he was, once called me on the phone and said, 'You were stabbed in the tenth grade—I have your records and know everything about you.' Another time, he called and said, 'I saw you leave your mother's bedside.' And it was true, I'd just visited her in the hospital, where she was having a thyroid problem. I felt someone was always watching me."

James's animus for Robert grew as the jury deliberated all the next day. "If he walks in here right now," James warned, "I'll choke him 'til he's pink. I did it once already, you know, the day I resigned as executor. My mother had to make me stop or I'd have strangled him. My reputation is ruined, and so is forty years of my mother's good works in the church." But his mother wasn't in the courthouse. She'd already flown home.

As we waited for a verdict, I lamented that Pastor John Alexander hadn't testified. Alexander had been arrested by Douglas County detectives in Georgia—initially for "operating as a used motor-vehicle dealer without a license." But when the cops learned his cars weren't so much used as make-believe, they found another charge to file: "theft by deception." Alexander told Assistant U.S. Attorney Dan Stewart that if he were called to testify in Kansas City, he'd take the Fifth on every question asked. Stewart saved the taxpayers the cost of an airline ticket.

"Alexander's unwillingness to cooperate was always a mystery to me," said Agent Gary Marshall. "I think his ego just wouldn't let him admit he had assisted Gomez in scamming so many people. Alexander's flock was quite a radical bunch, and he didn't want his image tarnished." Stewart left it up to Georgia's Sergeant Lamar Newborn to decide what to do with the Porsche-peddling pastor.

Hour after hour, there came no word from the jurors. I assumed they were debating what to do about James. Dan Stewart took my father's approach. "It's a waste of time to speculate," he said indifferently. The jurors deliberated for half of Wednesday, all of Thursday, and now it was time for lunch on Friday. I'd resigned myself to spending another weekend alone in Kansas City, eating barbecued pork and chicken. Kimberly Hall Nichols told me she hadn't slept at all the previous night and didn't expect to do much better over the coming weekend. She looked weary and defeated. For the first time, I noticed that James's sport coats and dress shirts were rumpled.

And then Stewart grabbed me in the hall and said, "They have a verdict."

I was amazed how many spectators and reporters suddenly materialized out of thin air. My friend Tanya Samuels, from the *Kansas City Star*, waved to me, and we sat together. Everyone was impatient to learn how this drama, conceived nine years earlier, would finally play out—everyone, that is, except defendant Gomez, who was apparently lingering over another double lunch two blocks distant. Attorney Bruce Simon apologized to Judge Laughrey, and a small expedition coalesced to fetch him. Robert returned out of breath but smiling and evidently sated.

The jury forewoman was in her early forties, but her hair was almost snow-white. I'd been prevented from speaking to her for three weeks and knew her only as the "gum chewer." She handed the verdict to Judge Laughrey's clerk, who walked it to the bench. "No Nonsense" took her time reading. Each defendant was facing twenty-three counts, and the judge wanted to study the outcome of each. It seemed like a cliché, but the tension in the room was almost unbearable. It surprised me. The outcome of this trial made no earthly difference to my life, yet my heart was pounding and my hands were clammy.

Judge Laughrey, as dour and stern-faced as the day she'd verbally demolished the wayward juror, declared she would read James Nichols's verdict first. The only sound in the courtroom was the reassuring whoosh of the ventilator fans. "On count number one," she intoned, "the United States government finds the defendant, James Randall Nichols, guilty as charged. On count number two," she continued, "the United States government finds the defendant James Randall Nichols guilty as charged. On count number three . . ." James sat as motionless as a marble statue, with one hand tucked under his chin. His wife appeared close to tears, but she—along with the rest of us—assumed the judge would eventually announce numerous counts on which James had been found innocent.

It didn't happen. Judge Laughrey pronounced him guilty twenty-three times in a row. With each recitation of guilt, her face more closely resembled a scowling mask.

And then it was Robert Gomez's turn. She read all twenty-three counts a second time. Gomez was found guilty on each and every charge. As the judge had begun reading, Robert had assumed his fearless F. Lee Bailey pose, but he wilted halfway through. He and attorney Bruce Simon said nothing, didn't even exchange glances.

There were no outraged howls from the spectators, no celebratory clapping, not so much as a peep. No members of the government's team smiled or slapped one another on the back. The room remained silent, businesslike.

Tanya Samuels and I had been unable to sit in our regular pew, directly behind Gomez's defense table, and now I realized why. The four burly men who had commandeered those places were, in fact, U.S. Marshals. When Laughrey had uttered the word "guilty" for the forty-sixth time, the men stood, walked around the railing, then flanked Nichols and Gomez, staring directly into their faces.

Assistant U.S. Attorney Dan Stewart asked Judge Laughrey to deny bail prior to sentencing. "There's still a substantial amount of cash missing, Your Honor," he said, "and Mr. Gomez paid $900 per week at the Plaza for his apartment. We believe he's living in this manner on monies obtained by fraud and will be dissipating further assets if he's free. There's every likelihood there's a lot of money out there that could be used to assist in flight."

"If it please the court and counsel," countered Bruce Simon, "the government never established that the funds that flowed to

Mr. Gomez for the purpose of gaming were fraudulently obtained. Mr. Gomez presents no flight risk. If he were going to run, he'd have done so by now."

"There's no evidence that Mr. Nichols knows where the missing funds even *are*," pleaded Tom Bradshaw. "He is a U.S. citizen, and he has no passport. We ask that he remain on bail until sentencing."

"No Nonsense" didn't hesitate. "Defendants are held in custody," she said, her voice a surly monotone. "With a guilty verdict now, there is a *substantial* risk of flight."

With that, two U.S. Marshals grabbed Nichols and two grabbed Gomez. The boys were frisked, their pockets emptied. Out tumbled keys, coins, pens, combs, and wallets. One marshal informed the court, "Mr. Nichols has $600 in cash. I need someone to sign for it." Kimberly Hall Nichols, wiping away tears, agreed. Then she was left standing in open court, holding a black camel-hair coat and a leather belt, as her husband and his former partner were handcuffed and shackled. James winked at her. Robert had no one in the courtroom to wave goodbye to. Both were led to a detention cell just to the right of the judge's bench. The marshals fiddled endlessly with keys and chains, and when the metal door finally slammed shut—slammed perhaps a little too dramatically —it absolutely made a sound of steely finality that was right out of a Hollywood movie.

"Wow," said my friend from the *Star*. "That, apparently, is *that*. I thought you said James might walk." She headed downstairs for the ensuing press conference. Dan Stewart, Curt Bohling, Agent Marshall, and Inspector Hamilton were all about to receive their fifteen minutes of fame, richly deserved.

I headed instead to the courthouse lobby, where I waylaid the white-haired forewoman. "The reason we deliberated so long," she told me, "was because we tried to find each man innocent on each claim. We worked backward to see if there was a document or if someone had a note that would contradict a claim of innocence. So we didn't wrestle with whether James believed the estate existed—there was a body of evidence outside that. There were no jurors who were substantially split on any issue after we worked through the evidence. There was a paper trail."

I asked what the jury had thought of James's considerable testimony. "There was no way his story could hold up," she replied. "He couldn't get around the witnesses. He is a very intelligent man. Smart, assertive—*too* smart not to have seen the truth. If he hadn't testified, we still had the evidence to break his story. We all had questions, small doubts, but there was no dispute among us on anything major."

I raced back upstairs to catch the last few minutes of the gangbang press conference, where U.S. Attorney Todd Graves was standing before an array of blinding TV lights. His blond hair and square face gave him the look of a California surfer. He was obviously enjoying the attention. "These two men stole $21 million from thousands of victims," he said to the cameras. "If there were others who were involved, I can't tell you. We're still looking for other participants, and we're still looking for the missing money. But we got the top two lieutenants. We cut the head off."

After the TV crews departed, the two prosecutors and two federal agents posed for still photos on the courthouse steps. I asked Gary Marshall if the four of them were planning to go out and hoist a dozen or so beers. "Dan supervises seven other attorneys," he told me, "and he has sixty open cases. So I doubt it."

It seemed like a dreary way to conclude twenty-nine months of work.

31

"THERE ARE NO WORDS"

Four months passed before Gwen Baker, fifty-three, returned to Judge Laughrey's courtroom, but her testimony against her "godsons" had evidently satisfied the prosecutors. Laughrey sentenced Baker to five years in federal prison without the possibility of parole. Furthermore, her properties in Memphis were confiscated, and she was fined $12,527,195, a sum representing the net proceeds of the scam. It was a fine that would have gotten the average citizen's attention. Baker was going to have to author quite a few successful stage plays to put her financial life back in order.

Still, five years in prison seemed trifling compared with the scope of the scam. I asked Baker's attorney, Lance Sandage, if his client grasped how close she'd come to spending each and every one of her golden years behind bars.

"She might have," he replied, "but only after hours of discussion." She remained defiant.

Corinne Conway was even luckier. Her attorney, Robin Fowler, argued persuasively and passionately at her sentencing. "Your Honor, this is dangerous ground," he admitted to Judge Laughrey, "because I was a prosecutor for twenty years, and I never liked it when defendants brought religion into the argument, when everybody suddenly finds God at sentencing. We're not going to hide behind that or use it as a shield. Corinne Conway should have seen this coming. But here is where the faith comes in. She believes God acts every day in the community, and it's no leap of faith for her to believe a wealthy person died and left an estate to help people of faith."

"No Nonsense" Laughrey must have been feeling merciful that day. She sentenced sixty-three-year-old Conway to a mere fourteen months in federal prison without parole. She also fined her $4,977,369—restitution for Conway's victims alone—and the government seized her beloved Virtuous Women's International Ministries, the glowing "church" on the hill that looked out over bucolic Higginsville, Missouri.

"She got off easy," reckoned police chief Cindy Schroer, who was the first cog in law enforcement to blow the whistle on the scam. "She did real damage to my little town. When people tell me she believed the cars were real—believed it right to the end—I say, 'No way, José.' You ask any cop in America what he hears day in and day out. It's, 'Oh, Officer, wait, it's not my fault. *I didn't know.*'" Schroer predicted Conway would eventually return to Higginsville, where "she'll have some explaining to do."

The boys weren't as lucky as the women. Not by a long shot.

During the trial, when James Nichols first stood to testify on his own behalf, Judge Laughrey had given him a memorable warning. She'd looked him in the eye and said, "Mr. Nichols, if you should be convicted, one of the things the court can take into account in evaluating your sentence is whether you have perjured yourself."

"All those never-seen lawyers, the gold bullion in the black Lincoln, the 350-pound Samoan—all that stuff sounded pretty farfetched," remarked Assistant U.S. Attorney Dan Stewart.

Judge Laughrey evidently agreed. She now explained to James that he faced a substantial "upward departure" from normal sentencing guidelines. For one thing, the law stipulated increased sentences for crimes involving more than fifty victims—in this case, there were *four thousand*—as well as an increase for defendants who "misrepresent that they are acting on behalf of a religious organization."

James was in trouble, and it was about to get worse. The judge said aloud what Stewart had predicted. "Mr. Nichols lied to this court and to the jury," she declared, "and it will count for an additional thirty months." But she was only getting warmed up, and now she really dropped the hammer.

She sentenced James Randall Nichols to *twenty-four years and four months* in federal prison without the possibility of parole. Like Baker, he was fined $12.5 million, and his remaining BMW and Ducati were seized. It was a gut-buster of a punishment. No one had expected it. James would be fifty-three years old—Gwen Baker's age—by the time he was released. If attorney Tom Bradshaw appeared shaken, Nichols was positively shell-shocked. He'd expected a sentence of sixty months. Instead, he'd received nearly five times that.

The irony of seizing the BMW and the motorcycle was not lost on prosecutor Stewart. "Year after year, these guys sold thousands of desirable vehicles that did not exist," he told me. "Looks like we finally found two that did."

Then it was Gomez's turn before the bench. For once, Robert appeared to grasp the severity of what might be in store. He had neglected to shave his head that morning, and he looked wan, doughy, and fearful. He had lost his trademark grin. The judge asked him to stand, then she similarly let him have it: twenty-one years and ten months in federal prison, without the possibility of parole. He, too, was fined $12.5 million, but at least he had a head start on paying it off. The government had already seized the $818,000 he'd been holding when he was arrested, and now he was also losing his jewelry, watches, and rings, as well as his Pete Rose and Hank Aaron baseball bats. And Laughrey still wasn't done. She added an additional fine of $8.7 million—the amount that was missing and presumed buried in someone's back yard or tucked into a tax-free shelter in the Caymans. What's more, Dan Stewart filed a motion alleging that $150,000 of the overall fees that Gomez had paid to attorney Bruce Simon had been derived from fraud. Gomez, in fact, had recklessly paid those fees using checks from the Bicycle Casino. That sum was now subject to confiscation.

Simon appeared disconsolate. "If it please the court and counsel," he urged, "this is a draconian sentence no matter how you look at it, and it is *more* than a deterrent to others who would follow in these young men's footsteps." When he said the word "more," his voice cracked.

"I agree," Judge Laughrey surprisingly replied. She looked angry. "It *is* draconian. And I'm interested in how America's clever corporate raiders, who are being tried for stealing similar sums [a clear reference to the Enron trial, then just beginning] will fare in *their* sentencing, versus the sentencing of these two clever inner-city boys." I wondered if Laughrey had perhaps been personally touched by the Miracle Cars tale. Several of the elderly and infirm victims had been financially wiped out, their retirement years ruined, and their testimony had been painful. Whatever had triggered it, "No Nonsense" was in no mood to suffer the two young Californians who'd spent seven years fleecing America's flocks.

At their sentencings, both boys had been asked if they had anything to say to the court or to their victims. James Nichols stood unsteadily, then meekly stammered, *"There are no words."* Then he sat down. The comment was perfectly in keeping with his character—solemn, serious, tight-lipped, introspective to the bitter end.

Not so Robert Gomez. When the judge asked if he had anything to say, at least two onlookers snickered out loud. Everyone knew what was coming. Robert *always* had something to say, and it wouldn't be brief.

Wearing bright blue sneakers, he duck-walked to the lectern in front of the judge's bench, gripping it as if holding on to a lifeboat. A chain encircled his prodigious waist, and it led down to shackles around his ankles. Just as he prepared to speak, he burst into tears. He cried and sobbed and heaved. He turned bright red and mucus flowed, which he wiped away with a sleeve of his bright-orange St. Clair County prison jumpsuit. I'd seen Robert cry before. He was notorious for turning the waterworks on and off. But this episode may have been heartfelt.

Then the words came in a familiar torrent. "My life changes after today," he began, stating the obvious. "I have lost dignity and respect in the gaming industry I once controlled and helped put together." It was a ridiculous claim, but the judge said nothing. "This prosecutor and his office, they won't admit to it, but they tried everything to bring me down. They wanted me to be an informant and snitch to something I could not help them with. I put my life in the hands of the Nichols family, and they put me where I am today—in prison. No more limousines, no free tickets to concerts and sports events, no poker tournaments. I've fallen from the king of the hill to the lowest of the low." He hesitated a moment, again on the verge of tears. "James Nichols's testimony in this matter was absurd, ridiculous," he continued. "The testimony from Gwen Baker was outrageous. I want this court to know I will not be Dan Stewart's puppet. I won't roll over on the casinos. I'm happy to pay any restitution, because I will eventually be free and will reach great success in my career. There's no excuse for what took place, but I believe in the old adage 'You can't cheat an honest man.'" It now sounded as if Robert were blaming the victims for their dishonesty, but, again, the judge held her tongue. "I gave Nichols and his family a lot of money," he continued, "not car money, but money I won. Why his family was not indicted is beyond me. People invested in this in order to get rich quick. I won't beg. I've never begged for anything, even when I was poor, living with my mother. But I ask the court to look at the fact that I did not put this together, did not preach in churches. My defense is that James and I should have had separate trials, and the government—sitting here to my left—is holding the noose for me. Now I may be ousted from the industry, barred, not welcome in the casinos, although Las Vegas is a different story." Half the spectators in the room smiled at this remark. Robert was already thinking ahead to his release. "The U.S. attorney's office sets out to hang a person when he doesn't roll over on his friends and business colleagues. Our Founding Fathers did *not* expect the judicial system to work like this, Your Honor. There's no excuse for the way the government did their job. I'll file an appeal, sure. I'll look forward to a second trial. Thank you."

Throughout his client's rambling tirade, attorney Simon glanced around the courtroom, as if hoping to locate a sky hook. Here before us was the reason Robert hadn't testified on his own behalf. He spoke with no thought to consequences, and Simon knew it better than anyone.

Judge Laughrey stretched her arms and paused for a minute. Then she said, "This has been a long and interesting matter." I admired her for not reacting to Robert's rant. "I believe that Mr. Nichols and Mr. Gomez should be treated similarly in this matter," she stated, "but sentencing guidelines lead us to odd outcomes. Now these two defendants are paying with most of their lives."

Later in the hall, Assistant U.S. Attorney Dan Stewart briefly questioned me about Gomez's various lunchtime rants, in which Robert had admitted he still had the missing money. Stewart asked if I'd be willing to say so under oath. But before I could answer, he changed his mind, pointing out that there had been no witnesses to my conversations and, in any event, the U.S. attorney's office was loath to subpoena reporters' notes. I was relieved.

I drove to the St. Clair County jail the next day and talked to Robert for two hours. We were separated by three inches of bulletproof glass, and the guards again relieved me of my tape recorder. "I hope I'm transferred to Lompoc [California]," he told me. "I hear they have a pool and a nine-hole golf course. That would be good for a nonviolent offender like me. I'm getting a million letters from casino people. Got a card from the Bike with two hundred signatures on it. The guards wouldn't let me keep it. I got my Christmas card from the big man in the golden wheelchair." He held the card to the glass. It featured a glossy photo of a red sleigh, but he wouldn't open it to reveal the signature within. "Larry's message is personal," he explained. "There's a guy in here who's charged with two homicides, and even *he* got a lighter sentence than me. I got more than some narcotics dealers get. It's hard to accept. You see examples of the judicial system being out of control. Well, this is one. This isn't what the Founding Fathers had in mind."

I wondered whether Robert could name more than one Founding Father and was about to ask him to give it a whirl. But he interrupted me. "Hey, as soon as I get settled," he said, sounding more upbeat, "I know a guy who can get Barbara Walters on the phone. I need to talk to her, get her to come down here and listen to my story. This whole thing, she's never gonna believe it."

32

AFTERMATH

To serve out his two-plus decades of stir, Robert Gomez was transferred not to Lompoc but to the federal prison in Anthony, New Mexico. It was warm there, and he was satisfied. He'd previously been appalled by the possibility of snow at Leavenworth. Corinne Conway found a home at the federal correctional institution in Greenville, Illinois, where the booming-voiced evangelist became as quiet as a church mouse. James Nichols was transferred to the federal facility in Victorville, California, not far from Riverside, close enough to his home that his wife could make day visits. And, by coincidence, Victorville was also where Gwen Baker wound up, although she and James were housed in separate quadrants.

In the early months of her incarceration, Gwen Baker and I became pen pals. She signed her letters "*Dr.* Gwendolyn Baker," referring to herself as "Gwen" only once. Her letters were pious, ethereal, celestial, sometimes immodest. "My spirits are up and I am staying busy," she wrote. "I shall not fall to pieces. I may shed a few tears every once in a while, but I will not weep excessively, lest I extinguish my light and not be able to see my way. I do need my light in this dark place. There are women young and old depending on me to be a strong refuge for them when they are at weak moments. When I walk in freedom, then I will do my crying. As for right now, only one or two tears will be allowed to escape from my eyes, and that in the dark."

Baker told me it was her role in life "to lend an ear, as always, and give words of wisdom to those in need." She said the light shining through the window "guided her hands and eyes across the page," and she wrote a song for a friend and cellmate "who, by the way, was F. Lee Bailey's last client." She asked, "Do I hear a story?"

Baker described herself as having been "involuntarily deposited in the belly of the beast who feeds off those captured— many have been consumed, staff as well as inmates." She discussed the "dissertation" she'd written for her mail-order doctorate, whose opening line was: "What other elements seep from light or darkness to fuel the human brain?" She added: "I will remain enclosed in my cloak of humility."

Baker claimed to have forgiven James and Robert but asked, "Do they have peace? I find it hard to believe they do. They have locked the truth up in their hearts and are refusing to set it free." When I couldn't locate a copy of her book, *Days on the Porch,* she revealed that it was "a poetic novel that made it only as far as an unedited test-market copy." She said she was still negotiating with a publicist in California and that she would mail a copy soon. It never arrived. A sequel to that book was in the works, she claimed, called *Laughing Ain't Easy.* As if that weren't enough, she was completing two musicals ("one Spanish, one Chinese"), a screenplay whose music and lyrics she was composing simultane-ously, and two dramas ("one African, one Indian"). Furthermore, she scolded me for publishing her oratorical admonition "God wants you to roll!" She claimed that her last word had been "grow," not "roll."

Of her head-on collision with America's legal system, Baker told me: "I forgive man for this unjust punishment. I forgive man for not being able to see the pure motive that was in my heart. How can justice come from a system composed of flawed minds? Where is our hope? Certainly not in the hands of man, who is so faulty. I love sunrises, sunsets, stars, clouds, the moon that shines in the dark sky, and the snow-capped mountains. Oh, the splendor of the artistry of God! When I stare out of my bedroom window or walk into the courtyard to cast my eyes upon the awesome seduction of the sky's colorful palette and His majestic mountains that surround me, it softens the harsh reality of this place where I have been deposited."

Then, suddenly, she broke off communication. She never explained why. Her lawyer told me, "Ms. Baker is trying to contact the author John Grisham, either to write the Miracle Cars story or to write her biography, I'm not sure which."

I forwarded a formal request to the Victorville Federal Correctional Institution, asking for permission to visit Baker in person. The executive assistant himself, Ed Gaunder, called back. He said, "Your request is denied, because it will reflect badly on the Bureau of Prisons." I never learned what that meant.

The last thing Baker wrote caused me to laugh out loud. "Sometimes the sky here looks as if it's on fire, and I watch in awe," she offered. "The world that God created is beautiful. His people need some work, though."

In Anthony, New Mexico—thirty minutes from Ciudad Juárez—Robert Gomez seemed to be having a far better time. For one thing, he'd catalogued his favorite luncheon fare: pizza, chicken patties, fish strips, tuna casserole, mac and cheese, corn dogs, chili dogs, and beans and rice. What's more, he had worked his daily food into a small business. "On Mondays and Wednesdays, we get a hot breakfast," he explained. "Pancakes, waffles, biscuits and gravy, and a cup of juice that tastes like Equal sweetener. But on the other three days, there's cold cereal sealed in a cardboard cup. I don't eat that. I just grab one or two and sell them later for $1. Not bad, huh? Selling something that's been given to me for free."

Robert had been handed Miracle Cars funds for free, too. Even in prison, he was running a scam, albeit on a scale he considered woefully beneath his station.

Back on Kemp Avenue in Carson, the Nichols family went into self-imposed seclusion. A neighbor told me that the few persons who had asked about "James's Big Adventure," as they now euphemistically called it, were met with icy silence.

Still curious about where the $8.7 million might be, Agent Elijah Zuniga drove to the Nichols home in April 2004. He knocked on the door and Rose appeared. Zuniga politely introduced himself and explained his part in arresting Robert Gomez. Then he asked, "Ma'am, would you speak to me a moment about your son James?" Rose slammed the door so hard that the front windows shook.

"I think they're hoping everyone will forget," said Dorothy Bell, one of Rose's former friends and also a victim. "Money changes people, separates them right away. They turn different colors. This whole Miracle Cars thing just turned me off the church, really. I found another church [replacing Christ Christian Home Missionary Baptist Church]. It took me two and a half years to get back on my feet financially, because I took out a loan for those cars. It messed up my relationship and trust even with my husband. A couple weeks ago, I went to a funeral and saw Rose there. I didn't talk to her. She didn't talk to me. She never once called to say she was sorry."

In May 2004, Agent Zuniga drove to Mercedes Flores's pink

house in Maywood, California. He found Robert's mother loading aluminum cans and cardboard into the bed of a pickup truck. "She looked like a woman who'd seen little luxury or rest," Zuniga reported. "She said her son had always had a room in her house, but he came and went at unpredictable times, and she rarely knew his whereabouts. She said, 'There's no way he took $21 million from anybody.' She blamed James Nichols and 'all those other black people' for that. She said, 'The *federales* put Bobby in jail because he wouldn't cooperate and snitch on Nichols and the casinos.' " It was Robert's standard lament.

Zuniga asked if Robert had given her money before he was arrested. "Bobby was *never* arrested," she corrected. "He went to Kansas City on his own to clear his name, but the police tricked him and kept him in jail." She said her son was then placed in a cell with Nichols and "other members of the Mafia, and he had to fight to keep alive."

Mercedes Flores was vague about Robert's career. "He gambled at casinos, mostly, but it wasn't his money," she offered. "Rich people like doctors and lawyers and actors would give him money to play card games, and he was so good he would double or triple their profits." She said Robert was perceived as being rich but "spent a lot of it on poor people and on the church, and he also had to hire a lot of bodyguards and armored cars to protect himself from James."

Her misperceptions were many, but their origins were clear.

Zuniga had hoped to talk longer, but Robert's stepbrother, Michael, suddenly appeared in the driveway. "He nearly dragged his mother back into the house," Zuniga recalled, "and he told me never to talk to her again, and he added, 'Mind your own fucking business.' "

Unlike Rose Nichols, Kimberly Hall Nichols had plenty to say. She was understandably bitter about being left alone to raise daughters Janiya Marie and Carmen Symone, and, just before the trial, James had impregnated her with a son. That boy was born on September 6, 2003, only ninety days after the trial. Kimberly sent me a birth announcement and a note. "In the past year and a half," she wrote, "I've watched the few people James called friends do everything imaginable to betray and con him out of his dreams. Most of all Robert. At times, Robert can really frighten me. There is no doubt in my mind that he is a complete nut. The problem is that he's a crafty nut. When the judge read the verdict last June, all I could do was stare at him. I can't begin to explain the rage inside me. To be honest, I feel that there was someone controlling Robert in all of this. I have no idea who, but someone."

James called me from prison, and I asked his opinion of the trial. "When Judge Laughrey saw the verdict," he replied, "did you see her eyes bug out? It was like she couldn't believe it. She thought I'd be found innocent. I think she denied the motion for a mistrial because she figured I'd go free and Robert would be sent up the river, as it should be. I sat on the stand for nine hours and did *not* lose my cool. I still find that somewhat amazing. They asked me Twenty Questions fifty times. I wish someone would show me the rule that says it's a crime to be naïve. Youth is for making mistakes. Sometimes, I sit and think how Robert kept that huge lie going for so long, right under my nose. My attorney tried real hard, but time didn't permit us to do too much. Other people should have testified in my behalf. We couldn't find a bunch of them. And, into the third week, I think the jury got tired."

After James read my magazine story, he wrote to say, "I can see that certain things did not add up on your cash register." He often had a turn of phrase like that, and it always made me smile. "My newborn's name is James Randall Nichols II," he added, "but everyone just calls him 'Deuce.'" James did not mention that Deuce will be twenty-four years old when he first claps eyes on his dad walking the streets of Carson. When James was twenty-four, he was regularly flying to Memphis to pick up sacks of cash and was swimming contentedly in Gwen Baker's warm pool. He told me it was one of the last memories he cherished.

National finder Kim Krawizcki was so totally mortified by the Miracle Cars scam that she fled her home state to become a nanny in New Jersey, working for minimum wage and attempting to forget the whole sordid mess. "I about had a nervous breakdown," she admitted, "and there was a time I contemplated suicide. But at least I'm over that. Still, I lost all my friends, my fiancé, my life's savings, and my dad still looks at me like I'm a dingbat." On the other hand, she learned a lesson that altered her personality. "I used to have a fear of confrontation, especially with Baker and Conway. Well, guess what? I'm not afraid to confront *anybody* anymore. I'm over it. After looking like a thief, I'm over it. After almost going to jail, I'm over it. The church is so big on authority, you know? Well, those people stole from me. They all got caught up playing this game, and they stopped being God's servants and instead became God's employees." Krawizcki still owes money to the IRS, and victims in Pennsylvania may yet sue her.

Linda Janowski, the former finance manager at South Bay Toyota, jettisoned her career in the car business and now serves as the vice president of a mortgage company. She is one of the few victims who started over and quickly regained her former financial glory. "I'm extremely careful about picking friends these days," she told me. "Nobody just waltzes into my life anymore, like Robert did. I subject strangers to pretty intense scrutiny. I had the plague once. Once was enough."

After Gomez was arrested, he occasionally phoned Janowski, and during one such conversation told her, "If they want to find the money, then they'd better start digging holes in back yards."

But Janowski was skeptical. "Robert only rented places," she pointed out, "and he's not going to leave millions in the yard of a house someone else lives in. Plus, he'd tell people anything. He told me he converted the money to diamonds and had hidden those. Then he told me he had an offshore account."

By coincidence, Robert Turner, the executive host of the high-limit poker section of the Bicycle Casino, moved into the same house in Downey that Robert Gomez and Richie "Fingers" Sklar had occupied. Turner was surprised to find every door in the house fitted with expensive remote-control locks, like those on a luxury car. He said he often jokes with his wife that he'll someday "go into the back yard or underneath the house and dig up the loot."

I asked Agent Zuniga whether Robert possessed the self-discipline to keep his mouth shut for more than twenty-one years if, indeed, he *had* hidden the money. "Not a chance," Zuniga replied, without hesitating. "Not only that, but Robert's casino friends all wondered who he could trust to watch over it. To a man, they said, 'If it was *me,* I'd dig it up and run.'"

After Gomez was convicted, freelance gambling writer Max Shapiro began researching the con for a story. He wrote a letter to Gomez and included a copy of the article that had appeared in *Car and Driver.* "Robert's response blew me away," Shapiro recalled. "He said that the writer, John Phillips, was his agent, and that the two were in the middle of a huge movie deal. Then he mentioned that the government was after his Swiss bank accounts, but he said they'll never find them. Robert is a smart guy, and I wouldn't put anything past him. He's not a street-stealing pachuco, you know? He's so complicated. Layers and layers. I remain impressed—if that's the right word—by his cunning."

Pastor John Alexander remains the object of scrutiny by a variety of law-enforcement agencies in Georgia, and he refused to speak to me. As of September 2004, he had not seen the inside of a courtroom. I called one of Alexander's cronies, a fellow Atlanta-area pastor named Frank Dennington. Pastor Dennington told me, "I don't talk to people like you. If you're poking your nose into this, you're an ass." Then he slammed down the receiver.

Elijah Buggs, the elderly victim in Long Beach whose brother, Houston, was the pastor of Christ Christian Home Missionary Baptist Church, today has no contact with the Nichols family and still blames James and Robert for hastening the death of his brother. "It was one of life's awful lessons," he said. "I always believed my wife and I were smarter than that. It's embarrassing." Buggs now rarely ventures out of his home. He added, "The next time a miracle comes along, I'll ask for proof."

In all, I interviewed close to seventy-five witnesses, victims, defendants, federal agents, lawyers, and prosecutors. As my final question, I made it a habit to ask, "Which of the boys, James or Robert, do you think came up with this scam?" About half said, "I don't know," and the remaining half were split down the middle, leaving the question unanswered.

"One thing's for sure," offered Assistant U.S. Attorney Curt Bohling, "the actual operation of the scheme required the talents and contacts of *both*." Dan Stewart agreed, saying, "I always believed it was a mutual creation."

California Justice Department Agent Elijah Zuniga, on the other hand, didn't equivocate. "It was *James*," he posited forcefully. "So much of the scam depended on the church, and which guy had the church connection? And if you compare the two, gave them a Mensa test, well, James is way smarter. Robert, he's all mouth. It was James's church, where people were allowed to get up and address the congregation, and the older members took what was said as gospel, if you'll pardon the pun. If it's said in the church, it must be true, right? Given how he was raised, how could Gomez know that? It was James's upbringing, his style. What crooks do is what's most comfortable for them. That's why, if a car chase goes on long enough, it invariably winds up where the guy lives. What did James see in Gomez? He saw a guy who had the gift of bullshit, of telling stories, a guy who could float the tale, keep it active and swimming upstream. When I worked undercover, I got close to a drug dealer in his late fifties. I had dinner with him, was in his house, he bought me Christmas gifts. He told me, 'You know why I succeed? Because I've learned that if you make up a good story and stick by it long enough, people will believe. They're *dying* to believe.' "

It still troubled me that the scheme was launched in James's own back yard, where it was sure to suffuse the neighborhood with the odor of fraud. Why begin there? "Because they had no choice," reckoned Agent Gary Marshall. "It's the only place on earth where anybody trusts them. They have to start somewhere, and one of these kids is black, the other Hispanic. What are they going to do, fly to Chicago and say to strangers, 'Hey, buy an invisible car from me'?"

And there was a third question that every onlooker asked: Why didn't the boys run when the feds began closing in? In fact, James Nichols *did* flee to Las Vegas and may have had travel plans much farther afield. But he got tangled up with his boyhood friend Steve Finnie, and the two rapidly squandered James's quarter-million-dollar getaway fund. In the end, James's net worth was equal to one BMW 323i and one Ducati M996. It wasn't enough to create a new life.

Robert Gomez, on the other hand, didn't *want* to run. He realized he could soak the Miracle Cars marks for an additional $3.5 million, even as the feds were swarming in the near shadows. Perhaps the money was so tempting that he simply expected to stash what he could and take the fall. "He told me he thought he'd only do five years," Linda Janowski recalls. "He's smart enough to know he couldn't earn several million bucks in the same period. So why not sit out a spell, take a rest, then come back later and have a little fun?"

"The other reason Robert didn't run," asserted Zuniga, "is that he began to believe his own con. The casinos were doing everything but having sex with the guy—food, junkets, jewelry—and he kidded himself into thinking he was actually this rich person who deserved it. Robert once said to me, 'You know, Inspector Hamilton is just jealous 'cause I'm a trust-fund baby and he's working for the government making fifty grand a year.' Even when we nabbed him, he told me, 'I'll do twenty-four months, be out, don't worry, the casinos will never bar me.' He came to believe his own lies."

That's certainly possible. Witnesses who were intimate with Robert and James—those who listened to them converse candidly, informally, and openly with each other—all confirmed that, for seven consecutive years, the boys spoke as if every element of the con were real. Never did they let down their guard. Never did they act out of character. Never did they refer to car buyers as "marks" or "suckers." Never did they joke about their "take" or the "back end." If they had tricked Baker and Conway, never was it a source of amusement or lighthearted banter. The women were National Finders and esteemed "estate representatives." The never-seen attorneys were always to be feared and respected. Their phone calls were to be answered promptly. Their bidding was to go unquestioned. James made that clear, even to his parents. Robert repeated it to James's wife, even when only the three of them were in the car and the con didn't need further bolstering. The scheme's theatrical aspect ran twenty-four hours a day, and that etiquette was conscientiously observed until James resigned as executor and Robert was handcuffed in the Hustler. It was ironic that Gwen Baker, searching for first-class actors for her San Francisco stage play, was already employed by two of California's finest.

The scheme had been replete with amazing details. For instance, instead of faxing the South Bay document from his home fax machine—where the letter could be prepared slowly, away from prying eyes—Robert had been smart enough to fax it from the *dealership*'s machine, which would imprint South Bay's name and number at the top, making the document appear genuine. And James worked psychological ploys that were endlessly clever. He'd warn buyers that they'd face $45-per-day storage fees if they didn't pick up their cars on the day stipulated. It had the effect of distracting victims from the troubling dilemma of "*When* do I get cars?" to "What do I do *when my cars arrive?*"

But their mistakes had been grand, too. The boys had created only one will, and it had been Robert's. On paper, James was merely the executor of the Gomez estate, not the Bowers estate. Technically, he'd have no power over anything until Robert died. In retrospect, however, it's easy to see why no will for Bowers had been created. Neither James nor Robert had the legal training to create a credible-looking will for an estate containing $411 million, 7,000 cars, and properties from coast to coast. Such a will could easily comprise a hundred pages and would be a nightmare to forge, even for a genuine lawyer. The boys were simply lucky that no one noticed. And, of course, Robert regularly tripped over his own ego, most famously in his acting debut, when he toyed with Detective Ayers, needlessly launching a civil suit that, by all rights, should have derailed the whole scheme.

"In principle, this was a classic confidence game," said Agent Zuniga, "and they *always* work. Watch late-night TV and study the infomercials. It's like, 'Buy this video for $29.95 and get perfect abs in six months, guaranteed, or your money back.' But in six months, the seller's gone. Imagine if the seller were a pastor from your own church. Then it's a cinch—*everybody* would buy, right? And the [white] accent that both boys developed? It was necessary to float the con, at least once it spread out of Carson and Compton. It's not so hard to learn to talk like that if you stay at home and watch TV, if you have a mommy-take-care-of-me kind of life, rather than hustling on the streets."

Zuniga *did* admit to being impressed by the boys' uncommon patience. Nichols and Gomez spent thirty-seven months formulating the con, making it sound credible before putting it into play. In their perception of what would and would not fly, the boys were uncanny, showing wisdom beyond their years. Whenever Rose Nichols expressed incredulity—about the delivery of gold bullion, about Vince McNeil's mechanical voice box, about engineering apprenticeships—the boys wisely backed off, letting the story simmer and settle in the background. By the time Gomez announced that cars were for sale, the broad framework of the scheme had already been locked in place for three years. Never did the boys force onlookers to swallow the story whole. Instead, it was presented in easy-to-digest increments, playing out as life itself plays out.

Asked to name what skills are necessary to become a professional poker player, the aptly named Chris Moneymaker, winner of $2.5 million in the 2003 World Series of Poker, said: "Lots of guts. No fear. The ability to read people. And a very good memory."

Without knowing it, he had described James and Robert to a T.

In January 2004, James Nichols called me on the prison phone. "My father taught me to work hard and not to have idle hands," he said. "By the time I was six or seven, he had two businesses. My work ethic came from him. But it's hard to stay busy in prison."

James was nonetheless trying. He said he was "submerged in several law books" and had adopted a nocturnal routine. "We eat our meals at five-thirty A.M., eleven A.M., and four P.M.," he explained. "In between, I sleep, and I don't get out of my bunk unless I need to make a phone call. There isn't much recreation here that appeals to me, but I do push-ups every night. Then I read between the hours of eleven P.M. and five A.M. I have peace of mind during those hours. It helps me think." James sounded depressed, except when he spoke about the pre-Gomez days—his teenage years. Not long after, he stopped phoning and his letters trailed off.

Naturally, Robert Gomez took the opposite approach. He called weekly, inundated me with letters, and continued to play handball with the truth. "I was talking to Larry," he stated, "and the Big Guy says my attorney robbed me, that it shouldn't have cost $165,000, which is what I paid. By the way, Larry says he was disappointed by how you portrayed me in the article. He says he'll run right over you with his wheelchair, sure." Then he let fly with the Gomez guffaw and a wet snort or two. Robert never had trouble amusing himself.

"Now a young guy named Jonathan is winning in pai gow, taking my place," Robert continued. "He writes me regularly for tips. I try to help. My mother was in Mexico recently for medical reasons, and she found out that agents were even snooping around down there, in banks where they think I stashed the money. Hah! They'll never find it. Never."

I asked if he'd heard anything from James. "Oh, sure, my sources tell me he's down, brooding," Robert replied. "I wrote him a note. I said, 'Let it go, man, move on, or you'll sour the deal for both of us.' He's strong, but now he's kind of an outcast from his family. They're embarrassed, it's a humiliation for him to be in prison. But in my business, in gambling, you know, it's common.

In my industry, people go to prison every month, then return a couple years later, and they're accepted back, no problem. It makes it easier for me."

Like Richard Nixon, Robert insisted he was no crook. "A money launderer is *not* a thief!" he self-incriminatingly suggested. "People like me will always be successful, secure, and at the very top. A friend recently told me, 'Buddha, I am convinced that the U.S. government will go broke before you do.' I'll always live the good life. The word is out to fellow inmates, and I'm a celebrity here, sure. It's great to be me!"

One of Harry Houdini's biographers described the magician as narcissistic, not above blatant power manipulations, and one of the most amazing exponents of bombast on earth, a shameless self-promoter. Houdini and Robert had plenty in common, although Houdini never offered fireworks and horses to mourners at a reverend's funeral.

Robert was keen on the prospect of a Miracle Cars book, "but only as long as I am the only character involved," he warned. "My story must be the largest part, sure. Of course, Baker, Conway, and Nichols can be brought up. But, ultimately, I must be the main character. By the way, what will I get out of this?" He told me he'd organized the inmates in his wing so that, at four P.M., they all sat down to watch Wolf Blitzer on CNN. "I've got them trained," he declared. And he said he'd received a tempting offer from "a major Las Vegas casino to work as a consultant," once his prison experience is concluded. "I told them, 'I'll need housing, living expenses, a limo, a driver, a yearly bonus,'" he boasted, "and they said, 'Well, sure, we very much want the Buddha name.' So they put my demands in front of their board of directors. After tax, I'd be clearing $3.5 million a year. What I want is to become a brand. You know, Buddha playing cards, Buddha T-shirts, Buddha poker cruises. But then I had second thoughts. I decided I'd rather be known as 'Buddha the pro gambler' than 'Buddha the casino exec.' So I told 'em to get lost. You know, there are three things I'll never have to worry about in life: going broke, going on a diet, or getting a real job."

The last time I talked to Robert on the phone, he said: "In court, I guess I rolled the dice and crapped out, but I've still got the nuts"—a gambling term implying that he's still holding a winning hand. He may also still hold $8.7 million. If so, it means he made a good living from the con. If, while nurturing the scheme, he worked forty-hour weeks from September 1994 through June 2002, then he earned $578 per hour.

"I'm gonna live 'til I'm eighty-five," he told me, "so I might as well give the feds some of those years. I'm in a quiet pod, have a TV to watch, phone calls to make. I stay in touch, make my rounds. It's not so bad. I'm in a cell with a real nice guy who's in for possession of a gun. I'll always be Buddha, the king of pai gow poker. I'll lay low for a while, but I'm Buddha the king. I'll get out. It's not the end of the world. The walls won't destroy me. Can I call you back? It's time for lunch."

Shortly after the Miracle Cars trial, Special Agent Elijah Zuniga resigned from the California Department of Justice to become a freelance consultant. He now advises the casinos on legal and compliance issues.

Six months after the trial, Agent Gary Marshall retired from the IRS following a distinguished thirty-one-year career. For his critical role in unraveling the Miracle Cars scam, he became a celebrity among the nation's 2,900 Criminal Investigation Division agents. In March 2004, he was formally summoned to Washington, D.C., where he was told he'd been selected as the "Special Agent of the Year." It was the first time a retired agent had been so honored.

"I couldn't pass up one more trip on Uncle Sam," Marshall joked. "They even paid for my wife to attend the ceremony, and we stayed in a nice D.C. hotel for two nights." It was an award he deserved. Marshall saved any number of future buyers from becoming victims, he helped Dan Stewart set up a fund for restitution, and he saved U.S. taxpayers far more than they were paying him in salary.

Further, Marshall was asked to address a convention of Certified Fraud Examiners, describing how he tracked the con. "I was hoping that some of those guys might have had a contact or two that would help us locate assets still maintained by Nichols or Gomez," he said. "On the other hand, I'm retired now. But it's hard to quit thinking about it." Out of the bowels of the Miracle Cars monster, it seemed as if Marshall was the only participant propelled to glory.

Inspector Steve Hamilton remained on the case. He returned to California to interview yet more of Robert Gomez's cronies, among them a gambler named Mark Betor, whom Robert always called "Mark Cash-Is-King." But Betor was afraid to talk, insisting that Gomez could reach out and inflict injury, even from the confines of a prison in New Mexico. Holding subpoenas, Hamilton returned to the casinos to search an additional five safe-deposit boxes that Gomez had reportedly rented. Rumor had it that one of the boxes contained a diamond-encrusted watch worth $1 million. All the boxes were empty.

To this day, Hamilton continues to search for the $8.7 million. It remains unaccounted for and is presumed hidden.

"The idea of crime based on wit is kind of wonderful," said Ricky Jay, an illusionist, pickpocket, actor, and celebrated card trickster. "There's not much admirable in a guy who comes at you with a gun and says, 'Give me your money.' But a guy who makes you sign a piece of paper, and then you find out you've bought the

Brooklyn Bridge—the con is enormously appealing. And it's theatrical. The con—the *big* con, especially—is an entire theatrical orchestration for an audience of one. It's both lovely and diabolical at the same time."

I asked James Nichols what he thought of that quote. He never responded.

I asked Robert Gomez what he thought of that quote. He said, "Risk is rewarded."

Notes on Sources

This is a work of nonfiction. As such, all of the characters are real. I have used no pseudonyms. Where I used dialogue, it was based on tape recordings, on trial transcripts, or on the recollection of at least one participant or eyewitness. Otherwise, the words were uttered in my presence. At the outset of every interview, I took care to announce myself as a reporter—first for *Car and Driver* magazine, for whom I was writing a feature called "The Miracle Cars" (October 2003), then for this book. Three sources agreed to speak with me under the condition their names not be used, but all agreed that I could publish their words. Only one source spoke to me under the condition that the interview was off the record.

The reporting for this book began in April 2003 and ended in October 2004. The summaries in the final few chapters represent the whereabouts and occupations of the characters at the time the manuscript was submitted to the publisher.

Chapter 1: Buddha and the Pornographer

The scene in which Robert Gomez gambles with Larry Flynt was a composite of eyewitness recollections. Most of the information came from Gomez himself, during an interview on December 12, 2003, at the St. Clair County jail in Osceola, Missouri, where he was being held temporarily after sentencing. At first, I had trouble verifying the identities of the professional poker players other than Flynt, because Linda Janowski, who was an eyewitness to one such game, couldn't remember their names. In a letter to me, Gomez specified the names Ted Forrest and Barry Greenstein. I showed those names to Agent Elijah Zuniga, who agreed that the two men regularly squared off against Flynt. I looked up the two gamblers' records in *Card Player* magazine. Then in a phone call in August 2004, I asked Gomez to repeat the names, and he had no trouble doing so.

I wrote six letters to Larry Flynt requesting an interview, either on the phone or in person. He never responded. His publicist, known only as "Kim from L.A.," said, "Larry is busy the whole year." Agent Zuniga told me that Flynt feared any connection, however tenuous, between Gomez's criminal activities and his casino. In all of my research, however, I never spoke to a single soul who possessed a shred of evidence of wrongdoing committed by any of the casinos. Flynt's lone quote was taken from a news story in the Los Angeles *New Times*. Flynt's movements within the casino were reported by Agent Zuniga, by Robert Turner (formerly the player development director at the Hustler), and by Raymond Garcia (then the director of loss prevention with the third-party banker Network Management Group). Garcia also testified at the trial in Kansas City in June 2003. In July 2004, Turner additionally confirmed that Flynt regularly played Ted Forrest and Barry Greenstein.

Linda Janowski's quotes and recollections were derived from a January 9, 2004, interview she granted in her Newport Beach, California, home, at a time when her life was still in turmoil. During that interview, she showed me a Sony TV and expensive jewelry that Robert Gomez had given her as gifts, plus photos of Robert gambling in casinos in California and Nevada. She spoke to me on the subject again on March 26, 2004. Eleanor Gonzales's quotes were derived from my handwritten notes following her appearance as a witness at the trial on May 28, 2003. Photocopies of the $518,731 check, written May 3, 2002, along with Pastor Alexander's handwritten note and various of the Hustler's payout vouchers to Robert Gomez, were all generously supplied to me by the U.S. Attorney's Office, Western District of Missouri.

Chapter 2: Security Guards in Long Beach

Details of the boys' early years were based on James Nichols's and Robert Gomez's recollections, collected during face-to-face interviews and during phone calls from prison. Other details were drawn from the sworn testimony of Rose Nichols, on May 29, 2003, and from the testimony of James Nichols, on both June 2 and June 3, 2003, during the trial in Kansas City.

Chapter 3: Roommates on Kemp Avenue

The U.S. Attorney's Office supplied me with a copy of the one-page undated letter James Nichols wrote by hand to the mythical John Bowers. For the sake of brevity, I presented only excerpts of that letter.

Chapter 4: Advice from the Pulpit

My description of Christ Christian Home Missionary Baptist Church was based on my visit there, on a Sunday in January of 2004. I ate lunch at the BBQ hut next door. I recommend the food, though not the scenery. Details of Robert Gomez's two speeches from the pulpit were supplied during a phone interview with a source who lived in a community outside of Compton. A long-time member of the church, that source agreed to be quoted but asked that I not use his/her name, fearing it would jeopardize his/her relationship with the Nichols family. Other details of James's and Robert's early church days were culled from the testimony of Reverend George Denton, on May 22, 2003, and via a phone interview with Dorothy Bell, on March 16, 2004. Through the church, Bell had known the Nichols family for fifteen years. A copy of an early handwritten list of estate cars and a chronology of negotiations with Gwen Baker were faxed to me by car dealer Greg Ross, following our lengthy phone interview on June 26, 2003. Assistant U.S. Attorney Dan Stewart provided a photocopy of the list of cars that included the 1996 Dodge Aries. Details concerning the early days of Miracle Cars sales were provided by Elijah and Rubye Buggs, during an interview at the dining room table in their home in Long Beach, January 10, 2004. At that time, Buggs also showed me the lists of cars given to him by Rose Nichols. The quotes from Gladys Milligan, Rose Nichols's sister, came from my notes of her testimony on May 30, 2003, in Kansas City, Missouri.

Chapter 5: The Gambling Life

The recollections of Robert Turner, formerly the executive host of the high-limit poker section at the Bicycle Casino, came from a transcript of a July 2004 interview conducted by Agent Elijah Zuniga in the casino's steakhouse. The explanation of pai gow poker is Zuniga's. Details of some of Robert Gomez's life in 1998— including his "Colombian" mother—were gleaned from letters written to me by James Nichols, in prison in the fall of 2003. Copies of all of Robert Gomez's Cash Transaction Reports (CTRs) were obtained by IRS Agent Gary Marshall and supplied to me by the U.S. Attorney's Office. Pauline Oliva's recollections were culled from her testimony in court, May 30, 2003. On September 12, 2003, Robert Gomez described to me his fight in the Bicycle Casino. Details of Robert Gomez's exceedingly peculiar "last will and testament" were supplied December 11, 2003, during my tape-recorded four-hour dinner with Assistant U.S. Attorney Dan Stewart, Postal Inspector Steve Hamilton, and Special Agent Gary Marshall. We ate at Jack Stack's steakhouse in Kansas City. I suspect the food was great, but I don't recall eating a single bite. Because the three men were federal employees, it was unethical for them to allow me to pay for their meals. In fact, they paid for mine.

Chapter 6: National Finders

Robert Gomez's transaction at the Las Vegas automobile dealership was verified by a receipt obtained by Special Agent Gary Marshall and Postal Inspector Steve Hamilton. Details of Rose and Sam Nichols's home-equity loan were divulged during Rose's testimony in court, May 29, 2003. Bits and pieces of Gwen Baker's initial phone call to Rose Nichols were related to me by Baker herself and in letters she wrote from the federal facility in Victorville, California. Baker's background, her job, and her religious habits in Memphis were divulged during her sworn testimony on May 21 and 22, 2003, during the trial in Kansas City.

Information regarding Pastor Holt was acquired from his May 26, 2003, courtroom testimony and from a subsequent phone interview, in the first quarter of 2004. Both David Harps spoke to me in the hall after they testified May 26, 2003. Months later, when I called David L. Harp, he refused to say anything further, suggesting I interview his attorney father. I did so on May 7, 2004, and David K. Harp described his trip to Memphis in detail. A copy of Gwen Baker's contract with Nichols and Gomez was supplied to me by the U.S. Attorney's Office. The details of Baker's Auto Emporium and of various office procedures were collected during a February 11, 2004, phone interview with Baker's daughter, Angela Arnold. Arnold also offered numerous insights into James Nichols's habits when he visited the Bakers in Tennessee.

Chapter 7: Ironing Out the Wrinkles

Details of Robert Gomez's gambling were obtained through interviews with Elijah Buggs (January 10, 2004) and Max Shapiro (March 16, 2004), but mostly from transcripts of Agent Elijah Zuniga's interviews with casino workers Robert Turner (July 2004) and Raymond Garcia (March 4, 2004). Information regarding Gomez's "follow-home robbery" was supplied by Gomez himself and by casino and police reports that were forwarded to me by the U.S. Attorney's Office. Agents Gary Marshall and Elijah Zuniga described the ins and outs of Cash Transaction Reports, and Marshall graciously supplied me with a list enumerating every CTR—including dates and amounts—that Gomez triggered within the U.S. Treasury Department. James Nichols's frequent trips to see notary public Juliet Lozano were divulged during her courtroom testimony, May 22, 2003. All excerpts from Nichols's various letters to Miracle Cars buyers were derived from photocopies of those letters, made available by the U.S. Attorney's Office. Details of the Reverend Houston Buggs's illness and subsequent funeral were supplied by his brother Elijah on January 10, 2004.

Corinne Conway's initial meetings with Gwen Baker were described during her May 20, 2003, courtroom testimony, or were supplied by her attorney Robin Fowler during my December 10, 2003, meeting with him in his office in Overland Park, Kansas. My impressions of the Virtuous Women's International Ministries were formed during three trips to Higginsville, Missouri, where I also interviewed a half-dozen citizens and victims.

Chapter 8: An Avalanche of Cash

Copies of monthly statements from the First Bank & Trust in Lakewood, California—the account belonging to James Nichols and Gwen Baker—were obtained by Agent Gary Marshall and supplied to me by Assistant U.S. Attorney Dan Stewart. The details regarding the automobiles and motorcycles purchased by James Nichols were culled from an "Auto Summary" prepared by Agent Gary Marshall on April 22, 2003, and entered into evidence. Throughout the book, I offered excerpts of letters from angry Miracle Cars customers. All were supplied by Elijah Buggs, Greg Ross, the U.S. Postal Inspection Service, or the U.S. Attorney's Office. During his courtroom testimony on May 21, 2003, investor Matt Jones described his experiences with Corinne Conway and Gwen Baker. James Nichols's run-in with Jim

Dugan was described to me by Assistant U.S. Attorney Dan Stewart and was fleshed out by Nichols's own sworn testimony on June 2, 2003.

Max Shapiro's recollections of Robert Gomez were related to me during a phone interview on March 16, 2004. At the time, professional gambler Barbara Enright—who played against Gomez on rare occasions—was in the room with Shapiro and, in the background, shouted out additional information and corrections to what Shapiro was saying. In particular, she helped clear up my misperceptions about third-party bankers. Patricia LeBlanc's comments were obtained from her June 2003 courtroom testimony. Details of the Reverend Houston Buggs's funeral were supplied by Robert Gomez on December 12, 2003, and were corroborated by eyewitnesses Elijah and Rubye Buggs during our meeting in Long Beach on January 10, 2004.

Chapter 9: Let the Celebrations Begin

I interviewed middle-school principal Ray Sutherland and his wife, Jill, on December 10, 2003, in the Mexican restaurant in Higginsville, Missouri, where Corinne Conway had often met with the Sutherlands' son. Details of the January 12, 2000, reception for Gwen Baker were supplied by the Sutherlands, by Davis Theatre owner Fran Schwarzer, and by the *Higginsville Advance,* whose reporters covered the event. Randy Lamb's involvement as an investor was corroborated during his May 21, 2003, courtroom testimony, and his estate-car purchases were enumerated by Agent Gary Marshall in a government summary prepared April 29, 2003, and entered into evidence at the trial.

Ralph Nunley's, Anna Sagato's, and Jack Rosenfeldt's recollections of Robert Gomez's gambling came from their courtroom testimonies. Robert Gomez's loans to Rouben Kandilian were verified via photocopies of checks shown to me by the U.S. Attorney's

Office. Throughout the book, details of Robert Gomez's various blowups and tantrums in the casinos were based on the casinos' security reports, on police reports, or on eyewitness descriptions.

Quotes from investors Ricky Siglar, Janice Siglar, Neil Smith, and Shari Smith were derived from their courtroom testimonies beginning May 21, 2003. Shari Smith then spoke to me on the phone during a lengthy interview May 6, 2004. Her insights into the scam were both helpful and touching.

Chapter 10: Coast-to-Coast Penetration

Kim Krawizcki's experiences as a National Finder were described to me by Krawizcki herself over the course of a two-day interview, February 5 and 6, 2004, in a hotel in Millville, New Jersey. I thank her deeply for the many hours she gave me. She was gracious, honest, and patient throughout. It was easy to see why Assistant U.S. Attorneys Dan Stewart and Curt Bohling had no interest in prosecuting her.

Chapter 11: A Civil Action

Details regarding the secondary sales of cars were revealed during Detective Kenneth Ayers's courtroom testimony, May 29, 2003, and the particulars of the civil action against James and Rose Nichols were obtained from documents supplied by the Superior Court of the State of California for the County of Los Angeles.

Chapter 12: Awards and Honors

Details of the Millennium Conference in Kansas City were derived from photocopies of promotional materials sent out by Corinne Conway and from the eyewitness accounts of Kim Krawizcki. The excerpts from speeches delivered by Gwen Baker and Corinne Conway were derived from transcripts of a videotape supplied by Assistant U.S. Attorney Dan Stewart. In a letter written to me,

Gwen Baker later denied she said, "God wants you to roll," claiming instead she said, "God wants you to *grow*." But I listened to the tape six times, and it was played yet again during a Certified Fraud Examiners conference in September 2004. Assistant U.S. Attorney Dan Stewart, Inspector Steve Hamilton, and Agent Gary Marshall attended that conference, and all agreed Baker said "roll." "So your title is accurate as far as we are concerned," Stewart confirmed in an e-mail on September 21, 2004.

Robert Fluellen's particulars were culled from his courtroom testimony on May 23, 2003. Greg Ross related additional details of his Miracle Cars experiences on May 22, 2003, in the hallway of the courthouse in Kansas City, following his testimony. On June 26, 2003, Ross and I talked extensively on the phone, and he subsequently mailed photocopies of the list of cars he purchased from Gwen Baker, plus various items of correspondence with Baker and a copy of his carefully crafted letter requesting a refund.

In the casinos, Robert Gomez forged numerous checks—not only was this the opinion of the U.S. Attorney's Office but also the sworn testimony of James Nichols—and copies of those checks were forwarded to me by Assistant U.S. Attorney Dan Stewart. As far as I know, none of those checks was ever presented to a bank. Stewart also showed me a copy of Gwen Baker's "diploma" from Friends International Christian University, whose entry requirements and whose failure to be recognized by the U.S. secretary of education are displayed on the school's Web site.

James Nichols's recollections of Robert Gomez were recorded during a phone call on June 18, 2003.

Chapter 13: Entertaining the Troops
The Las Vegas investors' junket was described to me by Robert Gomez (December 12, 2003) and by Angela Arnold (February 11, 2004). Further details were lifted from Melvin Hackett's testimony

(May 27, 2003). A government-prepared summary of Gwen Baker's real-estate purchases in Fayette County, Tennessee, was supplied by the U.S. Attorney's Office. The recollections of Richie Sklar were based on transcripts of an interview conducted by Agent Elijah Zuniga in March of 2004. Some details of Sklar's personal and criminal history were taken from a *Review-Journal* newspaper account written by Jay Richards. Corinne Conway's income and her tax liabilities were divulged during the sworn testimony of IRS Agent Gary Marshall and were corroborated by attorney Robin Fowler on December 10, 2003.

Chapter 14: A Dark Cloud on the Plains

The description of Higginsville, Missouri, was based on my visits there on June 7, 2003, December 9, 2003, and December 10, 2003. In her tiny office, Chief Cindy Schroer spoke to me for three hours on December 10, 2003. She gave me the names of several Higginsville victims, all of whom agreed to be interviewed. Neil Smith's Miracle Cars investments were enumerated in a summary prepared by Agent Gary Marshall, May 13, 2003, and entered into evidence. Raymond Garcia's statements regarding Robert Gomez were taken from transcripts of an interview conducted by Agent Elijah Zuniga, March 4, 2004. Kim Krawizcki's recollections were recorded by me on February 5 and 6, 2004, in Millville, New Jersey.

Chapter 15: Men in Black

The description of the Smoke House meeting was a composite of eyewitness accounts, principally those of attendees Greg Ross, who spoke to me on the phone on June 26, 2003, and Richard Gil, who spoke to me on February 18, 2004. Assistant U.S. Attorney Dan Stewart supplied a copy of a letter written by Matt Jones immediately following the Smoke House meeting, and James

Nichols also spoke to me about the meeting during a phone conversation on June 18, 2003. A copy of the so-called Smoke House letter was supplied to me by Gwen Baker's attorney, Lance Sandage, in Independence, Missouri.

Copies of Gwen Baker's expenses, including the purchase of a Camaro for her daughter, were supplied by the U.S. Attorney's Office. The recollections of Salvador Elias were derived from his sworn courtroom testimony on May 27, 2003.

Chapter 16: Innocent Bystanders

On January 9, 2004, Linda Janowski spent nearly an entire evening talking to me in her home in Newport Beach, California. She showed me jewelry and other gifts that Robert Gomez had given her. She patiently answered innumerable subsequent questions via e-mail. I admired her for her ability to forgive Robert Gomez and to bounce back financially from the crimes he committed against her. Copies of the South Bay Toyota and Payless Towing & Storage faxes were obtained by the U.S. Postal Inspection Service and were supplied by Assistant U.S. Attorney Dan Stewart. Gwen Baker's $208,000 withdrawal from First Bank & Trust was corroborated by photocopies of bank records and her own sworn testimony on May 21 and 22, 2003.

Chapter 17: Undercover Research

The recollections of Dan Stewart, Inspector Hamilton, and Agent Marshall were recorded during a meeting on December 11, 2003, on the fifth floor of the Whittaker Courthouse in Kansas City. The sums paid to Kim Krawizcki by Kenneth Copeland and the Kenneth Copeland Ministries were recorded in a government summary prepared by Agent Gary Marshall on February 5, 2003 (government exhibit 51–12) and supplied to me in the first quarter of 2004.

Kim Krawizcki's phone conversations with Gwen Baker were recorded by the FBI in August 2001, and transcripts were supplied to me by the U.S. Attorney's Office. Krawizcki knew the phone was tapped; Baker did not.

Details of Gwen Baker's stage play were supplied by Alphonso Slater during a phone interview on February 11, 2004. Descriptions of the various California stakeouts were based on the eyewitness accounts of Inspector Steve Hamilton, Agent Gary Marshall, and Agent Elijah Zuniga. All three spoke to me during numerous interviews, phone conversations, and e-mails beginning May 19, 2003, and continuing through October 20, 2004.

Chapter 18: The Casinos Have Eyes

A copy of Robert Gomez's tax-refund check was forwarded to me by the U.S. Attorney's Office in Kansas City. Agent Elijah Zuniga's recollections of this case, and his pursuit of Robert Gomez, were first described to me during a four-hour interview in Temecula, California, on January 9, 2004. We subsequently spoke on the phone or exchanged e-mails almost daily, right through October of 2004. Robert Gomez's recollections of his Las Vegas trips, plus the quotes he attributed to Larry Flynt, all derive from phone calls he made to me from St. Clair County Jail and from the La Tuna Federal Correctional Institution. On numerous occasions, I asked Flynt, as well as his publicist, if he could verify Gomez's statements. Flynt did not reply.

Chapter 19: The Partnership Is Dissolved

The heated conversation between James Nichols and Robert Gomez, on the occasion of Nichols's resignation as executor, was based on sometimes-conflicting quotes from the participants. I recorded Nichols's version during a phone interview June 18, 2003, and I recorded Gomez's version during a face-to-face jailhouse interview December 12, 2003. Nichols's expenditures in Las Vegas were enumerated in government exhibit 118–1, "Summary of Account Closing First Bank & Trust." Nichols's payments to family members were stipulated in government exhibit 109–13, prepared by Agent Gary Marshall on April 22, 2003. Sums quoted from the car-selling years were derived from Agent Marshall's summary, government exhibit 109–1, and supplied to me by Assistant U.S. Attorney Dan Stewart.

Chapter 20: Reinventing the Con

Robert Gomez's reformulation of the Miracle Cars scheme was based on accounts posited by Agent Gary Marshall, Inspector Steve Hamilton, Agent Elijah Zuniga, and Assistant U.S. Attorneys Dan Stewart and Curt Bohling. Their accounts corresponded with the opinions of James Nichols, who spoke to me on the subject in three phone interviews in June and July, 2003. Assistant U.S. Attorney Dan Stewart provided a copy of Pastor John Alexander's "Contractual Agreements." The U.S. Attorney's Office faxed me copies of most of Alexander's many wire transfers and checks, plus a letter Alexander wrote to Eldorado Enterprises on December 27, 2001. Despite my requests, neither Alexander nor his attorney in Atlanta would speak to me. Robert Turner's recollections were derived from transcripts of a July 2004 interview conducted by Agent Elijah Zuniga. Raymond Garcia's comments were likewise collected by Zuniga, on the evening of March 4, 2004.

Chapter 21: Good Cop/Bad Cop

A transcript of the tape-recorded phone conversation between Matt Jones and Corinne Conway was prepared by the U.S. Treasury Criminal Investigation Division on March 14, 2002, and was supplied to me by the U.S. Attorney's Office.

Chapter 22: Divergent Paths

Pastor John Alexander's sales proceeds and payments to Robert Gomez were calculated by Agent Gary Marshall in a government summary called "Computation of Car Sales (Gross and Net)" based on deposits to banks and direct payments made by Alexander. Similar sums were reported in a story by the *Kansas City Star*. The stories of various victims in this chapter were derived from newspaper accounts in the *St. Petersburg Times* and the *Kansas City Star*, recommended to me by *Star* reporter Tanyanika Samuels. Kim Krawizcki's conversations with Pastor John Alexander and with Alexander's wife were described to me by Krawizcki during my February 5 and 6, 2004, interviews with her in New Jersey. Details of the FedEx box stuffed full of car-sales proceeds were taken from the courtroom testimonies of Agent Steve Hamilton, James Nichols, and Kimberly Hall Nichols. Copies of the letters written by angry investors were supplied by the U.S. Attorney's Office in Kansas City and were corroborated by copies listed in the U.S. Postal Inspection Service's summary called "Items Given to Inspector Hamilton by Rose Nichols." Gwen Baker's so-called "For the Love of God" letter was forwarded to me by Assistant U.S. Attorney Dan Stewart, as was Baker's own April 2002 computation that she owed Matt Jones $443,500. Randy Lamb's purchases were enumerated in government exhibits 11–1A and 11–1B, both prepared by Agent Gary Marshall. Copies of Baker's April 2002 "IOU" letters to Randy Lamb were supplied by the U.S. Attorney's Office.

Chapter 23: The World According to Robert

Antonio Zaldua graciously agreed to speak to me via phone on the night of February 19, 2004. His claims of being unaware of Robert Gomez's criminal activities were persuasive. Robert Gomez's fictional Web site creations were first faxed to me by Max Shapiro, then duplicates were forwarded by Agent Elijah Zuniga. In phone interviews, freelance gambling writer Shapiro talked to me about Robert Gomez on March 16 and 17, 2004. A copy of the infamous $518,731 check was entered into evidence and supplied by the U.S. Attorney's Office, as was a copy of John Alexander's handwritten note of explanation. Agent Gary Marshall's statement that Alexander "had to know where the money was going" was made via e-mail on July 19, 2004. The $21.1 million sum, representing gross car-sales proceeds, was derived from numerous estimates, most reliably Agent Gary Marshall's summary, entered into evidence as exhibit 109–1.

The term "God's gravy train" first appeared in a story in the *Los Angeles New Times,* by Michael Gougis and Traci Jai Isaacs. It was an inspired turn of phrase, and an early favorite for this book's title. The sums that Robert Gomez laundered at individual casinos were tallied by Agent Gary Marshall and enumerated in government exhibit 109–2.

Chapter 24: The Feel of Steel

Details of Robert Gomez's arrest and the subsequent search of his home were supplied by Inspector Steve Hamilton, Agent Elijah Zuniga, and the Long Beach police. Property receipts were prepared by the Department of Justice Division of Gambling Control. Agent Zuniga supplied similar property receipts following the search of James Nichols's residence on Bankers Drive. The quote from prisoner Enrique Perez was lifted from his sworn courtroom testimony, June 3, 2004.

Chapter 25: Stonewalling in the Midwest

Corinne Conway's attorney Robin Fowler agreed to speak to me in a lengthy interview on the afternoon of December 10, 2003, in his office in Overland Park, Kansas. He believed in his client's innocence and worked tirelessly to obtain the light sentence she ultimately received. I interviewed Gwen Baker's attorney, Lance Sandage, on the afternoon of April 20, 2004. He was patient and forthcoming, and his opinions were valuable.

Chapter 26: Kansas City, Missouri

My accounts of events within the Charles Evans Whittaker Courthouse were collected during more than three weeks spent in Kansas City observing the trial, plus an additional ten days conducting interviews. Comments made by the lawyers, by Judge Laughrey, and by the defendants were based on my hand-written notes or on trial transcripts purchased from court recorder Kathleen M. Wirt. Robert Gomez's attorney, Bruce Simon, gave me more than one ride to the courthouse and was always open, honest, and willing to discuss the nuances of his client's defense. He was enormously helpful. U.S. Department of Justice Public Affairs Officer Don Ledford introduced me to Assistant U.S. Attorneys Dan Stewart and Curt Bohling and proved to be a master of courtroom logistics and scheduling. Ledford further supplied nearly one hundred pages of news releases emanating from the Office of the U.S. Attorney, Western District of Missouri, and was the first to supply copies of the indictments against all four defendants.

Courtroom etiquette prevented Judge Laughrey from talking to me about the defendants or witnesses in the matter of *United States* v. *Nichols and Gomez,* case number 02-00114-01/02-CR-W-NKL, although she graciously offered to clarify any points of law that confused me. I was in her courtroom so often that she sent an assistant to ask who I was, and she was amused when, at the start of the second week of the trial, I showed up with my own seat cushion. Judge Laughrey graciously took time to sign a decree allowing me to visit Robert Gomez in jail, when U.S. Marshals told me they wouldn't allow it. She was an iron maiden in her courtroom but was generous, considerate, and easygoing in her dealings with me.

Chapter 27: They'll Never Find My Money

Robert Gomez's comments outside the courtroom were lifted from my handwritten notes. Whenever I was in Robert's presence, I held at the ready both a pen and notebook. When I had to flip pages in that notebook, Robert would cease speaking so that I wouldn't miss a word. Comments he made while in jail were also recorded in my notebook, because my tape recorder was either confiscated or was of no value when we spoke through bulletproof glass. Shari Smith agreed to be interviewed on May 6, 2004, and Greg Ross faxed most of his Miracle Cars documents to me on June 26, 2003. Kimberly Hall Nichols e-mailed various observations and opinions for nearly a year following the trial and kept me current on James Nichols's life in the Victorville federal prison.

Chapter 28: Lying for Profit and Pleasure

Rose Nichols's comments were taken from court transcripts of her testimony, May 29, 2003, supplied by recorder Kathleen M. Wirt.

Chapter 29: The Main Event

James Nichols's recollections and opinions were culled from court transcripts and from his direct statements to me, taken from my handwritten notes. Kimberly Hall Nichols's words were uttered in the hall outside Courtroom 7A. Richard Gil's quote was not obtained during the trial but during a subsequent phone conversation in February of 2004. Gil was called as a witness at the trial but at the last moment wasn't needed.

Chapter 30: Deliberation and Decision

I interviewed the jury forewoman on the afternoon of June 6, 2003. She told me I could publish her comments but asked that I not divulge her name.

Chapter 31: "There Are No Words"

Attorney Robin Fowler's statements on behalf of Corinne Conway were obtained from a sentencing transcript supplied by Kathleen M. Wirt. Chief Cindy Schroer's comments were recorded during our meeting in Higginsville, Missouri, on December 10, 2003, and during a phone interview in August 2004. U.S. Attorney Todd P. Graves met with me in his office for an hour on June 6, 2003. Attorney Bruce Simon ate lunch with me in the Charles Evans Whittaker Courthouse on December 11, 2003, patiently and graciously explaining the government's position on the possible confiscation of fees paid to him by Robert Gomez. Gomez's colorful speech, made at his sentencing, was excerpted from my handwritten notes.

Chapter 32: Aftermath

Quotes from Gwen Baker, Robert Gomez, and James Nichols were derived from their handwritten letters, from our phone conversations, or from prison interviews. Ed Gaunder, the executive assistant at Victorville Federal Correctional Institution, denied my request to visit Gwen Baker on February 20, 2004, at 12:30 P.M. On August 3, 2004, I interviewed a neighbor who knew the Nichols family. That neighbor spoke on the condition I not reveal his/her name. Dorothy Bell agreed to be interviewed via phone on March 16, 2004. Mercedes Flores's comments regarding her son were derived from a transcript of an interview conducted in June 2004 by Agent Elijah Zuniga. Kim Krawizcki's comments were recorded in Millville, New Jersey, on February 5 and 6, 2004, during our face-to-face meeting. Max Shapiro's comments regarding Robert Gomez were recorded during a phone interview on the afternoon of March 16, 2004. Pastor Bill Dennington's comments were obtained during a brief phone exchange at 2:45 P.M. on April 7, 2004. He was not happy to be speaking to me. Elijah Buggs's quotes were recorded during our interview in his Long Beach home on January 10, 2004. The Chris Moneymaker quote was from a question-and-answer interview published in 2004 by *Sports Illustrated.* The Ricky Jay quote was excerpted from an excellent feature by Neil A. Grauer in the June 2004 issue of *Smithsonian,* and was reprinted by written permission of the magazine and the author.

As I write this—October 20, 2004—the appeals of Robert Gomez and James Nichols, as well as the government's rebuttal, have yet to be heard in court.

Index

About the Author

John Phillips III has written for *Car and Driver, Sports Illustrated, Toronto Globe & Mail, Harper's, Elle,* and the *Cleveland Plain Dealer,* among other publications. He was executive editor of *Car and Driver* for seven years and is currently the magazine's editor-at-large, contributing features and a regular column. He remains in touch with Gomez and Nichols, who are each serving more than twenty years in prison. Phillips lives in rural Michigan.